Timeshift

WITHDRAWN

Comedia
Series editor: David Morley

Timeshift

On video culture

Sean Cubitt

A Comedia book published by

ROUTLEDGE

London and New York

A Comedia book first published 1991
by Routledge
11 New Fetter Lane, London EC4P 4EE

Simultaneously published in the USA and Canada
by Routledge
a division of Routledge, Chapman and Hall, Inc.
29 West 35th Street, New York, NY 10001

Typeset in 10/12pt Palatino, Monophoto by Megaron, Cardiff, Wales
Printed in Great Britain by Biddles Ltd, Guildford

British Library Cataloguing in Publication Data
    Cubitt, Sean,
    Timeshift: on video culture.
    1. Videorecordings
    I. Title
    778.599

Library of Congress Cataloging in Publication Data
    Cubitt, Sean,
      Timeshift: on video culture/Sean Cubitt.
        p. cm.
      "A Comedia book."
      1. Video recordings. 2. Video art. 3. Mass media. 4. Popular
      culture. I. Title. II. Title: Timeshift.
      PN1992.935.C84 1991
      700'.9'04–dc20 90–8440

      ISBN 0–415–05548–2
      ISBN 0–415–01678–9 (pbk)

This book is gratefully
dedicated to my Mother
and in memory of Pat Sweeney
and
Steve Herman

Contents

Raids on video culture ix

1 The discontinuity announcer 1

2 Timeshift 21

3 Stars get in your eyes: How music became visible again 44

4 Box pop 65

5 How to watch video art: My father will heal you with love 86

6 An other and its others 108

7 Out of sight 128

8 Powerplay 149

9 Lost generations 169

Bibliography 188

Index 200

Raids on video culture

This book is a collection of approaches to a protean area of cultural practice, each of them less an essay than, in a term I borrow from Hans Magnus Enzensberger, a raid. Raiding video culture means hurtling in with malice aforethought, pillaging from the shiny emporia of images and activities, threading a way back out again, leaving a trail of anarchy and disappointment. It is a mode of attack that of necessity does violence to the matter in hand; the one thing it does not offer is justice. Suddenly, since the late 1960s, a new cultural continent has emerged from who knows what chthonic forces, uncharted, largely unformed. I have not wanted to map its contours, or to anthropologise its denizens, not even to colonise it in the name of some other, better established disciplinary island like film or media or cultural studies. These raids do not explain or contain. In all probability, they will be at best distractions and at worst unwarranted incursions into a pre-colonial Other. But they have been undertaken in the best spirit of the corsairs of old: desperate, arrogant but, I hope, completely involved, intellectually and emotionally, with the lie of the land, the strategies of its inhabitants and the rich pickings to be dragged back into the bazaars and pawnshops in the back alleys of dominant culture.

This is my first book, and there is a temptation to thank everybody I've ever known. However, I owe a debt of gratitude to my friends and colleagues in several organisations, one already defunct: the Society for Education in Film and Television, the Independent Film, Video and Photography Association, London Video Arts, Black Audio Film Collective, Albany Video, Circles Feminist Film and Video Distribution, Electronic Arts Intermix, the *Good Video Guide* and *Independent Media*. In addition I owe a special debt to colleagues and students at the Open University, Middlesex

Polytechnic, Central School of Art and Design, St Martin's School of Art and the West Surrey College of Art and Design. Earlier drafts of some sections of the first part of the book have appeared in *Screen* and *Undercut*, and I would like to thank the editors for their permission to reuse some of this material.

There are many individuals whose conversations and commitment gave me the idea for this book, helped me through it, or read sections: George Barber, Renny Bartlett, Jennifer Batchelor, Simon Biggs, Steven Bode, Steve Brockbank, Penny Dedman, John Dovey, Anne-Marie Duguet, Jean Marie Duhard, Kate Elwes, Terry Flaxton, Connie Genaris, John Goff, Dick Hebdige, Gavin Hodge, Nik Houghton, Tina Keane, Barry King, Karen Liebreich, Jean McClements, Jill McGreal, Mandy Merck, Tim Morrison, Peter Osborne, Atalia Shaw, Valerie Walkerdine, Jez Welsh, John Wyver. Thanks to Sarah Conibear for her painstaking correction of the manuscript. Over the last few years I have met many other activists in the video field, and though I may not have included everyone, I owe the inspiration for this book to them all: I hope they will enjoy it. My especial thanks to Alison Ripley for putting up with me during the process of composition, and to Dave Morley, than whom there can be no more meticulous and inspiring editor. Needless to say, the vagaries and mistakes that remain are entirely my own.

Chapter 1

The discontinuity announcer

The future is the becoming of possibilities. The present is the moment in which what has been and is disappearing crosses swords with what is on the brink of becoming. At its heart, this book is about video in its relation to the building of a democratic media culture. Video, with its instant playback and its ability to record sound and image simultaneously, thrusts the instability of the present in your face and shouts in your ear: 'It doesn't have to be this way.' Hence its option on democracy.

Video, it is already almost a truism to say, is not essentially any one thing at all. At root, 'video' might be held to be a recording medium, using the magnetic alignment of particles of oxides as a means of storing sound and images electronically. What I want to argue in this book is that this description is not merely inadequate, but that it is seriously misleading, even disabling. What is at stake is what I like to think of as video *culture*, that is to say, a set of relations around the uses of videotape, a set of practices and a set of possibilities concerning what these relations, uses and practices may become.

This step, towards thinking 'video' in terms of relationships, is itself fraught with perils. There is a serious problem in the description of culture in terms of relations, as the discipline of cultural studies has developed in academic disciplines over the last twenty-five years. In some senses this might be seen as a product of the double history of the emergence of cultural studies in academia and cultural journalism. On the one hand, sociological studies of the media and other cultural activities have stressed the institutional powers and organisation of cultural life. On the other hand, crudely put, semiotic approaches largely generated in the English literature schools, often in reaction to the influence of F. R. Leavis and New

Criticism, have stressed the inner workings of texts and models of their impact on readers – a general term used to cover all audiences for all forms of cultural life. Contemporary researchers and theoreticians have begun the enormous work of tracing the activities of the 'social reader', that is to say the actual living people who read, watch, listen to and partake in various cultural forms (Gray 1987b is a good overview of recent work). The move to deepen and challenge abstract sociological and textual models of what readers do is an enormous challenge, and will undoubtedly occupy researchers for a good time to come. This book draws heavily on the research undertaken so far. In particular it tries to look at the myriad ways in which people relate to each other and to themselves via video.

Any attempt to establish the democratic credentials of the medium has to begin by pressing the claims to equal privilege of all those involved in making meaning. The traditions sketched above, the sociological and the literary, privilege the producer and the text. I want to argue that the roles of many others are also in play: distributors, reviewers, exhibitors, traders, censors, technicians, engineers and, crucially, readers.

In English-language cultures, for many years, the privilege given to the text in literary studies demonstrated some of the worst aspects of western tradition. What was required of the act of reading among the major critics of literature this century was a demonstration that you had successfully given yourself over to the text. The mysteries surrounding the literary text still reek of The Book at the heart of western culture, the Bible: creation, inspiration, genius (a Roman local deity), being faithful to the text. The mysticism of this position has several adverse effects. It encourages a belief in the poverty and insignificance of the reader as opposed to the infinite richness and profundities of the text. In the same motion, the reader is reduced to a 'merely' subjective relation to the text, a secondary role subordinate to the text or, as the semioticians have it, 'subjected' to it. From such a position it is clear that the reader is inevitably incompetent to judge, alter or renew: a position with enormous consequences in the constitution of an individual reader's self-image: alone, limited, subordinate, alienated from others and, as psychoanalytic approaches stress, from large areas of her/himself. A visual expression of this is the practice of teaching young people to read silently. Reading aloud asserts the reader's active participation in the production of the text and affirms its social ownership: silent

reading is more like prayer, head bowed in silent and lonely subjugation.

This sense of the relative weakness of the reader's position underpins the ideologies of censorship addressed later in Chapter 8: qualities of good and bad are allocated – usually through the medium of an institutional discourse like Literature or Tradition – to texts which are presumed to affect more or less receptive readers. Readers are rarely credited with having effects on texts. When they do, for example in the writing of marginal notes, it is usually thought of as desecration – a blasphemy against The Book, for which the playwright Joe Orton suffered. I know only of one favourable reference to marginal jottings: Charles Lamb's recollections in the *Essays of Elia* of getting books back, very belatedly, from Coleridge, covered in the poet's philosophical musings. Though certain marginalia make their way into scholarly editions of writers' works, it is usually only when the authors of marginalia are as central – or more so – to the institution of Tradition than the texts on which they practice their palimpsests.

Although we learn to speak at home, we learn to read in institutions, either physical ones like schools or more abstract ones like the national language (received pronunciation, the Queen's English). Those institutions, though often staffed by genuinely committed people, still bear the scars of their histories in the structures and practices they have today, often despite the best efforts of teachers and students. The kind of media education I was involved with in the late 1980s with my colleagues in the Society for Education in Film and Television is a challenge to these constraints, because it begins with students' existing enthusiasms, pleasures and abilities, rather than a criticism of them. To a great extent, this shift has been made possible by beginning to unpack the notion that all reading – whether of books, plays, films or clothing – is the same. By privileging the reader's pleasures, it is possible to move away from the stranglehold of 'value', that mysterious core of the literary text. Instead this investigation will focus on what it is that people do when they use video.

Video's readers are already intensely 'literate'. The codes and conventions of moving-image media, now almost a hundred years old, are dense and complex. I would argue that there is a kind of Chinese Box effect in the history of twentieth-century media, TV subsuming film, video subsuming TV. Video viewers are already consumers of television, and through TV of film, pop, news,

photography .... Even very young viewers can tell the difference, say, between an action narrative and the news. Other viewers have little difficulty distinguishing a rented feature from an off-air recording. The major part of the population of the industrialised countries have grown up with moving pictures; many have grown up with TV and, throughout the industrialised and newly industrialising world, are increasingly familiar with the video deck and, to a lesser but growing extent, with video production equipment, especially portapaks, camcorders and computer graphics.

The domestic video cassette recorder (VCR) is itself a kind of production device, as it can be used for seizing moments from TV's incessant flow, compiling, crash editing. For example, while researching this book I've compiled several tapes of video work from the output of UK television stations, tapes which, were the laws of copyright less strict, I might be using as sources for lectures or backdrops for parties. However small my input, this kind of activity does seem to me to be adding value to the material which, unselected, remains just another blade of grass on the pampas of television output.

It's always easier to see a direct physical activity like domestic editing as an engagement in the processes of production. It is less in our cultural make up to recognise video viewing as a serious practice. By contrast, some of this book has been written on notepaper in public places – pubs, trains, cafés, waiting for a film or a meeting to start. Sometimes someone – a fellow passenger, the bartender – asks what you're writing. The same thing happens with video, the same question, what are you watching, but rarely with the same sense that you might be engaged in genuine emotional, intellectual or political activity. Writing is a visibly active process, and is respected as such, video viewing not so. On the other hand, in my experience, people are far more likely to take a few minutes to look at the tape you're viewing than they are to ask to read the notes you're writing. The silence that surrounds writing, as it surrounds reading, gives it a solitary air: video is noisier, more sociable, more open to intervention at this straightforward social level.

As I tried to indicate above, writing has an aura of privilege which has, certainly in English culture, been its own worst enemy. Isolated in silence, the writer's activity seems aloof and alien. Conversely, the very ubiquity and sheer noisiness of video delivers it over to

judgement – you don't need a degree to be bored, offended or bewildered by a tape. The viewer, remote control in hand, assumes a position of dominance over the flow of the screen.

Or is that the case? Is the video culture one in which viewer power dominates? Or are we potential victims of ideologies conveyed through video, and video itself just another mass medium? That question haunts this book, as it haunts the politics of media legislation in country after country. I am in two minds. Part of me wants to reject the trivialising impostures of broadcasting, low-grade features and talentless pop. Much of the culture I live in – metropolitan London under Thatcher in the 1980s and early 1990s – is ugly, violent, oppressive and hypocritical. I know that I watch tapes sometimes from a wish to forget the daily grind. But part of me also respects my own engagement in deciphering these messages from cultures I have never known in other forms – wildlife documentaries, aerobics, Hong Kong features . . . . I know too that my enjoyment of *Sergeant Bilko* or *EastEnders* is based in what I have learnt about moving images and the techniques for their remembrance. I have become competent.

The word 'competence' has a technical definition in linguistics:

the possibility of constructing and recognising the infinite number of grammatically correct sentences; of interpreting those among them, likewise infinite, which have meaning; deciphering ambiguous sentences; discerning that certain sentences, effectively very different in their sounds, nonetheless have a very strong grammatical similarity . . . the finite number of actual performances [of acts of speaking] does not forbid us speaking of theoretically infinite competence.

(Ducrot and Todorov 1972: 158)

In language, a competence is the ability to cope with the nuances and possibilities of a language or a dialect. In video, a competence is that set of acquired skills, so deeply embedded we scarcely know we have them and rarely stop to value them, which allow us to distinguish between a newscast and an advert in a split second, or to follow complex narrative structures of flashbacks and fantasy sequences, relating them back to the fictional present of the narrative.

These complex modes of storytelling in video – spatial orientation, time orientation, knowing who to believe and who to disbelieve – demand equally complex work on the part of the

viewers, whose competence in the practice of the medium, gleaned perhaps from older media but honed still further, in ways which I want to explore in this book, through video, is brought into active play as an interaction with the video text in the production (and critique) of meaning. This is not to belittle the skills of videomakers but to insist that audiences keep up with them, that the role of the audience is much more than simply paying for the cycle of production, distribution and consumption.

However, the production of meaning, in which the viewer is so active, is not necessarily a field of consensus. Cultural activity is not only intensively policed (as I've tried to argue below, pp. 157–64) on the macro scale of society at large, but also fought through at the micro level of the individual viewer and the domestic viewing situation so effectively analysed by, among others, Brunsdon (1982), Gray (1986; 1987a) and Morley (1986). The concept of democracy with which I began this chapter is also already the concept of struggle. By the word 'struggle' I intend a focus on the instability of meaning, and the impossibility of avoiding change. In a way the concept of struggle gives me an alibi – what I write now is only a moment of the struggle, a moment to be superseded, an intervention which may or may not be important here and now but which can only be one element of a larger historical process. But simultaneously, 'struggle' describes the way in which, under monopoly capital, cultural activity is undertaken in relations of dominance and subordination, but also of resistance, distrust and the active misreading of texts.

It is not that a given video is incapable of defining its own meaning. What I would like to argue is that any given cultural practice involves a range of cultural relations, many of which will act against or in different directions to the meaning which a particular tape seems to want to convey. The teacher setting up a classroom exercise on visual literacy, or the rental shop owner selecting titles to hire in a specific geographical community, have different ideas of meaning and knowledge which they bring to bear on their uses of the medium. At the same time, some meanings are heavily foregrounded in the processes both of production and of ancillary levels of meaning generated through reviewing, marketing and advertising. There is, as it were, a hierarchy of meanings, in which the intentions of the producing institutions may be dominant. At the same time, however, producers' intentions are never the only determining factors.

My VCR is playing back a drama production. During an advertising break something catches my eye, a heavily treated visual which looks like the amateur/art film format Super 8, advertising a bottled lager. I might have perked up here because I fancied the lead actor, enjoy billiards, like the product or, in this case, because a videomaker friend has been talking about this as an example of agencies raiding the avant-garde for techniques. But what also impresses me are the production values: deliberately cheapened and downgraded, apparently breaking the guidelines on engineering standards operating in Britain. In the hierarchy of meanings intended by the advertised product's manufacturers, product differentiation, giving their beer a special identity, reigns supreme. At the advertising agency, let's say for the sake of argument, this was perceived as a prestige account, allowing the 'creatives' a stab at recognition by their peers. That recognition heads their criteria for a successful advert, followed by the need to keep the client sweet. For the producers, then, recognition of their creative skills is the reading which they would prefer to be made of the text of the advert: its 'preferred reading'. But in my living room, I might be aware of these intentions while putting, for a moment, homoerotic desire and an interest in institutions of creativity in the front rank of my concerns. I haven't escaped the hierarchy – these possibilities inhere in the practice of advertising. Instead, I have privileged a subtext over the main message, anchoring my meaning there, while still absorbing the glamour and the product identity which the makers were after.

Such hierarchies are not autonomous entities which descend from the sky. Video practice, whether producing, viewing, distributing or whatever, takes place in a world where struggles over meaning rub shoulders with struggles over many other forms of control. The ownership of tapes and routes for their circulation, battles over standards and formats, struggles over the hard- and software between competing companies have damaged the development of the medium and threaten its future growth. Capitalism operates through a system of fragmentation, dividing one process away from another in the factory system, one form of knowledge from another, one skill from another and, in contemporary machine technology, dividing the skills away from the workers in order to invest them in machines. But this process, though in many ways strengthening economic development, is also a dangerous route to take since it divides capitalists from each other. This is good for

capitalism, in that it forces companies to increase the rate of exploitation of workers, but it is bad if it fragments the market so badly that the free flow of commodities and consequent economies of scale are impeded. Though the cinema managed, through the establishment of the Academy of Motion Picture Arts and Sciences, to set up a cartel to adjudicate on common standards (for example in the shape of frames or the system of sound reproduction), the same cannot be said of the electronic industries, who have produced a welter of different, mutually incompatible formats and the demise of some – like Phillips V-2000 domestic VCR format – which in certain respects were more attractive than the more successful VHS format.

There is no reason why domestic formats should not deliver far higher quality than the standard Betamax or VHS playback. These have been developed as the lowest common denominator and delivered in sufficient bulk, and therefore at low cost, to saturate the market and remove the possibility of other standards 'competing' for an improved commodity. Capitalism does not, cannot understand the delivery of quality as a central motivation: the profit motive alone provides its drive. In consequence, most domestic playback is poor, and the sound in particular execrable. We have paid for domestic convenience with a major drop in standards from the clarity and scale of sound and image in the heyday of the cinema.

Likewise we have lost the social experience of cinema-going, along with many aspects of the culture of the crowd which characterised the first half of this century. Audiences are not so much fragmented as atomised. Contemporary experience of the media is one centred on the individual, most vividly in the form of the personal stereo, and only then on the individual within a slightly larger group, family or peers. Video has contributed greatly to that movement, as McGrath (1985) notes. If video intervenes in the flow of television, and interferes in the here-and-nowness it seems to radiate, one effect of that is that people don't even see the same programmes at the same time, cutting off much of the possibility of gossip and chat based on a particular broadcast item. This is one of the serious discontinuities for which video is responsible.

At the same time, however, this fragmentation is also a multiplication of the number of sites in which the cultural struggle goes on, and to that extent opens new possibilities for a democratic model of communication and culture. Specifically, the increasing number of production sites, in the form of domestic editing and

domestic-format cameras, posits a democracy of antagonism, rather than one of consensus. At present, 'public opinion' can be identified with the extremely narrow range of interests represented by the press. But if it is possible that the 'public', no longer identifiable as a coherent market but taking on the role of producers of meanings themselves, is moving away from consensus broadcasting to diffused and intensely local practices, the meanings of the words 'opinion' and 'public' are also shifting as cultural practices.

The video is not restricted, like the television set, to the centre-out model of broadcasting which has become dominant throughout the industrialised world. The potential, as yet to be fully developed, for video to become a channel for all sorts of cultural work, is enormous, largely because it is so widespread and so accessible. On the other hand, the discontinuity currently experienced by *television* viewers between themselves and the sources of production frees them from responsibility for what is on TV. But that discontinuity also provides the possibility for a refusal of the consensus which broadcasting is so determined to create. Repeated experiences of refusal bring eventually a qualitative shift: alienation. This combination of an audience alienated from consensus broadcasting with the same audience empowered with the machinery for making their own work has led to a crop of new legislation aimed at controlling the flow of tapes. Likewise, if recent debates in parliament are to be believed, there has been a flowering of underground cultures – porn enthusiasts, sports fans, amateur vidéastes – circulating their own images.

It is in this context, a context of struggle and perhaps of the emergence of the terms for a new democracy, that I want to turn to the actual machinery involved in video culture: the technological relation. The key problem for technological analysis is the uneven distribution of access and control. This unevenness can be theorised globally as the concentration of access and power in what Paul Gilroy (1987) calls the overdeveloped nations. Locally, the appropriation of cultural, economic, technical and political skills and control over video in particular can be differentiated between individuals according to gender, class, race, physical ability . . . . The institutional settings in which people find themselves also have an enormous bearing on access and power.

The MacBride Report, a key document of the United Nations 'New World Information Order' policy in the 1980s, quotes 1977 figures that

In most developed countries, the number of [television] sets
approaches that of households. In the developing countries,
however, only a small minority of households can afford a
television set – in some 40 countries, only 10 per cent of
household units have a receiver – and programmes are available
chiefly in cities.

(UNESCO 1980: 76)

The concentration of ownership may be even more intense than
first appearances suggest when you take account of variations in the
definition of 'household', since the number of individuals making up
a household is likely to be larger in the southern hemisphere. The
situation does not seem to have improved over the decade since
MacBride.

Figures from 1987 indicate some interesting shifts: the UK is no
longer market leader in ownership of VCRs, trailing decisively, not
behind industrial nations of the northern hemisphere, but the
countries surrounding the Gulf and the newly industrialising
nations of the Pacific basin. The Japanese stranglehold on hardware
manufacture is no longer based on domestic but on 'offshore' plants
in nations with lower wage rates than their own. In a distinctive
shift of policy, some Japanese concerns have begun to license
Korean manufacturers, not only to assemble parts, but to
manufacture them too (*Screen Digest*, December 1987). Hardware
piracy – the fake Rolex syndrome taken across into electronic
consumer goods – thrives in Pacific and African markets, in an
uneasy relation with domestic software production, since the
imitation sells generally well below the cost of the original, freed of
the burden of footing the research and development bill. More
recently, US protectionism is impacting on the cost of chip-based
video equipment, starving East Asian hardware manufacturers of
the vast North American market.

National politics continue to play a role in the development of
media and related technologies. For example, a measure enacted by
the Mitterrand government in France routed all imports of VCRs
through a small bonded warehouse in Poitou for several years in an
effort to stimulate a domestic VCR manufacturing industry by
excluding cheaper foreign imports. However, whether consolidation of existing industrial bases or attempts to develop them are
in question, these industries rely to an increasing extent on the
labour of underdeveloped nations. Hundreds of thousands of

young women are employed in 'offshore' assembly plants at wages varying 'from about 5% of the US norm in Indonesia to nearly 25% in Hong Kong' (Siegel 1979, cited in Larsen and Rogers 1984: 194). Hispanic Americans and Filipino and Vietnamese immigrant workers are crucial within the American industry. Yet despite the importance of Third World and migrant peoples in the production of decks and cameras, the distribution of VCRs and computers in underdeveloped nations is even more sluggish than that of TVs. One reason may well be that the sites selected for offshore plants are chosen for the 'stability' of their governments and their friendliness towards the aims of transnationals – a situation paralleled by the absence of trades unions from North American plants.

Software – TV programmes, recorded music, films, computer programmes – is even more notably concentrated in the industrial north. Even major industries such as the Shanghai, Bombay and Hong Kong cinema studios have extreme difficulty matching the global penetration of Hollywood and the UK in software markets for broadcast and cassette distribution. On the other hand, it is worth bearing in mind Dave Laing's observation concerning the dominance of western musical forms in the recorded music markets of the world that 'while rock 'n roll was undoubtedly a moment in the expansion and technological development of the entertainment industry, it was also an instance of the *use* of foreign music by a generation as a means to distance themselves from a parental "national" culture' (Laing 1986: 338). The traffic in cultural uses which Laing singles out for attention here needs to be stressed. It can offer the beginnings of an understanding of the growth of local uses of media technologies – Jamaican dub techniques are a familiar example (see Hebdige 1986) – in which exported technologies are turned into the means for a new mode of cultural production at odds with the ideologies ostensibly intrinsic to the technology as such.

Turning to more local parameters, Cynthia Cockburn's trenchant observations of technological change and its gendered effects on workforces demonstrate in meticulous detail the scale and mode of operation of women's exclusion from technical education and employment. At 16 years of age in the UK, she notes,

> girls still had only 43.6 per cent of the passes in maths, 27.9 in physics, 27.3 per cent in the relatively new subject of computer studies, and 4.6 per cent in technical drawing in 1983. The

disadvantage is confirmed and deepened by 18 years of age. At A-level these percentages fall to 31.1, 21.0, 19.6 and 2.9 per cent respectively.

(Cockburn 1985: 18)

These findings are backed up by reports from, among others, Cockburn (1983), Linn (1985), Moy-Thomas (1985) and Turkle (1984). The division of labour and consequent proletarianisation of the working class noted by Marx in *Capital* (Marx 1976: 455–91) continues apace, and one of its contemporary avatars is the specifically capitalist exploitation of women and workers from underdeveloped nations. These unequal developments have their counterparts also in the more explicitly cultural practices of video, as we shall see.

The removal of skills from workers and their installation into the fixed capital of the workplace in the form, for example, of robot programmes, is a specific form of this exploitation: it takes the form, as Paul Virilio notes, of 'a paradoxical *miniaturisation of action*, which others prefer to baptise *automation*' (1986: 140). The division of labour and Taylorist principles in factory management has reached a point at which the extraction of the maximum amount of surplus value from a labour force entails a removal of skills from live workers and their placement in machines which, through electronics, are increasingly small: smaller because it takes less time for a signal to travel through a shorter circuit. A parallel activity is under way in the atomisation of elements of professional work and their displacement by video, in particular in the areas of training and personnel management. There is nothing intrinsically wrong with these shifts: they certainly have the potential for freeing people from repetitive tasks like health and safety lectures. What is disturbing is their production not in order to encourage the best use of personnel, but to make workers redundant and to increase the level of central managerial control over the content of instruction and staff relations. The Luddite position of resistance to technical change becomes more than understandable in these contexts.

Harry Braverman's study of the reorganisation of work in the office and retail trades is a case in point (Braverman 1974). Managers in industry justify automation in financial terms: automation produces redundancies, lessening the number of workers who have to be paid and adding to the reserve army of labour, the unemployed, to further depress wages. In the construction of

information and media devices, this tendency is backed up by the threat to move production from overdeveloped to underdeveloped countries. Yet automation actually threatens even this mode of neo-colonialism, by reducing the need for any kind of labour. Such developments, despite the rhetoric of 'global villages' and international networks for information flow, will undoubtedly widen the gap between rich and poor nations, and work to create technical elites within developing nations. Processes of design will remain in the power centres, while manufacture continues to divide labour tasks into ever more minimal, and therefore more machine-manageable, elements.

Clearly this bears out Marx's thesis that it is the factory system as such – not the individual items of machinery – which needs to be placed at the centre of analyses of technological change in industry. But it must be borne in mind that the specific nature of the technologies developed to perform these functions of capital is itself a product of capitalist relations, and that it is these relations which, for a materialist analysis, precede logically as well as historically the machinery in which they are fixed. Such technologies, especially in the productive sphere, are designed to extract the maximum surplus value from the labour power of the workforce, especially through removing skills from workers and rebuilding them as miniaturised gestures in the design of machines.

It is only by refusing to take the existing or predominant forms of technologies as absolute givens that we can offer explanations as to how people are able to use, manipulate or sabotage the technologies with which they come into contact. The growing challenge for the Left is not merely to appropriate the necessary skills to utilise the new technologies, but to create new modes of collective working around them, to bring social and cultural requirements to bear on the processes of manufacture. This in turn demands a political and intellectual act, the understanding of technologies not through what they are, but through what human purposes they might serve.

But what are the relations within which technology is talked about? If we want to break out from the stranglehold of actually existing states of affairs, in order to think about how new and better conditions can be attained, we have to disrupt the givenness of the terms. We have to think of the term 'technology' as a centrifugal net of interacting discourses, and as a function of them: educational, legal, aesthetic, socio-cultural, scientific. We are constrained by the

language we know to speak about technology as if it were a thing, solid, discrete, simply there. But existing definitions of technology not only exclude or marginalise some technical skills – for example, women's skills with sewing and knitting machines – they also give the impression of inevitability, since, as definitions, they *define* what is or is not possible. The first break is to rid ourselves of the prescriptive power of definition, and to think instead in terms of process and relations.

Marx writes in the 'Results of the Immediate Process of Production':

It is not just the objective conditions of the process of production that appear as its result. The same thing is true also of its specific social character. The social relations and therefore the social position of the agents of production in relation to each other, i.e. the *relations of production*, are themselves produced: they are also the constantly renewed result of the process.

(Marx 1976: 1065)

Capitalism, like other forms of social relation, has to replicate its patterns of dominance and subordination as part of the production process. The same is true of every moment of the circulation of commodities. And a characteristic of our epoch is that these relations should appear as objects, things which are simply and conclusively *here*, facts against which there is no arguing. Thus it is common, when employees rebel against new working practices, to suggest that they are reacting against the means of production, not against the relations of production which set up the new practices and machines initially. This was the burden of much of the UK press coverage of the Wapping dispute, in which print and distribution workers in Rupert Murdoch's News International operation refused new working conditions imposed on them without negotiation, while scab labour provided by the electricians' union 'proved' that old skills were no longer needed. The situation has emerged again in the dispute at TV-am, in which sacked technicians are accused of failing to live up to the working practices 'demanded' by new technologies.

Machines are often pitched in a binary opposition with the human (occasionally animal) body. The hinterland between human and machine is an abiding image in modern narratives from *Frankenstein* to *Bladerunner*, a fearful space where the truly human is lost to the machine, while the machine takes on the terrifying

attributes of the darker side of humanity. This nightmare seems to play in fascinating ways with perceived relations between people and technology. The machine can act in the place of all that we like to think we have displaced from psychic life – brutality, murder, revenge, torture (like the fantastic machines of Kafka) – or become the site of illicit desire, as in narratives of female androids from *Metropolis* to *The Stepford Wives*. Here the frailty of the human body is foregrounded, almost as a kind of biologically inbuilt generosity, which the machine can only violate.

The obverse of this appears in policy documents such as current legislation in the UK concerning the establishment of a national curriculum, in which art and physical education escape the strictures of testing, and are to be assessed only according to 'guidelines' (Department of Education and Science 1987: 10). While, on the one hand, a lingering gesture towards liberal education, this exception marks a barrier between the technical subjects and skills which will be tested, and the 'body and soul' which remain beyond it. Here the issue of control is raised in terms of a relation between a 'real' world of machines and an unreal, unstable and fearful area marked out as the world of the body. The play between these two positions – machine as embodiment of the rational, the precise, the organised or as the manifestation of passions unbridled by morality – suggest the complexity of the technological relation.

However, it only touches on one aspect of the relation, that between individuals and technologies. As I tried to stress before, technology is present to us only as the phenomenal form of a relation with other people. What we see in the conveyor belt is not a machine: it is a relation of power and exploitation between people. Like all meanings, the meaning of machinery is produced not individually, one man or one woman faced with a factory: it is created collectively. But this should not be read as a consensual view of the production of meaning. The relations into which we enter under capital are antagonistic: this much is clear from the brutality with which strikers and pickets are attacked, and from the the violence visited on women, gay men and Black people. The polite fiction of parliamentary democracy, that agreement can be reached through a process of argument and compromise, is simply inadequate to the process of living. The conditions of the production of meaning are that populations ostensibly sharing a language are divided by gender, class, region, sexuality and so on, and that these differences are expressed in hierarchies of knowledge

and power. It is also clear that those who have power will fight to keep it, and that those without are capable of taking action to redress their wrongs.

The fragmentation of communities into segments and factions is continued in the individual psyche. There is a great deal more work to be done in the area of interactions and continuities between psyche and the relations of production and reproduction first indicated by Metz (1977: 7), especially the new interweaving made possible in video viewing. Psychoanalytic approaches to television, for example, have yet to move far beyond the confines of Lacanian analyses of cinema, as Sandy Flitterman-Lewis has recently suggested (1987). Yet work on the 'liveness' of television, in particular Jane Feuer's work on segmented flow and Morley's work on the distracted gaze (Feuer 1983; Morley 1986), seems to indicate a play between institutional and intra-psychic in the viewing process which exceeds the relation evoked in cinematic identification. Our familial and social relations are very much in play in the uses to which we bend media technologies, as are the vagaries through which they become elements of psychic life. What is required is a conception of a relation, within which media technologies are constituted as such, which is simultaneously individual and collective, internal and external: a 'technological' relation which is both social and psychic.

Materialist study of video must begin with a questioning of the status of the object of knowledge. Semiotics in particular specifies that representation is a crucial factor in the constitution of the object. The givenness of the term 'technology' in the study of the technical dimension of human relations is part of the problem: in what historical motions has technology achieved the status of object? More particularly, why has 'video' now taken on an identity as, by and large, the least respectable of all the media? What steps link the identification of a body of practices as an object to its valorisation or marginalisation? If initially technology as the object of technicist discourse is at stake, ultimately the status of knowledge – of assumptions, norms, ideologemes, sememes – and finally of Truth is in play.

These are not postmodernist arguments. Postmodernism, in one of its more persuasive guises, problematises the organisation of knowledge, the modes in which truth can be reached. For a materialist, what is in play is the status of truth itself: is a true knowledge of any kind possible? Thus I would argue that materialist philosophy – too

easily cast aside by proponents of postmodernism as a notional *grand récit* of Marxism – is actually a far more radical enterprise than postmodernism's questioning of the 'master narrative', just as its politics is far more radical than to 'give the public free access to the memory and data banks' as advocated by Lyotard (1984: 67).

Yet Lyotard's formulation does raise the crucial issue of copyright, central to the politics of contemporary culture. The wars developing between hardware and software manufacturers – notoriously over the issue of digital audio tape-cassette (DAT) players, twin-deck VCRs and compact discs which can record as well as play back – indicate that capital is again entering a phase of intense internal contradiction. Bill Nichols (1988) suggests that the age of electronic reproduction also ushers in new subjective relations to media images and sounds. The copying hardware now in widespread domestic use – personal computers, tape recorders, VCRs – alters subtly but irrevocably the intensely personal relationships we develop with the sounds and images that form the lexicon of our audio-visual competences. At the same time both commerce and the state are involved in policing the electronic re-appropriation of sounds and images. We might well want to reserve the possibility of sympathising with the technicians, writers, musicians, performers and others whose stake in their product should be paid for as should any labour under capital. Yet we also know that it is copyright holders – by and large corporations – who receive remuneration for secondary use of material, and that, finally, the technology has outstripped the capacity of the current economic regime to cope with it. These sounds and pictures are our vocabulary, as necessary to us as words in spoken language. Structures of ownership and laws of copyright designed to deal with print piracy in the days of the bookshop publisher are simply unworkable in the electronic era (cf. Frow 1988).

Likewise it is clear that capital is incapable of providing software for its new machines. In an unpublished essay, Steve Brockbank charts the chequered history of computer software, concluding that only after over forty years of development has software design begun to be perceived as sharing with the building of machines themselves a major claim to research and development spending (Brockbank 1987). A visit to any video retailer will demonstrate that much the same is true of the market for video software: scarcely an item on the shelves offers any sense of an understanding that video might move beyond the same range of feature films which the

cinema has developed as a form for itself over the last seventy years. Public libraries in the UK are somewhat more adventurous: the DIY and aerobics tapes they stock show some understanding of the possibilities of the pause and rewind functions of domestic playback. Yet the market share of these kinds of tapes is, with the occasional title to break the norm, negligible. Again, the structures of contemporary capital militate against the development of video culture by concentrating on market consolidation based on homogenised product − principally in the form of the 90-minute feature film. So much so that the entire medium can now be considered as largely devoted to the distribution of Hollywood cinema films.

There is undoubtedly a movement within capital towards increasing centralisation and increasingly intensive capitalisation of distribution media. Since the 'Paramount Decrees' of the late 1940s and early 1950s, Hollywood has been disbarred from controlling vertically-integrated companies, controlling production, distribution and point-of-sale in the cinema business (Borneman 1976; Conant 1976). Vertical integration returns in control over electronic distribution, for example in Ted Turner's purchase of MGM or Murdoch's purchase of Fox, in which TV networks' ownership of studios' back catalogues allows them enormous power over releasing, pricing and marketing strategies. This consolidation of the US industry, allying film, TV and video distribution in single companies, works to maintain a stolidly homogeneous market, even while the technical opportunities for multiplying the number of genuinely different inputs into the system increase. In the UK a combination of deregulation of ownership with a manifesto pledge to control representations of sexuality and violence threatens a similar closure of heterogeneity. In the video retail trade, five major distributors established in 1987 a joint advertising scheme in which lead titles from Warner, MGM/UA, CIC, RCA/Columbia and CBS/Fox feature. Warner were explicit about one function of the campaign: to squeeze out the independent distributors, who might otherwise take a share of the market, by spending sums in advertising the Big Five's output which cannot possibly be matched even by companies of the size of Palace Pictures (*Screen Digest*, December 1987: 284).

Yet the saturation of continent-wide markets with homogeneous programming via cassette distribution and satellite broadcasting is as likely to create the conditions for increasingly local media and

language forms as to swamp them. With each new wave of capitalisation, the previous area is opened up for alternative uses. Photocopying, video cameras and edit suites, computing and computer imaging are available for community use already. But those who try to appropriate each newly available technology for new purposes seem constrained to reproduce the patterns of textual production which the medium seems to demand (cf. Ang 1987). Something of the 'technological' relation is deeply embedded, not simply as peer pressure, but as something far more deeply entrenched.

Class and gender relations re-emerge as professionalism, as new users find themselves lured by the glamour of the medium to reproduce not only similar programmes, but the same structures of decision-making and the same financial operations as their industrial and commercial predecessors. Reformist politics re-emerge as struggles for access clash with an emergent sense of what is 'good' video (and considerations of survival), while funding agencies in the late 1980s reassess their commitments to community-oriented, loss-making projects. The tyranny of 'good taste', of professional standards, of chasing festivals, prizes and reviews, become necessary attributes in the new mixed economy model of video production. But in a far more sinister twist, those relations also become thoroughly internalised. Relations to the cultural production of oppressed groups lose their liberality, and the work of women, Black groups or sexual minorities is commonly either dismissed or, now more commonly, patronised. Notions of what constitutes good practice are considered in the light of competition in the market-place: how closely can this piece of work approximate to the commonly held beliefs as to what such things should look like. Yet such a position entails a move towards the centres of power – of patriarchy, of neo-colonialism, of capital – not only in working practices but within the psyche at a fundamental level. Technological struggles demand personal politics. But those politics are linked inextricably with broader social questions: how are technological developments and psychic life to be thought through in relation to one another?

The video camera converts photons – elementary wave-particles in the visual wavelengths – into electrons – wave-particles in electromagnetic wavelengths. Tape lays these down by relying on the predictability of the effect of electrons on the magnetic orientation of ferrochrome oxides, in turn read back as electrons,

and converted via electron gun and the fluorescent screen back into photons, to be perceived by the human eye. But there is a scientific crux here: while we confidently expect an electron gun in a cathode ray tube to produce a foreseeable visual effect, the physicists are confounded. Quantum mechanics has no principle to explain why an electron or photon observed to be travelling at a certain speed in a certain direction with a certain charge should arrive at a given point at a given time. We have no accurate intellectual mechanism for predicting the activity of the major components of video, only the maths of probability.

According to Jean-Pierre Changeux (1986), the physical operations of the brain are even more obscure than the physics of quantum particles. The relationships we enter into with the VCR depend upon processes of which our culture is radically unsure. We cannot deal in essential characteristics and determinate truths, only in probabilities and processes. Such profound uncertainty, perceived in scientific discourse as part of the very fabric of the universe, could only emerge in a cultural context in which similar uncertainties circulate concerning the nature of meaning. But if science, culture and psyche alike, in the confrontation with technological aesthetics, stand at the brink of meaning, we also are freed from the constraints of a universe in which meaning is an absolute given: we have the choice to make our own meanings, though perhaps not under conditions of our own choosing. The remainder of this book attempts to understand the ramifications of this position, which I take to be the grounds for a democratic culture.

Chapter 2

Timeshift

To open a discussion of video viewing, I want to return to Althusser's schema for a materialist science: object of study; problematic; knowledge produced. Crudely stated the object of television studies has been described variously as institutional or textual, and the respective problematics as socio-economic analysis or interpretative models. The resultant knowledge might be even more crudely stated as cultural pessimism arising from an awareness of the enormous powers of televisual institutions, or viewer power as it is understood in the range of possible meanings to be derived from TV as a textual practice. The status of the televisual text (segment, programme, flow ...) and of the TV institution (local, national, global) need to be thought through simultaneously. The relations between the two pose a critical question about the nature of the audience: saleable commodity or, as theorised by *Screen* writers of the 1970s, an audience as an effect of the text. Would we today rephrase the dichotomy as one between consuming customers and critical activists?

A third tradition in TV studies, apart from the socio-political analysis of business and government involvement or the close analysis of texts, is that of technological determinism, a belief that the technological form of cultural production and consumption is itself determining of the kinds of product and modes of consumption that can be undertaken. The work of Marshall McLuhan, especially *Understanding Media* (1964) and its popularisation in *The Medium is the Message* (1967), is widely familiar, and retains a surprising degree of currency in video art circles, surprising because of the huge changes in TV culture in the last twenty years, and because the other TV and film-related discourses have abandoned McLuhanism for the last fifteen years.

Raymond Williams's critique (1974: 126–30) is almost as well known. McLuhan asserts that 'media, by altering the environment, evoke in us their unique ratios of sense perceptions. The extension of any one sense alters the way we think and act' (1967: unpaginated). Williams counters:

> If specific media are essentially psychic adjustments, coming not from relations between ourselves but between a generalised human organism and its general physical environment, then of course intention, in any general or particular case, is irrelevant, and with intention goes content, whether apparent or real. All media operations are in effect desocialised; they are simply physical events in an abstracted sensorium, and are distinguishable only by their variable sense ratios.
>
> (1974: 127)

Clearly such an approach cannot be reconciled with my insistence that it is relations, particularly of struggle, which precede the phenomena with which the world appears to present us. More recently, the work of Walter J. Ong has refocused attention on McLuhanite theses.

In *Orality and Literacy*, Ong posits an historical shift from spoken to written cultures which, in part because it draws on the fashionable 'grammatology' of Jacques Derrida (see pp. 29–30), has attracted a new generation of attention. Again, the emphasis is on form over content, and on the priority of technology over the social relations to which they relate:

> it is the oral word which first illuminates consciousness with articulate language, that first divides subject and predicate and then relates them to one another, and that ties human beings to one another in society. Writing introduces division and alienation, but a higher unity as well. It intensifies the sense of self and fosters more conscious interaction between persons. Writing is consciousness raising.
>
> (Ong 1982: 178–9)

Ong's mistake here is to subsume social relations within relations between objects, a distinctive quality of relations under capital, as I argued above. At the same time, technologies are invested with the status of historical agents: 'writing' is first homogenised, then made autonomous of both speech and social relations, and on that basis awarded the privileged position of an absolute given, from which

standpoint it can be said to act upon historically given individuals. This is precisely the kind of idealist philosophy, giving precedence to forms and ideas over people and their actual practices and relationships, which materialist arguments must counter.

At the same time, it must be admitted that a materialist project is in constant danger of slipping, through the acquired practice of a lifetime reading, writing and speaking the inherited language, into the kind of rhetoric which Ong demonstrates – a rhetorical form in which inanimate entities like 'writing' or 'video' are given the appearance of living historical agencies, able to influence the shape of history and of human lives. Post-structural analyses of television and, to some extent, of video are full of such infelicitous expressions, in part deriving from their roots in structuralism. Structuralist arguments, popularised in a political climate thirsty for an explanation for the collusion of the working classes in their own oppression under fascism in the continental European experience, propose that social formations are organised through structures, such as language, which pre-exist the individual who has to learn to speak that language. This pre-existence of social structures allowed to individuals only the option on which position in the structure they wished to occupy, not a choice of changing the structure. At the same time, as a theory, it had no model for explaining the social (and linguistic) changes which clearly characterise history. Post-structuralism began the task, on several fronts, of reworking structuralist thought, to a great extent fired by the libertarian and cultural-revolutionary elements of the events of 1968. Several lines of post-structural thought will emerge in what follows. One strand, itself internally very diverse, needs to be addressed in particular in the context of technological determinism: the theses advanced under the banner of 'postmodernism'.

Much of what emerges as postmodernism developed in response to the role of centralised institutions, like the Communist Party and national trades unions, seen as having betrayed the aspirations of a generation in continental politics since 1968. In the variety of work huddled loosely together as postmodernist, one consensus in particular emerges: post-war culture and politics are held to evidence the coming to equivalence of all signifiers, and their liberation from their signifieds, to such an extent that Jean Baudrillard (1983: 34) can talk about 'the dissolution of TV into life, the dissolution of life into TV'. Baudrillard's response to the problem of meaning as a structure based on binary oppositions

(active/passive, cause/effect, subject/object) is to claim that 'today', 'now', difference is abolished in the circulation of simulacra, entities which meld the sign and its referent ('reality') into a single, unanchored causeless effect freed from regimes of knowledge and power. For Baudrillard, fragmentation of meaning and the free play of simulacra are the only possible routes for reaction against his sombre vision of the totally administered society. Totalisation is the enemy, common to Baudrillard (see, for example, Baudrillard 1983) and the other key figure in the canon, Jean-François Lyotard (1984): any system, cultural (e.g. Marxism, science), political (e.g. police, fascism) or military (e.g. nuclear weaponry) is to be equated with any other system, and any non-systematic activity is to be prized as a response.

In the course of an analysis of Disneyland, Baudrillard observes that

> Disneyland is there to conceal the fact that it is the 'real' country, all of 'real' America, which *is* Disneyland (just as prisons are there to conceal the fact that it is the social in its entirety, in its banal omnipresence, which is carceral).
>
> (Baudrillard 1983: 16)

He notes that Los Angeles – a city subject to intense scrutiny among postmodernists – is surrounded by such 'imaginary stations' and goes on to claim that

> As much as electrical and nuclear power stations, as much as film studios, this town, which is nothing more than an immense script and a perpetual motion picture, needs this old imaginary made up of childhood signals and faked phantasms for its sympathetic nervous system.
>
> (ibid.)

This is the most extreme version of the technological determinist thesis, in which whole societies can be envisioned as effects of their characteristic media technologies. Baudrillard defends himself against the accusation of technological determinism by arguing that his philosophical abolition of the concept of difference – between active and passive, for instance, or between sender and receiver – allows him to say that TV is therefore capable of manipulation, and that TV audiences become a mere adjunct of the totalising practices of its endless flow: the 'presence' that TV seems to have to us reproduces its audience as themselves fragments of that eternal flow of disembodied signification.

The concept of difference, for example between sign and referent, is essential to an understanding of the regimes of power operated through discourse: discourse is always discourse 'about', i.e. it maintains a distance from its objects, and by maintaining that distance is able to impose structure, on 'perversion', for example, or on 'deviance', 'mental illness', 'disability', etc. This structuring operation is an operation of power. Baudrillard is interested in moving beyond the analysis of power, offering a vision of a world in which those acting and those acted upon are equally caught up in the whirling maelstrom of simulacra. The discourse and its subjects are united in an undifferentiated and indeterminate process (hence the word 'indefinite') beyond language, indecipherable as to its truth, somewhere between absolute freedom and absolute manipulation. In the Baudrillard analysis, TV is to the family – a construct which he cites as a cultural absolute – what DNA is to the living creature, a master-code which they are free only to accede to: freedom and manipulation are the same, under the tutelage of the absolute and anonymous Code. Clearly this avant-gardiste description of the workings of the media is a delight to those who wish to revel in their present forms: like the monetarist regimes under which they have found their greatest welcome, they allow no alternative. For us, this account is inadequate, misleading and impossible – in the sense that it denies rather than creates possibilities.

The postmodern use of 'now' is a problem in itself, both as a definition of an historical epoch (it was not this way before) and as a model of an eternal present, in which past and future alike are abolished – as differences – in the celebration of the eternal present. Likewise, despite Baudrillard's disclaimer, the media are still granted magical powers, not merely to influence ideologically, but, in Ong's phrase, to alter consciousness (Baudrillardistes would reject the value-system implied by 'consciousness-raising'). Inability to spot the internal contradictions of social formations leaves the postmodernist with the terrifying and final vision of the total society of unlimited power and range, within which subjects are merely momentary nodal points in a perpetual circulation of empty tokens, the ghosts of meaning. The lure of this apocalyptic vision on a psychoanalytic plane may well be on a par with the fascination we find in images of final destruction: the lure of defeat, the junky's nirvana, the return to primary narcissism. Its political attraction is that it removes the necessity to struggle, since justice and

democracy are themselves chimera and worse, totalising regimes of theory. The refusal of difference likewise overlooks the fissures that run through societies, devaluing material processes of living rather than revaluing popular culture. In a curious twist, the attempt to free theory of the weight of its own seriousness results in a deadening hypostasis – a rendering of ideas into objects – of the media as core agents of historical change and ultimately the agents of the end of history.

Following Peter Dews (1987), I want to argue that such an insistence that life-processes can be formed without the interaction of human beings is incoherent. Dews argues that:

> A human being can only acquire the competences which transform her or him into a speaking and acting subject through interaction with other subjects: the identity of the self is constituted through an entry into social roles, but these roles can themselves only be acquired through identifications, not with the actual behaviour of others, but with symbolically – above all linguistically – mediated models of behaviour.
>
> (1987: 198)

It is reciprocal influence between individuals that gives rise to social formations, formations which, however, in their turn, are the lenses through which we understand the actions of others. The special role of language needs to be stressed: there is always the struggle over meanings which distorts and distends language, so that it is never an utterly transparent channel for communication. Every message is a potential site of misrecognition within and between individuals. Thus for Volosinov, the Russian linguist of the early Soviet period, linguistic signs have the quality of 'multi-accentuality' arising from the fact that different class interests within a linguistic community use the same signs, but to different purposes: 'differently oriented accents intersect in every ideological sign. Sign becomes an arena of class struggle' (Volosinov (1929) 1986: 23). However, Volosinov goes on to argue that this multi-accentuality takes place within the established ideological domination of the ruling class of the day, and that 'The ruling class strives to impart a supraclass, eternal character to the ideological sign, to extinguish or drive inward the struggle between social value judgements which occurs in it, to make the sign uniaccentual' (ibid.). This struggle over the sign makes its meanings distort and refract, and we have always to remember that the sign is structured through the dominance of a

class – and through other power structures like those associated with gender and race. Power is exercised in hierarchies, in language as in the rest of social life: but dominance is never uncontested, and the dominant use of language can never be guaranteed to produce the effects intended or expected.

On this basis I want to move from some general comments on the state of play in the televisual domain as a social formation, towards some notion of how the individual is drawn into relationship with it. I want to start from local conditions, observations and accounts in the United Kingdom, and especially in England, as they relate to the widespread use and ownership of domestic video cassette recorders (VCRs). In particular I want to draw on my own experiences, an autobiographical account, if you like, of several years work in the video culture. This experience is not 'typical': its value lies more in a mode of writing in which, in common with many of the video artists discussed below (pp. 103–4), the performer has, through the first person, to mark out a kind of responsibility for what is written. The importance of the local in this argument is that it helps to circumscribe the generalisation of arguments to universal values, geographically or historically. In particular I would argue that the proliferation of VCRs in the UK has altered the terms of electronic – and possibly cinematic – viewing, but the same is not necessarily the case in areas like South Asia where, for example, communal viewing is the dominant practice, where broadcast is the dominant distribution mode, and where cinema is strong enough to reduce the entertainment functions of TV. Programmes or programme formats in world-wide distribution are viewed differently in various cultures, even within the same culture, or by the same person viewing at different times. These are the material circumstances within which I want to set out some propositions concerning first broadcast television and then video as cultural practices and attempt to see what differences there are between them.

Broadcast television is radically heterogeneous. Despite postmodern and technological determinist claims to the contrary, even small children differentiate between different domains in televisual flow (cf. Bazalgette 1987). Their relations to the screen, likewise, seem to be overdetermined by factors as various as number of siblings and regional loyalty. Although, as John Caughie (1980) argues, television derives strongly from radio, it also draws on a wealth of other forms: literary, journalistic, filmic, sporting . . . . The one domain it might be said to fail to contain –

both as a box contains its contents, and as the US army's strategic villages 'contained' Vietnamese revolutionaries − would be, paradoxically, television itself: not even the recent trend towards reflective programme-making on the history and practice of the medium in any sense contains the flow of programming (let alone the complex network of relationships devolving around the TV screen).

The modes of organisation of broadcasting in the UK are likewise heterogeneous, partaking of two classic forms − the regional network of commercial broadcasters based on advertising revenue, and the state-organised, licence-financed BBC − and two more unusual ones − Channel 4 as 'publisher' of independently produced programming, and the hybrid form of Sianel Pedwar Cymru. Delivery systems are similarly varied. Residual 405-line systems have only just given way to the 625-line standard. Transmitters and booster stations operate in a bewildering economy of ownership and rentals. Screens vary in size from wristwatch receivers to wall-mounted flat screens; black-and-white sets coexist, often in the same home, with colour receivers. Sound reproduction veers from the sublime (on TV/radio link-ups) to the ridiculous. Savage deregulation of satellite broadcasting conflicts with the residuals of British Telecom's monopoly on transmission, so that any signal destined for satellite relay has to pass through the BT-operated facilities of the Post Office Tower. Television is historically an impure medium. It is, I believe, impossible to say of TV that it is 'essentially' anything.

The condition of television showing us anything is that it cannot therefore show us everything. In particular it will not show us its means of production, except in a gesture that at once exposes and veils, using the cameras and lighting rigs as props behind and beyond which the real work of television remains invisible. As an institution in a world governed by racism and sexism and plagued with a dismal and outmoded system of exploitation, certain groups and activities will be shown rarely or never. The technology is such that TV cannot show us what is hidden from sight: in Rob Hof's film *Don't Eat Today Or Tomorrow* (Holland 1985) there is a pan shot of the Geneva skyline, while an on-camera speaker tells us that what is most important in Geneva, the subterranean vaults of the Swiss banks, is what you can't see. If TV produces knowledge, it also produces ignorance. A medium that specialises in giving to non-existent entities (ghosts, wombles, muppets) a local habitation and a

name also knowingly speaks to viewers of what it is not permitted to show (Official Secrets, 'naughty bits'). Thus there is also the constant belief that beyond what you know you aren't seeing lies the realm of what you guess you aren't seeing – The Truth.

TV manufactures invisibility. There are entities that do not lend themselves to photography – Britain, for example, or surplus value – which have to be inferred as second-order signifieds, and which as such are open to more detailed negotiations over the status of truth on television: what one person isn't able to see even if it is on screen but which another finds glaringly obvious. Television's categories of invisibility are necessarily bound up with its production of visibility: the programmes and adverts that we see are the tip of the iceberg of what we don't see – because TV is too all pervasive to be seen *in toto*, because some programmes never get shown, because some programmes never get made. What can be known about television is circumscribed by its partiality: in the global context, in what sense can anyone, or even any one discipline, grasp the whole of broadcasting? And how legitimate is it to specify television as an object of study when it bleeds into other broadcast media so constantly – into radio, particularly within broadcast institutions like the BBC and Independent Broadcasting Authority (IBA) or into print media and film in organisations like Rupert Murdoch's News International? How far can we go in taking audience sampling methods as providers of knowledge? In short, there can be no total knowledge about television.

Television is absent. Unlike cinema, the TV image is smaller, less well-defined, often watched in the light rather than the dark, and is generally a domestic or social leisure appliance, so that its messages are in competition with the rest of domestic or social life. Like that life (or those lives), it is ephemeral in its broadcast form: in the words of a pioneering essay on TV, it proposes itself as absolute presence, 'here and now, for me personally' (Heath and Skirrow 1977: 57). The characteristic flow of images noted by Williams in *Television: Technology and Cultural Form* (1974) is also a support for the ideology of presence, the imaginary presence of the TV's discourse to the viewer, itself logically dependent on the premise which Jacques Derrida identifies as the heart of western thought: the *metaphysics* of presence (Derrida 1967; 1976).

Derrida's major work addresses the question of writing and speech, one of those binary oppositions which underpin conventional modes of thought. Speech appears to be a full act, in

the sense that in it signifier and signified are united in one act. It is transparent, or so it seems, the speaker's voice confirming his or her self-identity, 'I speak therefore I am.' Writing, on the other hand, is usually considered to be a secondary representation of speech, a signifier of a signifier, a supplementary act to the original fullness of speaking. Derrida's deconstructive method begins by tipping the opposition upside down: what if writing is logically prior to speech? He argues that the absolute proximity of voice and meaning breaks down in this schema: there is no straightforward act of signification – every signifier is already a signifier of another signifier. Thus there is a gap, a delay, a difference and a deferral of meaning: in writing there is no present. What we have in front of us is always already past, sending us off to find some originating moment in another signifier, another act of signification. From this perspective, there is no fullness in the act of meaning: it is always part of a process, which Derrida labels 'différance', in which, for example, the subject that speaks is never present in the words spoken, there being an irresolvable difference between them.

The deconstruction of the pair writing/speech can then be used to mount a critique of the basis of western philosophy, an almost religious belief in the unity of sign and meaning which ultimately resides in a final, absolute signified, Being. Western systems based on truth rest on the theory of Being: that things, especially ultimate things like God, Knowledge and Truth, exist in and for themselves and can thus be present to us. For Derrida, there cannot be true knowledge because there is nothing there to mark as true, only the field of process.

It is this sense of the ideology of presence that underpins the practice of watching for company, especially among heavy media users like the elderly: the discourse of TV flow is 'present' in the sense that the viewer can enter into dialogue with the screen. Yet the broadcast flow is also a vanishing, a constant disappearing of what has just been shown. The electron scan builds up two images of each frame shown, the lines interlacing to form a 'complete' picture. Yet not only is the sensation of movement on screen an optical illusion brought about by the rapid succession of frames: each frame is itself radically incomplete, the line before always fading away, the first scan of the frame all but gone, even from the retina, before the second interlacing scan is complete. And because TV viewing is subject to constant distraction, and because 'it would be more accurate to say that television is constituted in a dialectic of

segmentation and flow ... that television possesses segmentation without closure' (Feuer 1983: 15–16), then viewing is also a process of missing. TV's presence to the viewer is subject to constant flux: it is only intermittently 'present', as a kind of writing on the glass, to the distracted viewer, and even in moments of concentration caught in a dialectic of constant becoming and constant fading.

Caught between the anxiety of loss and the desire for an ever-absent completion, television is simultaneously already over, and yet to become: its presence to itself is in question. Here we have to look to film theory for the beginnings of a concept of television viewing. Following Oudart (1977–8) and Dayan (1974), film theoreticians argue that in cinema the transition from shot to shot is the organising principle of 'suture', the psychic process through which the spectator is stitched into the imaginary space within the film like a surgical suture: but in television, the transition from segment to segment within the evening's flow is the organising principle of loss of suture, the loss of the subject to the televisual discourse. Editing between programme segments (station ident., credit sequence, announcer, advert, titles ...) is not organised for continuity but to mark segments off as distinct from one another, to reposition the viewer for a different kind of pleasure or attention. Film offers to take us out of ourselves and to provide us with a new imaginary identity for the evening: television is constantly seducing and rejecting us: no sooner inveigled into close attention than the segment is over and some new attention requested instead. TV, viewed with the kind of serious scrutiny which it rarely gets, would induce a kind of schizophrenia made up of constant transitions from one identity to another, one emotional, intellectual or aesthetic persona to another, its insanity redoubled by repetition. Luckily, distraction largely eliminates this frightening possibility. This self-same refusal on TV's part to take on a single identity allows us to escape constantly from it, especially at the point of the segment break.

Television's presence to the subject is a problem: so is the presence of the subject to television. The financial relations between audiences and the two media reflect this difference: the cinema spectator has to pay for a seat but the TV viewer has already paid: the presence of the former is essential to the movement from film (celluloid strips) to cinema (the spectacle). But TV doesn't need its viewers: like tap-water, it can wait indefinitely to flow. In its mode of address, television already assumes that you are watching: whole

programme formats, such as the chat show, are built on this premise. When we don't watch, it doesn't affect the nature of the programme, unlike the cinema, which, without an audience, is like nothing so much as a tomb. Cinematic suture creates the spectator without which it would not exist. Television, contrariwise, has already used up the viewer, and is left continuously asserting its own presence to itself with the obstinate repetitiveness of the hysteric. Internally and externally, TV is sited, to borrow the title of a recent BBC thriller series, at the edge of darkness. What is it that disappears in channel zapping but the entity television itself?

Because television is inexhaustible, it is exhausting. It is a cornucopia whose very wealth is its greatest weakness. As Serge Toubiana points out in his introduction to a special issue of *Cahiers du Cinéma* on video (1981), there are always two discourses in television, that of appearances, of the odds and ends of reality that struggle to appear on the screen, and that of the real, of the machinery and the televisual apparatus. In so far as it deals in appearances, it is open to struggle over meanings; in so far as it partakes of the real, it is transformable. TV is powerless: it is the object in play in a struggle over power, not the source of power itself. In one direction, television and the discourses about television in the UK have centred recently on the issues of ratings and of public service, for example around the BBC soap *EastEnders*. So that the question emerges: if the BBC have to deliver audiences like commercial broadcasters, who is it delivering them to? Do broadcasters serve the public, or is the public serving the broadcasters? A second direction can, however, be discerned in the struggle between the real apparatus and the appearance of reality it carries.

> This relationship of force [writes Toubiana] constitutes the basic canvas of television: sociological window always in search of more reality/ies, aquarium where the appearances of life unfurl *on the one hand*, principal instrument of a Ministry of Propaganda that won't own up *on the other*. In television, power is the impossible object, the object of an infinite quest: object little 'a'.
>
> (Toubiana 1981: 5)

This 'object little "a"' we will return to (p. 171): it is an element of the Lacanian theory of desire which might be translated through the title of one of Bunuel's last films, *That Obscure Object of Desire*. Suffice it to say here that desire, considered as the motor of human action and signification, is always desire for something, and that that

something is ultimately always beyond reach, since if we could reach it we would stop desiring, and therefore stop acting and making meanings. In television, Toubiana is arguing, power is just such an impossible goal, that which motivates the continued engagement of people in this bizarre medium because it is a quest that can never be completed.

In the light of what has been said, we can conclude this set of propositions about broadcasting with an assertion: television has to be produced as an object. In some senses television as discourse produces subject positions from which it is to be understood, yet its own status as originating point of that process is in question. Institutionally, as broadcast flow and as viewing process – even as the object of discourse about television – television is a site of struggle, and one of the stakes in that struggle is the existence of TV as a discrete entity. This is clearly not to argue that TV doesn't exist, but that its existence has to be produced in relation to the subjects which, institutionally and discursively, it is said to produce. If the subject is produced as subject in the television discourse, why should we presume that television is not produced as object in the same relationship? I'd argue that the status – ontological, epistemological, political – of television is produced in the individual viewer, in the micro-culture of the living room, in the local, national and global cultures variously, as a kind of ghost, a frightening, comforting, harmless, powerful, informative, debilitating, entertaining, boring matrix of contradiction which requires the faith of its viewers in its presence to them as object before it can take on the aspect of producer of meaning. The unstable dialectic of the real and the apparent, the present and the absent, the visible and the invisible is the condition under which TV enters into the social. The viewing of – and the writing about – television has as a primary function the task of producing TV as an entity. Simultaneously, the relations around TV are inter- and intrasubjective: they are relations within and between subjects.

In his discussion of the fallacy of seeing humanity in the abstract, Marx demonstrates in the 1857 Preface that there is a fundamental problem in attempting to reduce people – and for our purposes the same is true of TV audiences – to an undifferentiated mass, one which inflects any subsequent attempt to define the relations around the commodity form:

> To regard society as one single subject is . . . to look at it
> wrongly, speculatively. With a single subject, production and
> consumption appear as moments of a single act . . . . In society,
> however, the producer's relation to the product, once the latter is
> finished, is an external one, and its return to the subject depends
> on his relations to other individuals.
>
> (Marx 1973: 94)

Relations of distribution and exchange – the relations between
production and consumption – are relations of race, class, gender,
age and the other factors that overdetermine the divisions in the
social formation. They should themselves be understood, not as
concrete, self-sufficient entities, but as polarities produced in the
struggle over ownership, control and meaning. As Marx went on to
argue in the first chapter of *Capital* (1976), capital has, as one of its
effects, that relations between people appear as relations between or
mediated through objects. Capital produces the object status as a
function of its institution of property and class relations, just as we
saw above that the ruling class will attempt to swing the sign into
its own, 'uni-accentual' domain. But as with the multi-accentual sign,
the object remains a site of struggle. It is in this context that we have
to see the problem of the object status of television. That television
exists as an object is so natural an assumption as to appear
unquestionable. It is towards the unquestionable that critical studies
should always direct their most questioning gaze. The struggle over
meaning, over institutional control, and in the sphere of discourses
about television is also the struggle that places the subject in
relation to the object. We should no more countenance a Cartesian
object of knowledge than we countenance the unitary, centred and
autonomous subject of the *Discourse on Method*. What matters is not
the entities between which we fondly imagine relationships, but the
relation between them which defines their status. There are no
positive terms: we must deal in difference.

The term 'difference' has an important place in the linguistic
underpinnings of the social and cultural theories I have been
looking at in this analysis. The Swiss linguist Saussure changed
linguistic science radically in the early years of the century by
shifting attention from the historical origin of languages (diachronic
analysis) towards the study of language at a single moment in time
(synchronic analysis) as a system governed by rules. Among his
early theoretical discoveries was the realisation that signifiers, the

material forms taken by language, such as sounds or letters, are arbitrary, in the sense that they have no necessary connection with the things to which they refer. This realisation of the gap between signifier and signifier leads him to a second important discovery: that the quality of signifiers which allows them to signify is their *difference* from one another. Language is a rule-governed system which relies for its existence on the irreducible differences between its component elements. The relation, for example, between one brush stroke and another is crucial to the way a painting is made: the same stroke in the same place merely obscures the first stroke. But rough blocks of colour, meaningless in themselves, can take on a meaning when seen in their relations with each other, just as you can see a face in the moon or figures dancing in the flames of a log fire. Advance on your TV screen with a magnifying glass and observe the meaningless flecks of fluorescence: it is their relations – of difference – which allow them to make up a meaningful image. Even a single frame or a split second of noise from the soundtrack will make no sense unless understood in relations of difference to what has gone before and what will follow after. This perception of difference between terms being more important than the (arbitrary) terms themselves should be borne in mind in what follows.

With video, television enters the age of mechanical reproduction. Recently the leading Scottish TV and stage dramatist John McGrath wrote:

> Drama has lost the quintessential quality of television – that of being an event brought to us as a nation simultaneously. Ten years ago, I think television drama was still primarily created as an event specially tailored for the one-off moment of transmission .... This was the quality that made it different from film, and linked it to the heroic unrepeatability of the experience of theatre.
>
> (1985: 52–3)

The aura of live television, the uniqueness, the here-and-now-ness of the broadcast event, is demolished by the use of the VCR, as Jane Feuer observes (1983: 15). Perhaps it is McGrath's name that gives this quote its particular resonance for me: when I was a student and without a TV, I remember persuading a communal household down the street to watch the televisation of one of McGrath's and British television's most significant drama presentations, *The Cheviot, the Stag and the Black, Black Oil*. In a basement crowded with the

commune and their neighbours we watched and then discussed into the small hours. Communal viewing and live TV are contrasted later in McGrath's Edinburgh article with the atomised, 'dead' viewing of video in tones of nostalgia. It is a nostalgia that seems closely related to that of Rousseau and Lévi-Strauss as analysed in Derrida's *Of Grammatology* (1976): timeshifting stands in the same relation to 'live' TV as writing does to speech. What underlies McGrath's nostalgia is the acute perception of the presence, the fullness, the self-sufficiency of the broadcast event. Compared to it, videotape appears belated, fragmenting of the audience, incomplete and unsatisfactory. Liveness in a sense serves to mask the fragmentary nature of television, we might argue in reply: videotape forces back on to broadcast its own incompletion. Transparently recorded, video establishes a new relation with the audience, one that alters, I believe, the way we watch now. Because even if you have forgotten to switch on the timer, there is always someone else who may have, the aura of irreplaceability is eliminated – much as Margaret Morse has argued that the 'action replay' alters the viewer's relation to 'live' sport (1983: 48–9). Through video, TV can cease to be a slave to the metaphysics of presence.

If television's characteristic mode of address is the pretence of dialogue (the ubiquitous 'we' of presenter-speak, the 'Thank you for inviting us into your home tonight'), it is so only because of the metaphysics of presence. Timeshifting obviously alters the viewer's relation to the referent of 'tonight', but also to the complementary particles 'we', 'us', 'you', 'your'. That is the anxiety which video brings to the viewing process: it would be rash to watch a video for company, in the way you might watch TV or listen to the radio. And if Ann Gray's research (1986; 1987a) has uncovered a gendered, guilty viewing of timeshifted tapes among her sample of women viewers in the north of England, surely that may be read as a function of the demise of presence, thus of the contingent quality of 'watching television' as opposed to watching a specific programme, and thus of a complicity between screen and viewer. I return to the issue of guilty viewing below (pp. 41–2).

We now have video to thank for extending the viewing day, freeing viewers from the tyranny of the network schedules, freeze framing, fast forward and reverse vision, the chance to go back and forth in a tape and thence to disturb the diegetic hold of broadcast, the chance to watch in bite-size chunks, and thus for multiplying the available programme formats. But all of these we gain only at the

expense of the gamble of solipsism: videotapes don't talk back. The removal of broadcast's (mendacious?) 'we' is the condition of entering a different relation with the screen, one which places back on the viewer responsibility for the item viewed and for the uses to which it is put. Because it takes issue with the presence of television, it alters the possibilities of identification with the screen, the implied unity of the audience, and even with ourselves.

You cannot watch a video for the first time. Like any recorded medium in Benjamin's age of mechanical reproduction, video shifts out of the ubiquitous present. It makes the present contingent on the replication of the past and the plotting of the future, as timeshifting absorbs the eternal present of TV flow into bite-size chunks, saved for future viewing. Though video finally contains TV as TV could not contain itself (more powerfully even than the way in which TV subsumes film and radio in its insatiable hunger for programme materials), it does so by reproduction, stealing the aura from TV in order to include within itself the property of infinite repetition. In this sense video joins the other recording media not simply as supplementary memories of events and sensations but as the possibility of their replication. So: we have to see in video viewing that it is always already the repetition of a process that has, for the viewer, no origin, no initial presence from which to obtain a guarantee of its own authenticity or presence. This property has become an investment: not only can a series, programme or segment be held for study (removing them from that complex and unstable entity 'television'), they can be held for rescheduling across a variety of distribution media in a way that has fundamentally altered the economics of TV production. The balances of power between institutions, texts and viewers are radically unsettled. *Pace* Andy Lipman (1985: 3), time has shifted.

Video is out of control. The history of video technology (see Armes 1988; Keen 1987) has an intensive relation with surveillance technology and an important military input. Broadcasting began as a telecommunications technology with Marconi's transatlantic 'S' in morse code: but it became subject to struggle over the control of telecoms, and was reduced to a monodirectional medium for the most part. Video's surveillance uses bring with them the property of immediate playback. There is nothing natural or essential about these technological variants: they too are produced in social and cultural contexts characterised by the struggle between end-users and producers. Like many of late capitalism's inventions, they

exceed attempts to control them. In the case of video this has led to the extremely clumsy Video Recordings Act discussed below (Chapter 4), through which government has attempted to make up for the lack of institutional control of the medium by direct legislative intervention. Likewise, the current copyright legislation is in serious disarray. What has happened here, why has video managed to become a familiar domestic cultural form without the usual institutional practices that tend to cluster about such innovations, is perhaps to do with the problem of defining, again, what it is. Hardware manufacturers seem to have carried the day thus far, needing a new commodity to sell into the domestic leisure market as television sales and rentals bottomed out. Now they must struggle with software manufacturers, and with the paternalistic elements of the reproductive process in capital – moral campaigners, the intelligentsia of the ruling faction of the Tory party. But it would be rash to say that video, because it is beyond normal forms of institutional control, is in the sphere of viewer control. Video has made more complex the struggles over media power: it has not healed the wounds or even shifted the balance, except as a production medium. If current moralist discourses have directed attention to the masturbatory functions of video viewing, they have done so consistently through a broader political involvement in the crisis of the family as institution (in line with other Tory policies to place social welfare in the 'private' sector). The VCR has entered as a new factor in a strange and at times almost violent new set of circumstances. As Jeremy Tunstall observes, 'The VCR is not just a wild card: it seems likely to be a rogue that will deal a whole handful of wild cards, which in turn points towards a very chancy game of poker' (1986: 178).

The metaphor of the poker game seems particularly evocative here. John Fiske (1987: chapters 12 and 13) has a useful discussion of the routes through which psychoanalytic approaches to television can be moved from a problematic of pleasure (characteristic of cinema theory) to one of play, which might yet prove more relevant to TV and which, with provisos that will become apparent, I believe to be even more useful for video culture. The theory of pleasure, as it has been developed in film theory, begins to open a door between the public and private spheres, between what emerges from the social and symbolic universes which are our common heritage, and the deeply personal reactions and involvements which we have

with them as individuals. How does the social structure of the game enter into the psychic structure of the player?

Debates on cinematic pleasure are long-running and too complex to enter into in detail here – the reader is referred to Ellis (1982), Fiske (1988) and Laura Mulvey's seminal 1975 essay, 'Visual Pleasure and Narrative Cinema'. None the less, it is important to future arguments to give some kind of resumé of psychoanalytic approaches to cultural studies, approaches which, for all their weaknesses, offer an opportunity to investigate the relations between ideological production 'out there' and their reception 'in here', in the inner life of the viewer.

The psychoanalyst Jacques Lacan uses the metaphor of a mirror to describe the crucial transition between the inchoate world of the infant and the self-aware world of the adult. The child that recognises itself in the mirror for the first time, sees that what is in the mirror is both like itself and yet more so: more clearly defined, apparently better co-ordinated, more distinct. Yet it is itself. Mulvey describes this as 'the beginning of the long love affair/despair between self and image which has found . . . such joyous recognition in the cinema' (1975: 10), since it is the first identification, an identification with oneself, yet one which is cut across by the illusion that you could be better, more than you are; by the splitting of the psyche which that incurs; and by the inevitable sense of loss that comes with the end of that period when we were at one with the world. This range of experience, which remains deeply entrenched in the psyche, the domain of relations to oneself, Lacan calls the Imaginary.

This is the first of a series of splittings which produce the decentred, unstable subjectivity of the adult psyche. Beyond the mirror phase, the subject has to internalise the rules of language and the social from toilet-training to dress codes, table-manners to school discipline, which Lacan calls the Symbolic. The core of linguistic analysis of such systems is, as we have seen, the concept of difference. Lacan argues that the first entry into the Symbolic, the first rules internalised by the child, are the rules and structures of sexual difference. This stage of development is marked in Freudian discourse as the Oedipus Complex and its attendant castration anxiety, enormously powerful emotional upheavals whose legacy can be seen, for example, in the savagery visited by the heterosexual hegemony on gay men and lesbians. The first frightened discovery of the meaning of difference furthers the

splitting begun in the shock of discovering one's separate identity from the rest of the world. But these processes of loss and splitting are essential if we are to become social creatures.

Language is then learnt in the context of a psyche already internally differentiated as well as differentiated from the world beyond. Lacan insists on the separation of ego from the other constituent elements of psychic life: ego (Das Ich in German, the 'I') is the place of the subject *in language*, the route through which the social and the personal can intermingle. Cinematic pleasure is said to engage both the Symbolic and the action of desire, but also, crucially, to invoke that moment before the mirror when the child first became aware of itself as separate from the world and internally divided. Identification, in particular, rests on our Imaginary ability, learnt at that stage, to respond to ideal images, like ourselves but more so, which the star system supplies in such abundance. The problem in the psychoanalytic account derives from a problem in the societies in which it has developed: it is heavily biased towards masculine identity, with women an adjunct: difference emerges in the theory as a power relation in which femininity is the masculine's Other, subordinate and alien. On the other hand, this imbalance makes psychoanalysis an amazing tool for the exploration of patriarchy and male pleasures.

Many recent scholars are moving towards the theory of carnival associated with Mikhail Bakhtin and games or play theory as a way of moving beyond the impasse of sexual difference posited in psychoanalysis, towards a theory which might both account for women's pleasures in the cinema and be more appropriate to the scale and flow of broadcasting. The sense of risk and danger associated with Tunstall's poker game is here moved to the level of subjective relations. Gillian Skirrow's important analysis of video games (1986) throws another wild card into the deal and ups the ante again. Drawing on Bakhtin among others, she raises the question of gender in a particularly male-dominated practice, the arcade and domestic video game. Her approach uses the relatively unfamiliar psychoanalysis of childhood developed by Melanie Klein.

Skirrow's 'Hellivision' argues persuasively that the narrative outlines of video adventure games underpin a player-relation which goes back to infantile fantasies explored by Klein in her analyses of children. For Klein, children's play involves an 'acting out', through which can be read the infant child's symbolic representations of

anxious relations with the mother's body. The child is unable to cope with its own destructive impulses save through a series of symbolisations which allow it to make retribution for its violent wishes, symbolisations which may include fantasies of its own violent destruction. The video game, with its built-in probability of 'death' as a narrative closure, not to mention searching for treasure in underground vaults, replicates these infantile symbolisations of the male.

Like the Lacanians, contemporary heirs of Klein's practice emphasise that sexual difference is internalised by the child in so far as the biological differences of anatomy takes on meaning. The signifiers of sexual difference are no less arbitrary than any other: there is no reason why they should signify a polarity between power and its Other, save that those meanings have been produced in social process. Clearly sexual difference is marked out in our society as a central − some would say *the* central − instance of signification and through signification as an exercise of power. For the analysis of video viewing, the critical factors are desire and anxiety provoked through the establishment of sexual difference.

At the same time, there are intense − and less intense − pleasures to be derived from play, from sanctioned and therefore trivialised games at the edge of darkness. Freud's analysis of the fort-da game, Klein's play-technique and Lacan's remarks on dice, alongside a vast literature on carnival and game-playing, indicate an abiding fascination in play which adults maintain long after childhood. What is most important here is the evidence that the process of socialisation, of subject-ion, is evidently incomplete in most people, and that a relation of struggle emerges within and between individuals in play which, like jokes, carnivals and many forms of sexual activity, rejoices in the transgression of rules, the risk of guilty feelings and/or retribution, excess, risk and danger.

The craft of cultural activity is to tread those boundaries, limits, edges with the mathematical precision of the fetishist. It is such a mode of pleasure which I believe to be in play, precisely, in video viewing: a retreat to a pre-Oedipal relation, prior even to Lacan's mirror phase, in which identity and sexual identity alike are, precisely, in play. It is the sensation of guilt that brings this into play, along with the masturbatory functions of video, Ann Gray's (1986) observations of male power being signified by hanging on to the remote control even when out of the house, and the question of solipsism raised above. Morley's work seems to indicate the use of

the TV *set* as a medium through which family issues are negotiated: video seems more likely to be used for solitary or slightly illicit viewing – by housewives during coffee-breaks, by teenagers late at night – which suggests to me a relation closer to that of the gambler to the game than of the nuclear family round the set. It is the use of the video as an alibi – not a surrogate for company but an alternative to it – for more or less intensively introverted pleasure.

The act of timeshifting a programme off-air is itself fairly insignificant: it is the extraction of time from other duties for this severely undervalued and marginalised activity that adds the frisson of the forbidden to the promise of pleasure. Horkheimer and Adorno suggest that 'The history of civilization is the history of the introversion of sacrifice; in other words, the history of renunciation' (quoted in Michaelson 1986: 111), a formula in which 'civilisation' is to be understood as both western culture and what a child in our society acquires when s/he acquires language and gender. In Kleinian terms, it is the introjection of those destructive impulses which the child could not otherwise support. Perhaps a Kleinian analysis offers the clearest route: these tiny manipulable figures on the video screen can be made to suffer, to repeat, to stand still for minutes on end, to be inspected, judged and spurned. Through video, the predestined and predetermined flow of the outside world, of the televisual Symbolic, of civilisation, can become subject to the subject. As such, they are voided of their 'real' referents and become instead manifestations of internal states. Through video, you can play with yourself, renegotiate the terms the world has imposed through your entry into the social, invoke the time before time was so ineluctably uni-directional, play among signifiers freed, at least partially and for a moment, of the social necessities of signifying something for someone.

Lacan offers a critique of Klein's treatment of Dick, an autistic child, suggesting that the human world is constituted through an interest brought to bear on objects as different from but equivalent to one another and functionally infinite in number: qualities of language. Dick's world is non-human (not pre-human) because he cannot share in these perceptions: his world is non-linguistic. We, however, as adults, cannot return to such a state, nor can we invent one. What we can do, however, is evoke the non-linguistic within 'language' forms, such as videotape, in our viewing, something I believe the modes of illicit viewing I've mentioned encourage. The little rituals that accompany viewing – dousing the lights, collecting

beers and cigarettes at arm's reach, taking the phone off the hook — mark out the time of viewing as one that is removed from the normal organisation of time, a time for oneself, in which the external struggle can be shifted to an internal plane. How such internal work might relate to the cultural politics of carnival is an issue to which we now turn.

Chapter 3

Stars get in your eyes
How music became visible again

Music became invisible in the nineteenth century. This was not at first a technological achievement: it began in the realm of aesthetics, classically in Walter Pater's expression: 'all art constantly aspires to the condition of music' (Pater 1912). From this statement, it seems legitimate to extrapolate that Pater was of the first generation to shut their eyes during a performance, since it is the purity of music, its distance from denotative meanings, its abstraction, to which the other media (as was the case with Greenberg's vision of modernist painting (Greenberg 1983)) aspired. Until then, music had been unthinkable without the presence of the performers. From this principle is derived the possibility of both radio and the gramophone – as sources of musical performance which lay no claim to the eyes. The purity of sound had to be conceptualised before it could be invented as technology.

The 'purity' of music is the condition of its becoming a commodity: before it can be exchanged and consumed under the aegis of capital, music must first be divorced from the moment of its production. The labour of performance has to be subsumed into the autonomous status of an object before it can be understood as product, standing free of the material practice of its production, both steps essential to its circulation as commodity, organised into the forms of communication and profit-making which the social formation of capital demands. The technology of recording emerges only within this nexus of aesthetic and economic determinants in a mutually-facilitating conjuncture. The gramophone and the wireless, as Armes indicates (1988: 12–38), were produced in a period characterised by struggle over the direction of flow of information: both technologies were invested with the possibility of two-directional uses, recording/playback,

broadcast/telecoms. But produced they were, and in a manner which, in Benjamin's analysis, removed the aura characteristic of the unique performance, replacing it with the infinite replicability of mass reproduction.

Residual elements of performance-oriented work remain: Pierre Boulez and Andrew Gerzso have written recently of Boulez's computer-aided composition, *Répons*,

> a tape recorder lacks the suppleness in timing that is so crucial in live concerts. Give and take with the tempo of a piece is one of the basic features of music. Moreover, prerecorded material may also disappoint people who enjoy seeing musicians playing their instruments on stage.
>
> (Boulez and Gerzso 1988: 27)

Musical performance preserves (or, as Jacques Attali (1985) would argue, prefigures) an order in which events are not merely replicable. The contemporary concert tour, however, occupies an ambiguous position in this respect, since it is already the object of its own replications in videos and 'live' albums, so much so that the Grateful Dead reserve a section of their auditoria for home tapers, and Bob Dylan's company documents every tour with a live album as a way of beating the bootleggers at their own game. Concerts, on the massive scale on which they are organised today, lose money unless they generate revenue in areas other than ticket sales.

Given the escalating costs and demands of live performance and the risk of diminishing profits through pirate recordings, it is not surprising that the pioneers of the modern pop video, the Beatles, entered into the filmed-performance and proto-pop video format as an alternative to touring. In this sense we can revert to a formulation of the previous chapter, that video cannot be watched for the first time, and say the same of concert performances: whatever else they may be, they are already the possibility of their reproduction. For example, the use of giant video screens in stadia noted by Steve Connor (1987) pinpoints the relation of performance to its 'immediate' mediation as representation. A related effect seems to be emerging in opera, notably in the big-screen 'live' reproduction of Luciano Pavarotti's performances at Covent Garden outdoors in the Piazza to enthusiastic crowds in the summer of 1987. Ironically, the Boulez piece referred to above as a model of the interrelation of electronic and live effects was commissioned for radio – for an invisible medium, and its later life as the subject of an INA (Institut

National de l'Audiovisuel) video by Robert Cahen foregrounds, not the live quality spoken of by its composer, but the technology of audio and video recording.

However, though there are general qualities to be perceived in the specific mode of circulation of music under capital, there are also many factors involved in both the nature of specific songs and the different ways in which they are consumed: issues of meaning which cannot be subsumed under technical determinants of the means of reproduction. In particular, it has to be insisted that music does have meanings. Trying to uncover a single use-value for music is a chimera, but that there are use-values (plural) is undeniable. These can be generalised as meanings and pleasures, and among the meanings we need to be able to distinguish the referential qualities, for a contemporary western audience, of specific combinations of sound: a nasal reed in a modal scale connotes the Orient, a wurlitzer Blackpool and the old cinema, accordions France and so forth.

Music *video* is heir to both the referential qualities of music and older visual elements of performance and spectacle. Though specific videos recruit images from the musical, it is not usually the cinema which has provided the legacy of techniques that video draws on. There are exceptions: Richard Lester's Beatles films, the *Memo to Turner* sequence in Nic Roeg's *Performance*. Roeg, in particular, plays with the relations of sound and image in the cinema – the usual privileging of image over soundtrack – and with the opposite effect in music: by cutting across the diegesis, breaking down established character traits of the protagonists, turning dramatic and sinister players into humorous dance performers and throwing two plot-lines together in a way which would disrupt the normal functioning of narration, Roeg has the song reorganise, if only temporarily, the nature and status of the fiction. The image is impure compared to the purity of the sound alone: Roeg produces a deliberately impure image track that becomes, unusually for cinema, subordinate to the sound. The song and its meanings dominate the vision track, not as commentary, chorus or spectacle, as in the musical, but as determinant of the visuals.

It cannot be stated often enough that TV originated in radio (Caughie 1984; Poole 1984). Broadcasting is a sound medium with images. Music video, though typically shot on film before being edited on tape, works in the same way, which is why, as a time slot or programme segment, it finds a natural home in the 'segmented flow' of televisual images, sounds and events. At the same time, this

helps to explain the lack of success, aesthetic and financial, of pop video as a programme filler in the cinema, and of 'films' oriented to the video market – Prince's *Under the Cherry Moon*, Culture Club's *Electric Dreams*, the Pet Shop Boys' *Wish You Were Here* – as cinema.

Popular song – and it is typically songs and not instrumentals that have dominated the pop market – is forged in a dialectic between clashing cultures and musical forms: diatonics pushing against modal forms of blues and European folk music, the linear time of melody clashing with the circular time of rhythm, industrial modes of production in conflict with cultural traditions that antedate them, audience demands for a recognisable formula faced with an equal demand for novelty. In these conflicts is the germ of pleasure in listening, the sense that something is in play or at risk, that a note might not be reached, that a melody might not be resolved. The clearest example of this is in improvised music, but in any experience of listening to melody there is a momentary, pleasurable hiatus or tension before we greet a successful resolution to a tune with the sense of satisfaction that accompanies a satisfactory ending to a story. Melody offers a 'narrative' structure of tensions and releases which enact or represent the tensions of teenage growing up or of adult compromise and loss in a resolvable form (and therefore also a fictional one: real life rarely if ever offers such resolution). Song is particularly successful in this respect because it operates a privileged site of identification, and thus a route into the narrative structure, through the amplified singing voice. Just watch a group of people dancing: if they're having a good time, you'll find they are also singing along with the lyric. In singing we are guaranteed a place in the language of song, identifying our 'I' with the singer's 'I'. And yet this can only come about because of the paradoxical absence of the singer from the song and from language, in recorded and also in live performance.

Singing is an activity that traverses one of the boundaries which I discussed in the previous chapter (pp. 29–30): the line between inside and outside of the body. The voice proceeds from the viscera (Barthes 1977: 181–2), is deeply marked as individual as well as by marks of dialect and timbre that denote race, class, gender .... And yet the singer is marked as an absence in the song, a product of the slippage between the presence to language and the presence to self of the singing subject: a familiar demonstration is the way in which we often fail to recognise our own voices played back on tape. Beyond this lies the art of the microphone, which merely

foregrounds this paradoxical relation of presence and absence. The amplified voice promises intimacy, nowhere clearer than in the use of the microphone as an instrument by singers as various as Frank Sinatra, Elvis Presley and Sade. The promise of presence is counterpointed with the actuality of absence, of unattainability which marks the relation as one of glamour, poignancy, the match of love and despair characteristic of the moment of identification.

Like cinematic identifications, singer–listener identifications allow us to enjoy, without responsibility, areas of experience that might perhaps otherwise be forbidden. The act of singing posits an ideal listener, the one true person for whom it is sung, someone who is never us. Such a tension mimics the pleasures of other tensions and paradoxes, allowing both the enjoyment of risk and danger produced as component elements of the song's signification, and for the excess of meaning (*signifiance*) which creates a space for multiple and often contradictory readings. It is in this way that popular song has maintained its commitment, despite its organisation in global capital, to sex, rebellion, freedom and anarchy. At the same time, these are representations of authentic emotion, not unhindered communicative acts transferring emotion unmediated from singer to listener. Of all the musical techniques drawing on these paradoxes, perhaps the most emotive is the fade-out, the failure of narrative closure within the text of the song. Originally forced on engineers by the time limits of the 78 r.p.m. disc, by the time Chuck Berry was recording for Chess in the early 1950s (see Cubitt 1984) it had become an aesthetic device, one which draws us into a vortex of incompletion.

This account of the failure of narrative closure forms a kind of homology with capitalism considered as a social order rooted in the abolition of the past, the plundering of the present and the shifting of gratification into the future. As early as the eighteenth century, Dr Johnson noted in his edition of the plays that 'Shakespeare huddles his endings'. In contemporary 'consumer' capital in particular, narrative, identification and representations of emotion and rebellion are capable of providing both subject positions and the possibility of exceeding them. We need, more precisely, an understanding of the ways in which songs function in broadcasting, playback and the cultural formations of viewers. Following Mandel (1977), two qualities seem to govern the emergence of a fully global capitalism since the Second World War: atomisation and consolidation. Under atomisation I would include: Virilio's

conception of the miniaturisation of labour cited above (p. 12); the cultural evacuation of the ground of history; the multiplication of nodes of power in deregulated cultural markets; and the process of suburbanisation. Characteristic of each of these is their inability to sustain a lasting resolution of contradiction, as witnessed in the fade-out. The cult of the broken, fragmented and jagged image characteristic of the pop video, its reduction of the past to a supermarket for poses and its insistence on removing the present from contact with past or future, each devolve from these conditions, just as its sites of consumption are, most commonly, in domestic living rooms ostensibly removed from the hurly-burly of history and social struggle.

Consolidation draws together apparently opposite but mutual developments: the growth of corporate identity, networking and syndicating as routes to homogenised markets, homogenisation, again, in 'lifestyle' marketing, marginalisation as a new mode of oppression, 'colour-blind' race policy and the concomitant insistence on ethnic absolutism in the construction of national identity (e.g. in the Education Reform Act), the imposition of the monopoly of 'consumer choice', in which market forces and centralisation of state power go hand in hand. An instance: pop videos take their formal positions in the segmented flow of broadcasting on the same terms as news. Like news, pop on TV relies on novelty, on the elimination of analysis in favour of sensation, on the dominance of the soundtrack over the images (one bombed city, one guerrilla, is much like another till we learn that they are Beirut or Belfast, terrorists or freedom-fighters). Eye-contact is a crucial mode of address for both. Like news events, pop acts are criticised for preparing themselves for the camera, for using the media, for irrationality and abnormality – the very qualities that make them newsworthy. 'Sexy' is a term applied commonly to news stories and videos. Like news, pop TV uses the mechanism of marginalisation to void the present of its historical formation, to indicate the boundaries within which normality can be expected to continue to perform in the indefinite present, to homogenise. Alternatively: everybody has a different living room, but they are all living rooms.

If modernism was the culture of the cities, postmodernism is the culture of suburbia. I use the term 'postmodern' to describe, loosely, the cultural formations of the 1980s, as opposed to the cultures of, in particular, the first half of this century, though I am by no means

as convinced of an absolute disjuncture between the two as some commentators. Perhaps the most characteristic cultural form of the modernist period is the cinema – not film as such, but the mass audiences for communally-viewed films in places of public entertainment. The recurring obsession of modernist artists was the crowd. The era of mass strikes and demonstrations, of revolutionary communism, of the battle for the streets among fascists, anarchists and socialists, was also the era of mass entertainment and recreation in spectator sports, cinemas, concert halls and ballrooms. Postmodernism is characterised by the domestic consumption of leisure, a process of suburbanisation often incorrectly read as embourgeoisement, the marketing of Victorian middle-class domesticity to the mass of the people.

The 'mass' audience delivered by broadcasting is a mass in the sense that, from the broadcasters' point of view, it is differentiated only by its spending patterns, but it is no longer a mass audience in the sense of something that could be seen, participated in, enjoyed for its sociality. With falling gates at spectator sports, rock concerts are almost the last bastion of mass entertainment. Like carnival, football has become more known for its policing than for its cultural aspirations: while there are still moral panics over rock culture – the most recent over acid house – the rock concert has escaped the worst of that policing in the UK, most visibly perhaps through its participation in unificatory events like Live-Aid. Yet elements of carnival, with the dangerous permissions to riot which it entails, remain in the culture. The problem for pop video, indeed for video culture as a whole, is that carnival is the defining instance of the urban crowd. Yet video must work, especially as a domestic medium, in a world in which crowds are no longer an inspiration but an object of fear: the culture of suburbia.

One quality which marks off the experience of the suburbs from that of the city is the possibility of excluding 'alien' cultures from the purposes of the built environment. One of the most significant absences of MTV, the North American cable station devoted to pop (certainly through 1985 when I last watched it), was that of Black musicians. Certain artists do emerge – Michael Jackson, Tina Turner, Aretha Franklin, the Pointer Sisters – as Kaplan (1987) notes. It might also be noted that these stars are among those who most successfully approximate mainstream white forms. The histories lurking behind these artists are those of Quincy Jones, widely in demand with film and TV companies, Allen Toussaint,

hit-maker since the days of 'Ain't Got a Home', Tina Turner's return to performance since her work with British group Heaven 17, Aretha Franklin's position as Queen of Soul refocused by her association with George Michael and the Eurythmics. What is not being addressed, with the rare exception of occasional cross-over hits, is the product of Black urban America. The North American 'Academy of Video Arts' annual award ceremony has changed the title of the award for Black artist of the year three times in five years, landing up in 1988 with the term 'Urban Video'. This would indicate that we could generalise from Davis's (1987) argument that there are two kinds of city within the geographical boundaries of Los Angeles, the postmodern city of the sprawl and the Third World, modernist cities of downtown still characterised by cultures lived, not in domestic units, but in public, on the street.

For MTV, the existence of a culture of the mass is deeply problematic, since it questions the fundamental mode of its distribution and consumption. The domestic, rather than the mass, is the given on which MTV predicates its signification as well as its business practices. Its racism is not a simple prejudice but a product of a struggle over the mode of circulation of meanings in the suburban, atomised and monopoly-dominated model of cultural formation. British pop TV is somewhat more eclectic, but the pop video market is as much a prisoner of this kind of marginalisation as the US cable system. Its racism does not deal with race as a skin colour: it is a political relation, a relation of power and exclusion. Kaplan and most commentators on MTV don't look to the possibility of mass cable or broadcast delivery of music cultures already deeply embedded in North America, such as salsa, let alone the marginalised cultures of Europe and North America: no flamenco, no Celtic music, nothing from Quebec, from the working-class women singer-songwriters of the south, no native American music (though see Fenster (1988) and Easley and Rabinovitz (1988) for accounts of specialist Country and Western and salsa stations respectively). There are no representatives at all in the States, and precious few in the UK, of the diverse musics of the southern hemisphere. (Although the market breakthrough of world music in the UK has had some effects on broadcast pop, it has yet to reach pop video markets.) Consolidation of 'rock' as generic means the consistent marginalisation or occlusion of cultural forms that might effectively question the Anglo-American cultural domination not only of the recorded music markets, but also of the terms in which

such markets define their consumers. The emergence of a market for
world music appears as an addition to the mainstream rock or pop
markets, no more and no less important than the jazz, folk or soul
markets with which it overlaps.

These motions of capital – atomisation and consolidation –
constitute undoubtedly the terms on which we will have to develop
our futures. They can be sung uncritically, as they are by both the
lunatic fringes of the right-wing parties in power in the US and the
UK, and the nominally 'Labour' government of Australia. For
example, the enormous world-wide drive towards deregulated
media markets, in a move from paternalist models of public
broadcasting to intensively centralised but free-standing
transnationals, combines the consolidation of power and capital
with an ideology of multiplication of consumer choice through
intensification of domestic technologies. The same movements can
be criticised, but it is an inadequate critique which works from the
nostalgic, mythic humanism of the paternalist state, as is the case
with the British Labour Party: a backward-looking and ultimately
reactionary critique. We need to begin from a standpoint in which
the present is not an inevitable and indefinitely extensible moment,
in which the past is not canonised but analysed for the roots of the
current historical conjuncture and for reasons and routes for
changing it. In its celebration of an eternal present, pop video
colludes in the exercise of power by ruling elites on an increasingly
global scale. Instead, armed with a critical understanding of the past,
we need to work on theses concerning the future as a field of
possibilities which pop video, among other forms as presently
constituted, either denies or modulates into forms which can be
marginalised.

These exclusions and modulations tell us about the nature of the
audience which pop television and the music video aim to capitalise
– an audience with spending power, an audience with access to
cable, a middle-class audience. Within these parameters, such an
audience may well represent a homogeneous market. The genre
conventions categorised by Kaplan (1987: 55) do not do justice to
the smoothing out, not to say denial, of difference in the flow of
music television: as idealist categories, they fail either to account for
the formal workings of pastiche as a compositional mode or the
industrial production of novelty as a major institutional signifying
practice in pop video. Similarly, the celebration of 'style' in Fiske's
account of music video (1987: 250–5) omits an account of what is

absented from the world of the televisual: an elision of difference which, in some respects, produces the homogeneous culture on which it premises itself. A brief foray into art history may illuminate this problem.

Andreas Huyssen (1987) begins to indicate the importance of Andy Warhol's work in the relations of high and low culture. Signifiers of a signifier (silk-screens of a photograph), the serial Marilyn Monroe portraits centre on their reproductivity more even than the work of Norman Rockwell. As illustrator, Rockwell plays on the reproducibility of his paintings, in the main designed for magazine reproduction: in *The Connoisseur* he reproduces a Pollock canvas with, in the foreground, the photo-realist figure of an art collector peering earnestly into the canvas. The composition, contrasting the represented Pollock canvas with the symmetry of the frame within the frame, the parquet flooring and the almost military bearing of the connoisseur, pastiches the artist-as-wildman ethos of abstract expressionism, just as the *Triple Self-portrait* of 1956 jokingly plays on postcard reproductions of the great self-portraits (Rembrandt, Durer, Picasso) as reproduced by Rockwell for further reproduction as cover-art for the *Saturday Evening Post*. Like Rockwell, but with the higher seriousness of an ex-commercial artist, Warhol boasts the vacuity of his images in the same breath as asserting their commodity function, equal to all other commodities – 'All is pretty', 'Everyone will be famous for 15 minutes'. Not profundity or challenge but superficiality and cleverness, not technique but technics. Of all things, Warhol's studio, 'The Factory', despised, and in its despising hid its fear of, passion. It is the celebration of celibacy, the carnival of the minimal, the style obsession of suburban culture. In this instance, art prefigured economics: in our era, the trading of shares takes precedence over the creation of wealth – as witness (since we are speaking of cans) the space between the Bolivian or Cornish tin-mines and the traded options in tin futures which crashed on the metals exchange in 1985. The reality of tin-mining is voided from its commodity status. Warhol just got there first.

There is a limit to the subversive effects claimed for the textual disruptions praised by many commentators (Chambers 1986; Fiske 1987; Kaplan 1987) in pop video. In particular pop belongs, however uneasily, in the domestic mode of consumption in which the flow takes precedence over the individual 'text', the overall discourse over the utterances of which it is made up. That discourse

in turn is subject to the overdeterminations of the politics of living room power. With its particular address to the 'young', pop video plays to a set of concerns which sit uneasily in the family circle: it speaks to the sexually active (or would-be sexually active) in a site where such activity is forbidden. It centres on star images derived from the role of the singing voice in recorded music outlined above (pp. 47–8) but adding a new dimension of spectacle to the possibilities of identification. It speaks often of community as an alternative to family – the community of the studio audience, of the young, of youth cultures, of rebellion . . . . It speaks to adolescents of the torments of adolescence in front of their parents. There is a politics of embarrassment around pop on television, one which the video deck offers to anneal. Parents are too firmly anchored in their identities to share the problems of fine-tuning the personality which is the basis of teen angst. The VCR has the capacity to atomise cultural consumption *within* the family, removing those vital signifiers of hope, role models in the *Top of the Pops* studio, from the searching and unanswerable critique of parents.

Certainly there is an argument to be made that MTV actively seeks to produce and/or reproduce homogeneity as a reality-effect, precisely by evaporating images of their content, subordinating them in a hierarchy of modes of address in which record sales are the overarching and absent principle. Music video makes all things visible (Grossberg (1988: 321) can even speak of 'the eighties, when no image is forbidden'), yet there is a hierarchy, witnessed, for example, in the economically-derived prominence of the star image – even in the *absence* of the star, as in Michael Jackson's *Bad*. At the same time, the analysis either of style as surface without depth, or of marketing motives as the core of the music business, is inadequate to the understanding of meaning-production among video viewers. Madonna acts in this context as an important example for many commentators on pop video, especially as it relates to the culture of adolescent girls. Describing her *Papa Don't Preach* video, Kaplan writes:

> As the video's rapid and broad success suggests, Madonna has here touched on issues confronting many teenagers today, particularly those in the lower classes, which her video (set as it is in a section of New Jersey facing New York City's skyline) obviously addresses.
>
> (1987: 132)

This reading seems to miss much of the complexity of the viewer relation to the 'mature' image of Madonna. The representation of a working-class milieu does not imply an address to the working class. My own reading is that the address is to the wealthy child, toying with the adventurousness of being street-wise, just as her shift from jumble-sale chic to designer corsetry signals a shift from identification with what Kaplan identifies as 'bordello Queen/bag lady' to a kitsch expropriation of working-class modes of expression. The same problematic emerges in *Desperately Seeking Susan*, in which Madonna's character arrives in New York on a bus called 'Freedom' and tells a colleague she hasn't died, just been to New Jersey. Her opposite number in the film is, precisely, a New Jersey bourgeoise longing for the imagined freedom of the street life.

The issue of 'rapid and broad success' needs to be raised as a question: how do we gauge the 'success' of a video? Aesthetically? In terms of record sales? Sales of striped T-shirts? If representation cannot be identified with address, nor can address be identified with reading. Yet this account has almost become a truism of cultural studies vision of Madonna. Judith Williamson writes 'She does in public what most girls do in private, like a little girl in an adult world with no one to say "No". This gives an enormous sense of released energy, which is itself positive' (1986: 47). Fiske quotes this approvingly before going on to write

> Combining the crucifix with the signs of pornography is a carnivalesque profanity, but the new combination does not 'mean' anything specific, all it signifies is her power over discourse, her ability to use the already written signifiers of patriarchal Christianity, and to tear them away from their signifieds is a moment of empowerment.
>
> (1987: 252–3)

What each of these descriptions fails to do is to point out the gap between the act and its representation, imbuing a two-dimensional image with the attributes of a human being. Thus, apparently, they allow a special transparency of the TV screen in girls' culture that exists nowhere else in televisual discourse, an immediacy of signification and a generosity of identification which are otherwise always analysed in terms of their framing, ideological formations, constructions and so on. Their enthusiasm is infectious, but it is essential to recognise that it is not carnival but the representation of carnival that is at stake in pop video.

Fiske in particular loads into the music video all the meanings and functions which might, optimistically, be associated with carnival. For him, carnival is not only the licensed outrages of a special – usually brief – season, but the trace of enduring popular oppositional and disruptive forces. But since historically there is no TV discourse that recognises this abiding strength, he is constrained to argue that

> In the postmodern world, style performs many of the functions of carnival. It is essentially liberating, acting as an empowering language for the subordinate. Its similarities to carnival lie in its insistence on the materiality of the signifier, in its excessiveness, its ability to offend good taste (bourgeois taste).... Style is a recycling of images that wrenches them out of the original context that enabled them to make sense and reduces them to free-floating signifiers whose only signification is that they are free, outside the control of normal sense and sense-making, and thus able to enter the world of pleasure where their materiality can work directly on the sensual eye, running the boundary between culture and nature, between ideology and its absence.
>
> (Fiske 1987: 249–50)

In turn, this allows Fiske to remove the image of Madonna from the voyeuristic mechanisms of the patriarchal gaze, a wonderfully cheerful analysis which misses entirely the production of visibility, the signification for someone which her display, lyrics, marketing and photography clearly involves. Surely Madonna's more recent persona is to be read as an attempt to emerge from the impasse of the DIY sexuality: in particular her recent videos work on the mythic reconciliation of socially-constructed and individually-invented sexuality, through the contradictions of self-presentation in a cultural mode, the music video, which is more capable than any other of assimilating the disruptive into itself. Madonna's videos do not subvert bourgeois taste, they reconfirm it by tinkering at the edges of the permissible: with kitsch, which I understand to be the parodic modulation of the Oriental, the alien, the ugly (the Other) into the cute, the patronised, the homogeneous (the Same). What is in operation here is the containment of the potential of populist disruption, not its irruption into an unwilling system. The excess of personalities in the process of becoming – identified by Williamson (1986) as the lure of Madonna – is traded in for an excess of signifiers of wealth: Bacardis, yachts and jewellery. The

metaphysics of presence returns via the star system.

Benjamin's (1969) description of the disappearance of aura is incomplete unless we see that in some way it returns in the star system: the mythical application of that engagement with an original returns, attached to the figure, in this context, of the singer. Singled out for identification, but also for homo- as well as heteroerotic and narcissistic pleasures, the star takes on the role of originator of the work, the absent centre of its production, the core of the economy of desire established in the tape or the body of work mapped out by the artist as *auteur*. Like the singing voice on record, the singer's face, body and movements appear as the originating presence of the video – even in a tape in which the singer doesn't appear as such: the all-seeing sexual eye of Duran Duran's *The Chauffeur* for example. It is only in politicised strategies, like those adopted by Cabaret Voltaire, that the rigorous search for origin is meticulously played back to the viewer, in the disruption of star as author, as an obsession without end, one produced and reproduced in the video. Generally, though not exclusively, stars also serve to hide the act of production of the tape, precisely because they serve as ego-ideals in whom, to all appearances, the struggle of becoming has never taken place, and for whom personality, style and identity are unitary, solid, given, unchallenged.

Angela MacRobbie's work on girls' culture (1977) suggests that between childhood and being an adult lies a space in which alternative options on socialisation can be explored, in particular the development of community in a variety of guises. TV's constant address to its audience as a community, pop video's constant representation of community as an alternative to either romance or parental authority and the link through to subcultural identifications all suggest that a Bakhtinian dialogic reading has an important part to play. In particular, there seems to be a dialectic at play between carnivalesque postponement of assuming individuality and the narcissistic identification with stars which offers an illusory achievement of individuality. It is this dialectic which is mobilised in late capitalist cultural formations as a vehicle for more complex negotiations of the interdependence of individual and community, though both terms are deeply troubled, even to the point of absence, in the decentred subject and atomised city of contemporary suburbia.

It is interesting to note that both Fiske (1988: 231) and Kaplan (1987: 94) refer to the fort-da game, both in contexts of discussions

of pleasure, neither in the Freudian context of the repetition compulsion, with its conclusion that there exists a mental function 'whose business it is to free the mental apparatus entirely from excitation or to keep the amount of excitation in it constant or to keep it as low as possible' (Freud 1961: 56). Heavy rotation, the repetitive use of individual tapes in programme flow, not only points to the prehistory of MTV as pop radio programming done with the distracted attention of the audience in mind; it also indicates a shift between broadcast and cable which we can illuminate further through looking at VCR playback. TV poses the moment as irreplaceable, as 'live' and therefore subject to irreversible fading. Cable and satellite channels put tapes into heavy rotation (play-lists of tapes to be shown most frequently), thus inventing a cyclical time far more insistent than the seasonal schedules of television. Apart from the occasional seasonal novelty hit – and the term 'novelty' gives the game away here – MTV and similar formats break with the polite fiction that there is a link between TV schedules and the rural calendars of a bygone age. Closing the circle of time in the rotation of floating, history-less signifiers may solve a major philosophical problem faced by 'postmodernist' critiques of cultural theory: the teleological problem of basing historical analysis, including analysis of the present, on an Ideal moment, present or future, by which preceding moments can be judged. But it does so only at the expense, however circumscribed, of cultural–political action. Such a critique is all too easy in a society in which modernism – if anything at all, a series of strategies for coping with the novelty of urban life – gives way to the ahistorical culture of suburbia. Postmodern celebration of the eternally-cycling present represents and colludes in that ahistoricism: it does not critique it.

Video deletes both scheduling and rotation. In their place it offers repetition as radical alterity: that which can be repeated is already history. Timeshifting (the most poetic word to enter the English language in the last twenty years), fast-forward, vision-rewind and freeze-framing reintroduce television to the qualities of writing ('the disappearance of natural presence' (Derrida 1976: 159)). But after the metaphysics of presence that underpins the liveness of broadcasting, after the closed organisation of time on satellite and cable with its promise of being always there (if not always here), video has no such guarantees. Video poses its difference as the potential for silence.

The most emotional telephone calls, to return to my earlier metaphor, are the ones that contain the most silence: 'Are you still there?' The telephone gives no guarantee that you will be answered. There is that vertiginous feeling of a conversation going on in the void, out of which, from time to time perhaps, the speech of another arises. Television guarantees an answer, but without dialogue it is also without the sense of risk that the telephone can engender. Video, freed of the ontology of the 'live', reintroduces the risk that there might be no one out there after all, that no voice, no friendly eye-contact, will thank you 'for inviting us into your home'. Video reintroduces the possibility of silence into the electronic media – not the representations of silence that you get, so movingly sometimes, in the cinema, where it is a silence communally experienced, a silence in the film but not of it (for film, silence is a sound effect). Cinematic silence is a presence, video silence an absence, a breakdown in that most garrulous of all media, television: like the forlorn 'Do not adjust your set' message, pathetic as a message in a bottle. Video silence puts speech at risk and puts its radical absence into play. By these tokens, by the offer of the blank and silent screen, it has the capacity to challenge television's replacement of dialogue with chat, its representation. As a result it challenges also the dominance of narration over diegesis, since video viewing is unconstrained by voice-overs and the order of images imposed by broadcast. Likewise video disturbs the processes of identification – how can you identify with the 'do not adjust' message, with the person who has not answered the phone, with alterity? – questions, through shifting time, the very grounds of dialogue, the presence to itself and to the viewer of the programme.

Video's narratives play out an anxious scenario in which the teller of the tale, the Other of the telephone call, isn't there to guarantee the fullness of the speech. Video's potentiality for producing silence feeds the solipsism of capitalist individualism and disrupts, even as it tries to ensure, identification with the singing voice. The horizontal space between screen and speaker, unlike cinema's carefully created illusion of depth through the siting of speakers behind or in stereophony around the screen, helps to disrupt the unity of sound and image in a way that even playing video sound through a hi-fi system fails to remedy completely. Here is none of the suturing effect of cinema, the invitation to enter the fictional space of the image. The glass screen, and its role as light source in

the living room competing with other light sources, seems to offer a relation to, not a relation within, the image; yet the provenance and presence of the image to itself and the viewer is never complete, throwing the viewer back on to his/her own devices. The video viewer runs the constant risk of solipsism, of an irreducibly self-directed relationship, the narcissism of the infant convinced of its omnipotence and its oneness with the world risking becoming a closed circuit. But without running this constant risk, there is no possibility of sociality or dialogue. Without the condition zero of the lone and self-reflexive viewer, there is no possibility of plurality; no communication without isolation. Video is that profoundly dialectical medium which pits the viewer *against* the world of discourse in order to reach a new mode of community.

Does the focus on Madonna as high-priestess of post-feminist postmodernism perhaps engage something of this relation? Fiske, in this connection, speaks of the carnivalesque 'style' as a liberating effect: 'The subordinate, in a reversal of incorporation, steal the discourse of the dominant and use its signifiers for their own pleasures, their own identities' (1988: 253–4). I remain sceptical as to whether incorporation is actually being reversed here: or whether, in fact, the opposite is still not at least equally the case – that through the commodification of Madonna as image, 'wannabe's' are being imbricated into the social reproduction of femininity under the alibi of Madonna's apparent control over her representations. It concerns a possible confusion between star, star image and the practices surrounding viewing: Madonna not as image but as practice, a point of departure from which to emerge into a *different* space is an attractive, but, I fear, unduly utopian reading precisely because it remains a *reading*, implicated as a reading in the replication of sameness, unable to differentiate between textual production and social effects of meaning. While Fiske works hard towards a two-way model of TV culture, he is still a crucial step away from music and video, not as texts for consumption but as sites for action, performance, making. Williamson's image of the teenage girl dancing for herself in the mirror prior to the enforced advent of womanhood seems to be closer to the point I want to make – the centrality of the relation to self of the viewer in the video relation.

Capital requires the active participation of its subjects in the cultural reproduction of their subject positions. However, it must at the same time produce the means of reproduction – including

camcorders, VCRs and tape – all of which absolutely require active subjects. It is the absolute in this imperative which creates the contradiction: individually we are all maladjusted. We cannot be trusted with reproducing ourselves culturally – whence the necessity of policing – and yet cultural industries rely on the origination of new product from inadequately 'socialised' sectors, which means that they must both take the risk and develop methods for containing aberrant productions. In particular the commodity form, as analysed by Marx, serves to reify cultural production, to turn a process engaging social relations into a thing to which viewers are asked to relate, as a preliminary step towards control in the viewing act. The challenge to pop video is less how to get 'better' product than how to produce new modes of distribution and engagement beyond the commodity relation.

There is a mode of cultural policing which operates on a fear that music video curtails the range of associations that a song can evoke, restricting the breadth of operation of imagination in a paradoxical motion, through which the addition of image to sound is seen as an effective diminution of individual engagement and action. As in Derrida's description of the role of writing, in which the supplementary role of the written is taken to be a painful abstraction from the fullness of the spoken word, music video's insistence on the visual elements of music is read as a denigration of the magical role of music as a feeder – and to some extent a guarantor – of the individual's imagination. In many instances the video is offered as an apparent anchor for the meaning of the song, but there is a startling quality of language, including video and music, which asserts that the attempt to anchor meaning by supplementing additional codes to the initial message is doomed to multiplying the possible routes of interpretation, rather than narrowing them.

TV, we know, does not so much describe as add itself to the real: to sport, drama, cinema, news events, theatre, light entertainment and to song. Pop video specifically adds itself to the discourses of youth, supplementing both the language youth uses to speak of itself and the language deployed around youth as a problem. It is characteristic of the dialectic of capital that it would produce two discourses: a speech from and a speech to/about the Other which it has itself consecrated – youth as category of existence. On the one hand, the discovery of puberty is articulated – in the sense that an articulated lorry is articulated – with the discovery of sexism and injustice, in such a way that in later discourses of adulthood the cry

against injustice can therefore be easily dismissed as merely a stage in the process of growing up. On the other hand, paternalistic discourses of education, ambition, sowing wild oats are simultaneously tipped upside down – especially education, a constant target for satire – and earnestly embedded in the discourse. Ambition is peculiarly situated in the mode of video which deals in wealth, from Ultravox's *Vienna* to Madonna's *Material Girl*: ludicrously overblown images of wealth and power at once satirise and glamorise the imaginary world of the wealthy. This is not so much ambiguity as having your cake and eating it.

The one factor which is elsewhere predominant in discourses of youth, indeed virtually all narrative formations in contemporary society, the family, is everywhere absent in pop music, except in the form of the wedding. But weddings – representations of weddings – are narrative figures, elements of a rhetoric of storytelling rather than flesh and blood events. Angela MacRobbie (1977) argues for a consideration of the space between the 'family of origin', from which the youth departs, and the 'family of destiny' posited in the romantic discourses pitched at the teenage market, the family into which they will grow through the procedures of love and its narrative trope, marriage. It is not pushing too hard, I think, to envision this phase as a liminal one, a threshold between two states which, momentarily, shares neither of their presuppositions. Pop music has continually played to and on that liminal phase, its potency, its urgency, its anger, its anxiety, its unsettled and unsettling sexualities, its willingness to re-evaluate all values, its nihilism and its optimism.

The problem for broadcasters is not that pop video pins meaning down too definitely: it is that it must, under the kinds of guidelines and legislation operating in most if not all western states, try as much as possible not to show what songs are about. Sexual anxiety, growing pains, violent fantasies, Oedipal trauma – none of these things are permissible or desirable in broadcasting, and are illegal on video in the United Kingdom. Yet alongside the careful targeting of the adolescent market, some consensual, hegemonic operation must be carried out if the vital youth audience, with its important present purchasing power, is to be delivered to advertisers as also future purchasers. Youth must be targeted in its rebelliousness, but within an overall system which maintains itself and their future roles in it. Pop video must at once follow the music with its appeal to excess and transgression, while at the same time ensuring that such

carnivalesque improprieties remain safely on the inside of the cathode ray tube. Hence both the fascination and the constant disappointment of music video: generically we expect it to deliver; in the specific instance it almost never does.

The repertoire of effects deployed in music video, not so much in the individual tape but in the expectations raised by the discourse of pop video, are effects supposed to lure the youth audience, a response to the necessity to produce excess as pop itself produces it. For instance, teen narcissism can be addressed and engaged through a series of strategies, among them parody, achieved narcissistic identification, multiple role-models, images of the star as power-centre (e.g. in performance videos stressing audience adulation, or tapes like Billy Idol's *Rebel Yell*), images of the star as centre of interlocking networks of desire, or again star as agent of a refusal of desire and power in the figure of the loner. This is not an exhaustive list, and its constituent elements are not mutually exclusive. In their turn, such elements bleed across into other lists in the rhetoric of affects: sexy images, usually built out of nostalgic and paternalistic notions of what constitutes 'sexy'; images of rebellion and violence; images drawing on the shallowness of daily life to produce a mysticised need for depth in some poetic/religious form. However, these are all elements of a rhetoric: pop video cannot *be* sexy, narcissistic, violent or rebellious – it can only *represent* glamour, eros and anarchy.

None the less, within that nexus, I have tried to indicate that there is a special role to be played in video viewing between the narcissistic position and the function of community as, in turn, a mode of the carnivalesque. I will explore this theme further in chapters on artists' video and campaigning uses of the medium (Chapters 5, 6 and 7). Here it needs to be said that the options open to music video are strictly limited by the terms of playback, even when playback is instantaneous and on the grand scale, as at stadium concerts. The premium is still participation in the community of pop via a gamble on the solipsism of video, channelled in dominant forms by an encouragement to participate in the production of the star performance. The gamble is always the attraction: the knowledge that we will usually lose is the risk; the principle that we still could win is the lure – as in the hunter's and the psychoanalyst's vocabularies, the lure is a decoy, one that definitely exists (therefore not unreal) but which is not what we *really* wanted. There is all the difference in the world between the

genuine passions which this dialectic invokes and the impoverished and impoverishing ideological packaging in which it is inevitably embroiled, to such an extent that it is impossible to extricate the passion from the wrapping.

Part of the problem lies in the conceptualisation of 'youth' as an audience. Clearly young people are as riven by class, race, gender, sexuality, disability . . . as the rest of society: sharing a birth-year does not make for common ground. Dick Hebdige (1983) offers a useful history of the anthropological conceptualising of youth, from Mayhew's investigations of darkest London in the 1850s to the documentation of subcultures in the academies and the style magazines of the 1980s. From sociological surveillance to the market researchers of today (a transition most clearly marked in the history of Mass Observation, originally a unique attempt to document the life of the working class, now a commercial research outfit), youth remains typically without a place from which it might speak with its own voice.

Of course, within the narrative which guides our understandings, the discourse of pop always produces positions from which the appearance of authentic speech is made: positions marked as 'John Lennon', 'David Bowie', 'Bruce Springsteen' or 'Madonna', for example. Or alternatively, authenticity − fullness of speech − is marked as a specific style, sometimes even a specific moment in the history of a style, as in current reportage of acid house; often marked by race, occasionally by gender, frequently, in recurring cycles, by proximity to 'folk' roots. This is partly a reaction against the perceived capitalising on a cross-over act (Aswad, Ruben Blades and Papa Wemba are recent subjects of such critiques as they attempt to break out from devoted cult followings to the mass market), in which the loyalty of fans needs to be repaid by an equal loyalty on the part of performers in a subcultural contract which guarantees, precisely, the authenticity of the voice as one that can be identified with, *viz.* one which accepts its part in the contract between individual and community. With the video, though, authenticity of this kind is impossible. There is only the star as anchor: and not even the star − only a representation, a mediation, in which the immediacy of authentic and full speech is manifestly not there. The video echoes and re-echoes the absence of that full dialectic: that is why it can so fully articulate the dialectic of community and *solipsistic* individual, the voice that doesn't speak at the end of the telephone line.

Chapter 4

Box pop

The conclusion of the last chapter suggests an anxious dialectic of solipsism and carnival. In this chapter I want to move further into these issues. To do so, and to take some responsibility for a method which centres on the process of reading rather than on the textuality of the tapes, I will be using myself as a guinea pig, trying to watch the details of my own enjoyment and dislikes. At the same time, the rapid turnover of tapes (and the probable gap between writing and reading) makes an appreciation of the way in which tapes traverse biography not only desirable but ineluctable. That intrusive and disturbed word 'I' derives, in this usage, from a greater writer covering a related field: 'This *I*, nicely accused of impertinence in many cases, implies however a great modesty; it encloses the writer within the strictest limits of sincerity' (Charles Baudelaire's essay on 'Richard Wagner and *Tannhäuser*' (1861), in Baudelaire 1968: 267). My aim is to read from the uses of videos their position in the process of making meaning: like Yeats at the close of his search for images, such an analysis must begin 'where all ladders start,/ In the foul rag-and-bone shop of the heart' (Yeats, 'The Circus Animals' Desertion' (1939), 1950: 392).

At its best, pop video dives straight into this fearful dialectic and uses it as a space to party in. The tape for George Clinton's *Do Fries Go With That Shake* has been a personal favourite since first sighted in an otherwise sleepy Brixton pub one Saturday evening. This tape plays on the kind of carnival of excess. Clinton is the overweight short-order cook enamoured of the girls he has met the night before. The boss is a glamorous woman in black with a magic mirror which she asks 'Who is the fairest of them all?' Discovering her place usurped by the (also big) Fly Girls, she puts rat poison in the salt shaker used by Clinton to prepare the Girls' fries. Among

the outrageous costumes and food-fights, singing buns and grotesquely coloured food, one of the Girls goes into a psychedelic dream, from which she is awakened with a kiss by our hero. Apart from the cartoon graphics, cheap computer effects, quotes from photo-romances and visual gags, what I always like about this tape is the way that 'sexy' is equated with big. This promise of sex has everything to do with body-hair, grunting and funk, one of whose meanings is precisely sweat.

Showing this tape to a day school on gender, I was brought up sharp for suggesting that the equation of sex and food, and of both with the devalued forms of each (junk food, sweaty sex) as mess or dirt (psychoanalysis might want to add shit: in context, I didn't), was fun because it demonstrated a healthy disrespect for the correct functions of things. At the same time, I argued, while playing on stereotypical images of male desire, it both frustrates its operation (in the dream sequence, what threatens to become a wet tee-shirt/ mud wrestling bout at the bottom of a milk shake becomes a perilous moment in the fairy-tale narrative as the witch-figure starts to drink them up) and deflates it through parody, both in the figure of the unmanned man (the wally, the nerd, a type of masculine representation as common in the mass media, if not more so, than the macho, here worked through in the interestingly positive light of fairy-tale) and in the equation of food and sex ('B-b-b-b-b-b-buns'). In particular, I was enthusiastic about the move away from the deodorised, ethereal, unreal, disembodied and passionless sexuality of the sex toys, male and female, generally paraded for adolescent male consumption in pop's visual discourses.

What I presumed I had ignored was the strength of feeling among the women attending the school concerning the representation of women – any women – as sexual beings, since any such representation was almost inevitably generated within patriarchal discourses and as such must necessarily reproduce sexist values. Certainly there was a degree of such feeling in the room – a revolt against the status of women as signifiers circulated by men within a patriarchally organised Symbolic domain from which they were therefore denied access. In the wake of 1968's foregrounding of the political importance of cultural struggle it was the women's movement (and to an important extent the Gay Liberation Front, but with less widespread effect) which maintained that cultural struggle at the forefront of their concerns. I had thought that the carnivalesque intrusion into and questioning of sexual identity

which I was cheerfully reading from the tape would come across as a serious choice in opposition to the stranglehold of imposed socio-cultural individuality, and lead the way towards an understanding of some form of pan-sexuality as a possible future mode of activity.

My reading of the audience was that they were refusing a model of fluidity and process, a vision of sexuality in the carnival as superfluous, unbounded, as ready to take a milk shake as object as it is to take another human. I felt that they were clinging to a binary model of sexuality whose ultimate terms of reference are to genital – biologically given – difference: there is male and there is female, irredeemably different. To have one kind of body is automatically to partake in the gendered structures of power that characterise our society (see Merck 1987: 7). I was ready to assert, with Derrida, the irreducibility of difference as a founding relation. Difference antedates those elements which it will be taken to differentiate: social systems demand difference, but they do not specify difference between what terms, which is why the war between those who open their eggs at the little end and those who prefer the big in *Gulliver's Travels* rings so true. The second step is to assert, with Barthes, that the multiplication of difference upon difference – just as, in counting, the great step is to get from 0 to 1, after which 2, 3 and 4 are a cinch – produces a far vaster range of possible modes of relation than the initial binary opposition. Sexual difference cannot be denied, but it needs to be multiplied beyond the oppressive regularities of the male/female duality.

This allows an escape from the impasse noted by Andrew Britton in which insistence on the givenness of sexual difference as such dooms women to their oppression (and men to their anxious and guilty wielding of power), an oppression which is then 'perpetually rediscovered in the objects to which theory addresses itself' (Britton 1984: 42). Having confidently diagnosed the women's dis-agreement with (not my reading but) the tape, I had also a theory as to why I was so impatient of the argument – this was another sex-essentialist argument, pinning the essence of masculinity in such a way that no change can be thought of, let alone brought into being.

What in retrospect was at fault was my misunderstanding of the situation in which I and my audience, differently, watched the tape. A large, cold lecture theatre, far too large for the audience, with two monitors for playback and the acoustics of a swimming pool; a visiting male lecturer with little knowledge of the people he was speaking to; an audience made up of groups who knew each other,

jointly involved in a short-lived little community of intellectual endeavour of their own, in which sexuality was in play only as the object of discourse . . . and crucially, a lecturer on adrenaline rush, and therefore with a higher stake in finding something to get excited about. What effectively I was doing was to expect that a video tape could have major effects on a disparate group of people regardless of their prior and present commitments, experiences and cultural formation.

At Cambridge Circus in the heart of London's West End is a converted chapel housing one of an international chain of nightclubs called The Limelight. Despite the scale of the building, the dance-floor is a surprisingly small area, most of the delights on offer involving other activities, within which the dance-floor operates as a kind of alibi for some, a backdrop for others. One wall of the floor is made up of a bank of video monitors playing in sync., with one or two other monitors rolling in unison from the facing pillars. They do not sync. with the music. On display one night late in 1986 when I was there (ostensibly to see a new photographic exhibition) were a selection of already rather dated George Barber scratch videos (see below, p. 68), a handful of nondescript pop videos and a Chuck Jones road-runner cartoon playing in heavy rotation.

Video in the nightclubs plays a special role in the world of sexual expectancy. Perhaps this is only in the West End: a world where carnival has become a continuous round of commodity fetishism, in which the marketing of consumers to consumers in the big clubs is the interplay that sells relations as objects, but objects also as the forms through which relations can be mediated. The Limelight at one level markets punters to other punters through the mediating factor of videos, food, music and an environment suitable for dancing. At a second level, the club provides an organised form for sexual encounter, otherwise in the city a potentially dangerous activity. This level should not be taken lightly: 'violence', 'risk' and 'excess' are bandied about as concepts and as terms of rhetoric in English-language academia with little reference to the real violence visited on gay men, women, Black people, Asians, Irish, the elderly. The city-centre nightclub has a relation to such violence which you have only to sniff at to understand: the violence of the crowd, of the city, of masculinity, deployed within an established format that suggests a short-term resolution – partnering up.

Industrialisation of carnival? Or transcendence of the commodity form, since nightclubs in essence sell people to people, not things to

consumers? And in this nexus, what is the function of video? In many respects, the reduction of tape to the merest wallpaper is a suitable role: an alibi for the coincidental presence of the sexually active on the look-out in the same space. Here video serves as little more than a light source: lightly flickering, a wall to look away towards in moments when other modes of communication break down. At the same time, nobody who has danced on this kind of floor can have missed the difference between monitors, how there is more than an angle of vision differentiating one monitor from another in the dark space of the nightclub – or the gallery, when multi-monitor set-ups are used.

Multiscreen exhibition gives special attention to the replicability and the fallibility of the video image, and to the simultaneously familiar and unfamiliar nature of its electronic production, at once the familiar of the hearth and the dangerous entity unplugged in electrical storms. At home, you might turn off the TV when guests come round, but not in the clubs. In a public space – which is where virtually all multiscreen installations are likely to be – this produces a specific tension. Which is the true image? The loss of the original noted by Benjamin (1969: 217ff.) in modern art is foregrounded for the viewer as the multiplication of similar but distinct (and distinguishable) images on a wall of monitors, which divides attention between them. Cinematic identification is weakened and the colour, luminance and grain will be different on each monitor. How am I to know which one is addressing me? In the flick of an eye from one screen to the next, the address to myself is lost, and with it, to push the metaphor a little, the coherence of my Self as well, subject of so many simultaneous addresses.

A video wall has the opposite effect to the famed 'wall of sound' pioneered by Phil Spector's series of 1960s hits 'You've Lost That Loving Feeling', 'River Deep, Mountain High', etc. Much subsequent production practice in pop has derived from this strategy of massing resources behind a basic R. & B. beat (subsequently disco has been added as an option) to produce an epic emotional soup. Stadium rock from Pink Floyd to REO Speedwagon is full of such devices, as is a great deal of FM rock. The relentless solidity of such sound tactics is motivated by a single factor: to convince, to charm, to impassion its audience, and to determine their reaction. It is a mode of address which strives to enforce a single, definite subject position. The 'b.p.m.' thesis – that a specific number of beats per minute can produce a specific audience

response – is a totalitarian version of behaviourism which takes Spector's technique to a new order of significance in disco production. The video wall operates in a different direction, dismantling the fixity of the subject, offering, very precisely, distraction: tending towards a kind of multiplication of difference within the subject. (This line of contrast might lead to another style of conspiracy theory: why do multiple-monitor set-ups figure so heavily in big shopping malls and Virgin Megastores? Are we being put off balance at a prior moment to the resolution of purchase?)

As it approaches the state of writing, video also becomes a form of supplement, an addition which disrupts the nature of its 'original', especially the immediacy of its address. Video representation, like its narrative forms, is partial, so we have to ask, what is it partial to? Are we dealing with the production of objects or partial objects of desire, or the anxious products of loss? Or both? And how do these relate to the reproduction of self in the dialectic of consumption?

Pop, as identified in mainstream broadcasting, is a homogenised and homogenising field. But what is so impressive is that it is subject to sudden surges of vibrancy, not just among single artists, regions or styles, but in sudden blasts of energy which seem to galvanise everyone involved: punk was one such moment, the emergence of world music seems to promise something equally forceful. It is such energising for no apparent reason, a statistical catastrophe materialised as a new mode of music's use, which gives the lie to merely personal accounts of pop. There is more here than a relation within the listener, or between the listener and the song. The social construction and circulation of desire emerges within the individual relation to the individual tape: some of the interpersonal grounds for carnival. For video, this relates to the specific nature of the social field of the visual (given the sharing of audio technology with cinema) in combination with the peculiar nature of the video apparatus.

As Simon Biggs remarked in a talk at the AIR Gallery, London, in 1987, video remains when the artwork is gone. The blank apparatus lingers on even when the tape is over, so that the medium persists in the absence of its message, belying the identity of medium and artwork in other forms. A painting cannot be separated from its physical carrier: you cannot remove the painting and not remove the paint and canvas too. But the video screen remains after the tape is finished. Cinema, by contrast, is an experience which involves darkness and the special preparation of the viewing space: part of

the experience is the occlusion of the apparatus that facilitates it. This is not true for video: since screen and tape are separately visible, we have the possibility of a new kind of dialogue between them.

The sadness of empty cinemas is to do with the absence of the crowds for whom they were built, the harshness of the cleaners' lights illuminating stains on crushed velvet seats, shining in cruel democracy on the remnants of romance and fantasy, last night's broken dreams: dreams of strangers in the fantastic intimacy of cinematic fascinations. Not many living rooms will hit you with the same poignancy. Thomas Hardy, with the eye of the newly bereaved, could identify 'the look of a room' by the absence of a loved one (Hardy (1912–13) 1978: 105), but for most people, an empty living room expects to be filled, where an empty cinema has the emotional *avoirdupois* of an unanswered telephone: the sheerness of absence, unalloyed with semblances of presence. Because it is everyone's space when full, it is no one's space when empty, a space almost of bereavement.

Is it because cinema deals so much in illusory presences? That the star system and the discourses of glamour rely on the dialectic of what's both here and not here? In the absence of those gorgeous but uncertain existences that pass across the screen, the quotidian is marked out with the obstinacy of spilt orange juice against the transience of the dream of passion on the silvered screen. There is nothing unreal about either the optical effects or the emotions that we feel in the cinema, but an opposition between the screen and the 'real world' continues to shape our sense of cinema: the persistence of video's apparatus after the experience is over opens up a new relation. The great totalitarian wall of the cinematic apparatus belongs, like the Spector wall of sound, to an older aesthetic than televisual media.

Yet one factor does remain common, though differently inflected historically in cinema, television and video, and that is the relation of the viewer to vision itself. In the process of learning to speak, we have to learn also how to be spoken to. Language embraces us and everyone around us, pre-dating our ability to speak and structuring its possibilities. In just the same way, the look which we learn to focus and to direct, the look over which we have a measure of control and which is full of meaning for us, is also a structure which pre-dates us and shapes what we can do with the gaze. Our looking is always already presumed in and presumes another look or set of

looks, more precisely the look of others. In this structuring net, the actual looks are the equivalent of *parole*, acts of speech or enunciation, while the whole field of the visible, like *langue*, is the structure of vision. Just as there is no coherent language without the rules of word-formation and syntax, so there is no looking without the field of the visible. To enter that field, to take on the act of looking, is also to put yourself into the field of the visible. To look means also to be seen, to relate to yourself as visible: even when there is no one there to look, we exist in the visible, just as we remain 'I' even when there is no one to speak to. To be visible is to be inscribed into such rule-governed structures as the mask, for example, or the returned gaze.

This field of vision has to be understood as a field of relations. First, to distinguish it from light as such: light flows, as wave-particles, more or less in every direction, filling the space which it creates by moving through it. Light is a tool in cinema and video, a ground which facilitates the structures of the visible, but which is not the same as them. The look, the socially-acquired organisation of the instinctual pleasure of the eye, is the instance around which the visible is structured; it 'is not a look which I have seen, but a look which I imagine in the field of the Other' (Lacan 1973: 79). To look is to inscribe oneself into the field of looking in which the look you give is conditional on the look which you receive: a field of relations between self and other marked, let us say, by embarrassment, by shame, by a blush, by an attempt to 'cover up', a communicative nexus as full of deceit and of beauty as that of language.

Looking is therefore as bound in the dialectics of desire and anxiety as any other field of human life. Pop video in particular deals with the inscription of the star image into the field of the visible as a movement between star and fan which generates a complex set of relations of visibility in the viewing. Like Williamson's 'wannabe' (1986: 47) dancing for the mirror, the pop video offers a space in which a spatially circumscribed relation to oneself via the medium of the video is also and simultaneously a relation with all looks. Caught in front of the mirror – say by a parent – the self-enjoyment of that look is curtailed by anxiety. What is disrupted is partially a special, imaginary relation to the star and partially its mediation through the dancer's imaginary relation with her own body, itself an other, both looking and looked at. Yet it is almost the consummation that the situation demands, certainly as narrated in endless teen comedies. The closed loop of looking is inherently

unstable within existing structures, the narcissistic gesture only a step down from the Oedipal scenario. Such an unstable structure must break down from the weight of its own instability, but in doing so it will involve the surrounding politics of the living room, the peer group and the community.

Unlike pop records, with their invitations to dance or song, pop video makes no *explicit* request for action: only that you watch. People can and do dance to pop videos in the sort of spaces identified above (p. 68): private spaces or spaces of public entertainment, where the solipsist/communard relation is fantastically resolved in the magic unity of exhibition, and where the impulse to move between self and others – precisely the function of party dancing (as opposed to couple dances) – is more easily accomplished. In domestic use, the pop video lives both more and less dangerously: in an exchange which plays through a special series of relations which it shares with other viewing experiences, but to which it adds its own inflections.

The pop video is subject to intense scrutiny in at least some instances: a scrutiny of fashion, of dance steps, of pose, of *mise-en-scène*, of accessories and the human milieu. The serious fan will want to get as close as possible to learning by heart the image of the star and perhaps also – as immortalised in the film *Hairspray* – to imitate dance routines and so forth. Aerobics tapes, to use one example of the DIY mode of video culture, constantly invite, request, even demand a very specific set of activities. Jane Fonda introduces *Jane Fonda's Aerobic Lesson* with the injunction: 'For this session, you will need a chair, some shoes ... weights'. Yet despite the contrast between this explicit call to action and the implicit invitation of pop video, there is some parallel between the two modes of address. Both propose a narcissistic identification with the star, even though one positions the subject more obviously than the other within a pedagogical process. Yet both partake in peculiar and complex ways in the process of teaching, of passing on information from screen to viewer. In both cases, the nature of this information is heavily coded due to its proximity to the body, which has had such a problematic history in twentieth-century culture. Dancing to a pop video and performing aerobics exercises at home with a tape are specifically coded through the discourses of youth and age associated with pop video and aerobics, and to the narcissistic motivations which each poses as the entry point to commonality.

Pop video speaks to the self-image of its audiences through

images of stars as working models of style for adolescent sexuality. In some respects, Williamson's comments (1986: 47–88) on Madonna are very apposite: that Madonna lives out in public the private fantasy of the girl dancing in front of the mirror, a moment of self-indulgence before the onset of other-directed adult femininity. Yet it is essential to stress the term 'acting out': this is not an invitation to be Madonna but a representation of an ideally inward performance which is, however, also within the field of the visible and the chain of signification: an outwardly-directed display. The dialectic pleasures come from the performed models of how to be 'private' in 'public', how the experiences of self relate to presentation of self, how the gap between experience and presentation take on a social form both as inner speech and as performance. Each of these reacts in turn dialectically on the organisation of images in the overall culture which the adolescent inhabits: the commonality for whom the field of the visible exists.

The 'feeling good' discourse of aerobics tapes deflects the possibility of voyeurism – though whether that is totally achieved in the social audience I doubt – through an appeal to self-enjoyment supposedly held in common between the women on screen and the ideal female viewer in front of the set. At the same time, however, as Margaret Morse argues persuasively (1988), the pitch of these tapes is tied very strongly to processes of ageing and fears about it. The stars of the genre are women like Fonda and Raquel Welch, women who have reached *un certain âge* but who are 'still' beautiful. Such an anxious relation between self as body, self as image and self as ageing subject of the look of the Other plays again a fruitful and, in this case, physiologically motivating role in the viewing process.

The relation of screen image and self-image emerges not simply as a necessary address of screen to viewer, but as coincidence. Coincidence might either be a cause for rejection (like but unlike) or for approach (like but not like enough). The processes of recognition of the similar and performance as a way of approaching it helps make the gap between our own body and the screen image of achieved beauty less unbearable. Through the pedagogy of the star turn, we are presented with a programme of work, a discipline, through which our dislocations of self and self-image can be annealed. Just begin by subjecting yourself, not to the text of the tape but to the discourse of which the tape is but one utterance: not just to *Like a Prayer* or *Jane Fonda's Workout Tape* but to the discourses of beauty, age, femininity which they draw on and

reproduce. (Equally gender specific would be examples such as Heavy Metal videos or *Keep Fighting Fit with Number 2 Para*.)

Here we witness another quality of the field of vision: it is, like language-based discourses, organised hierarchically. When Charles Laughton, in Korda's film *Rembrandt*, asks his model to imagine his look at her as being as innocent as the water she washes in or the air that surrounds her or the light that shines in through the window, the poetry of the speech is powerful precisely because it is untrue. The scene is bathed in an erotic glow, the more sensuous for its very chastity. The artist's 'innocent' eye in the scene is an eye endowed with power: he is master of the house in which Saskia is a servant; he is old while she young; he is an artist, she a peasant; and he is a man. It is not the star that is necessarily imbued with such powers in the relation with the viewer, but the viewer who subjects herself to the tyranny of the achieved body, most vividly in aerobics, but also in another star discourse prizing physical prowess, pop video.

What is at stake is a Lacanian imaginary figure, as Morse (1988: 33) expresses it: 'We construct the imaginary of wholeness, of bodily perfection.' Such perfection is both a protective armour and a disguise for the frailty of the 'real' body, a socially-constructed ideal version of the body made for both self and, crucially, Other, in the image of wholeness and completion. Morse goes on to argue that this process is undertaken within an order of looking governed by the male, as defined psychoanalytically. In patriarchy, the phallus circulates as 'symbol of perfection and sign of exchange value' (ibid.: 39): as the signifier of masculinity, the ultimate arbiter of patriarchal relations, the phallus connotes power, wealth and male desire. Thus the term 'phallic' applied to a woman denotes the use of her as a signifier of male desire and power, and Morse can argue that

> Our relation to the imaginary produced in the aerobic realm is one which is described as 'male' in psychoanalysis. Nor does the feminine silhouette we produce, a phallic woman adjusted for us with a few curves, give the women we are an easy space in representation and exchange.

> (ibid.: 39)

Even without taking on the problematic issues of gender specificity in psychoanalysis, it is quite possible that, in the pursuit of 'aerobicity', wholeness is just as much a fantasy project as it is in the fan's longing gaze at the star. Again, the glamour and excitement of the pursuit is based as much on anxiety as on desire.

Beyond this, the aerobic tapes that have made the most impression on the market are also manufactured within a regime of pop music. The original name of the practice is 'aerobic dance exercise', with the implication that aerobics can be a legitimate use of unpaid leisure time, even though it is implicated in the economy of sexuality within which women's beauty is subordinated to the requirements of a heterosexist world. Pop is frequently used, as it is in the home-worker oriented daytime radio stations, for a specific address to women. At its worst, pop radio is a daily regimen, like aerobics, designed to comfort by mobilising and assuaging, in rapidly-closed circuits, fears and yearnings concerning loss, ageing, child-rearing and perhaps death. The mapping of time through broadcasting, especially for home-workers, might perhaps be disrupted through video use, but does the programmatic side of exercise tapes threaten to return to cyclical, time-bound regimes? It is in these terms that the worst-scenario model of video culture nears realisation: to quote Morse again: 'Empowering media such as the VCR can also represent a new stage of rationalisation, allowing more aspects of socialisation to be sytematised as commodities in a market system' (1988: 42).

Marketing self-image is not restricted to the teenage zone. Becoming somewhat belatedly aware of Madonna in the year I turned 30, in the throes of a small emotional upheaval over my age, the strains of *Material Girl* rang like a plague bell: too old, too poor and too far away. The pastiche of Monroe in the accompanying video did not speak to me of fluorescent self-organised sexuality: it spoke of desire, of loss and of a shame that I should even want to be desired within a fictional world packed to the gunwales with the symbolism of wealth. My shame became tied in with the perception that the passionless, affectless world of commodity fetishism operated exclusions: 'the boy with the cold, hard cash is always Mr Right'. The cluster of unwelcome emotions orbited around a sensation that at last I had left my youth behind, and with it otherwise disorganised fantasies that had never emerged as such for me before – a fantasy of wealth, in particular, of which I had never before been conscious. I had the unpleasant experience of becoming at first the other of this textual other, and in the same movement, the other to my self. The desire to be desired is, I believe, fundamentally human. To have it spelt out in such a specific, fiscal and 'post-feminist' way filled me with despair. I could rationalise it as sorrow for a dead pop culture of commonality and revolution,

but only at the expense of the seriousness of the emotion as I felt it.

I am quite happy to accept a reading, such as Kaplan's, of *Material Girl* as in some way a magical recovery of feminine strength. That it is expressed through pastiche seems to me less interesting than its insistence on money as motive and emotive force. Yet even this disagreement seems less captivating than, at last, knowing that more than one reading is possible at all. But below this lies a more powerful realisation still: that the self that desires to be desired is actually constituted as a self in the act of mutual desire – that the core of self is the relation to another: only in that relation can one exist for oneself:

> In a word, I discover the transcendental relation to another [*autrui*] as constitutive of my own being . . . . Nor is another in the first instance a certain existence which I meet in the world – and who wouldn't know how to be indispensable to my existence, because I existed before meeting them – it is the ex-centric term which contributes to the constitution of my being.
>
> (Sartre 1979: 290)

The production of a self is a social phenomenon: we do not start as selves waiting for society to occur to us. Before the social (and, therefore, before language) we do not exist. The social field of the visible awaits our arrival, and we are unable to look, to see or to be seen, until we enter it. On the other hand, society and language absolutely require human agents as their supports. The process is not symmetrical: the relations into which we are born are relations of power in which the *individual* subject is at a serious disadvantage. Yet it is possible, as *social* subjects, to engage in the production of ourselves, since subjectivity is itself always already a function of human interaction. This ex-centric formation of the human subject is what leaves us open to social interaction. Even if a message is imposed, as a text, from some nodal power source within the discursive architectures of the social formation, its readings remain in play in a dialectic between speaker and listener: the word is itself a product of that relation, and even after its production remains in play, even when power exercised across the relationship refuses to allow dialogue between parties.

The pedagogic relation of teacher and taught in the star-vehicle pop video or aerobics tape might appear to deny social interaction in the production of meaning through precisely such an exercise of power. What has not emerged so clearly here is the possibility for

disruption in the distance such a text has to travel between point of origin and point of consumption. Across that distance, there are two sets of changes: first, a kind of relativity effect due to the unalterably and irreducibly different trajectories of sender and receiver, so that the message always arrives, as it were, at a tangent; and, second, multiple sets of contingencies that weigh upon every transmission and every reception. Even thinking about these things, say, at the level of their impact on our individual consciousness, is a social act: the words, images and tunes through which we think, in a still moment of their circulation, are waiting for us to add the next signifier in the endless and social chain of signification. Looking within, we look through and into the eyes of another.

The boy who dances in front of the mirror moves to a different position socially to the contemplative one outlined above (p. 59): he may go on to execute the same gesture in (specially marked out) public places like discos. While he dances, the dance is *for* an Imaginary audience created in his own image. But that image is itself socially created, and as such still itself in play and at risk. The step into public performance involves a further step: an inflection of the dance's address, so that it is now *for* a more clearly demarcated and more manifestly social audience, and therefore subject to the rules of the Symbolic concerning where and when dancing can take place, what at any specific historical conjuncture constitutes a suitable mode of dancing, what constitutes a peer group for which kind of dancing . . . .

In so far as pop video shares in the star discourse of the cinema – and it is important to recognise that videos are only one among many circulations of the image of the pop star – it engages the viewer in the circulation of ego-ideals, those imaginary images of the self through which the viewer finds both a space in the visual, narrative and auditory world of the tape, but which also serve as alternatives to the fixed quality of the ego we mainly experience in adult life. That pop uses many media, and that audio is no longer the privileged site of performance (as film is for the film star), means that the audiences for pop video are more eagerly engaged in the *production* of ego-ideals than in the cinema. The fact that they are alternatives to the ego makes them particularly powerful as motivators for fantasy and identification for the adolescent, still open to options which adult life will largely close off. Such identifications can slip across age, race, class and, at least occasionally, across gender too: pop video constantly addresses the

possibility of being Black for white audiences (Michael Jackson), of being mature for the young (cock rock), of being working class for the bourgeoisie (Bruce Springsteen). Male-to-female identifications can be generated through two mechanisms: either by allowing the male viewer a chance of identification in narrative situations with a woman protagonist (e.g. through the possession of Truth, melodramatic tears become available to either sex in the video for Tina Turner's *Private Dancer*, which plays on the secret thoughts of a dime-a-dance 'companion'); or alternatively through the generation of a homoerotic gaze underwritten in the diegesis as the gaze of a female fan, as in a host of videos centring on dance routines by male stars. What seems important here is that it is possible to identify, at the same time, both with the singer and with the fan, to be both the looker and the looked upon. This double identification is a splendid visual parable of the working out of the narcissistic moment in video viewing: controlling the look as both subject and object.

Self-image is both a projection for external consumption and an inward turn of desire. Such desire is historically bound: the desire for music which is satisfied with Whitney Houston records is different from that which requires a guest to sit at the piano after tea, just as the hunger satisfied by ripping apart dead animals with your teeth differs from the satisfaction available from french fries and a milk shake. Desire is organised, like the languages in which it expresses itself, as a social structure. 'Watching star videos' is then a description of a mode of watching, not of a genre of video: a mode of looking in which the desire for style expressed in mirror dancing (or for a 'perfect' body in aerobics tapes) is enclosed in a loop through viewer and screen, but with a common address to an imaginary audience. That audience, historically and in practice materially absent, is the atomised audience of suburbia, decentred in the social construction of the subjectivity, but without any collectivity but an imaginary one in which to work and influence, to open out the reproductive cycle. This closure leads, potentially at least, to Morse's worse-case scenario.

A very powerful example of work that attempts to reach beyond the closed loop, especially in the context of the discussion of aerobics tapes above (p. 74), is the sell-through video 'concept' album *Savage* made with the Eurythmics by Sophie Muller in 1988. The opening track, *Beethoven (I Love To Listen To)*, begins with a suburban interior dominated by a reproduction of Landseer's *Monarch of the Glen*, icon of Victorian Scotland and the most

popular print of the Victorian bourgeoisie. Beneath its paternal crown of antlers, lead singer Annie Lennox, herself a Scot, arranges flowers in the costume and wig of a *bonne bourgeoise* while an orchestral backing circles through a pastiche of a horror film's suspense motif. After the title animation, Lennox reappears furiously knitting while, without music, she says in BBC English, 'Some women believe that they don't count. You have used that against me.'

As the initial beats of the first song, *Beethoven (I Love To Listen To)*, restate the ominous theme of the pre-credit sequence, a steady-cam shot accelerates up a flight of stairs, bursting through a door into three-quarter-shot of Lennox as the first chords break in. Lennox gives a startling performance as a woman on the verge of breakdown, conducting the mean tasks of housework and child-rearing with a passion and intensity counterpointed with the insistence of the music and classically clipped phrasing of her soundtrack singing (un-lipsynched). In the background, a demonically-teasing daughter scribbles on walls and throws bric-à-brac on the floor. The transformation which the horror themes on the soundtrack have prepared involves Lennox taking on a whorish travesty of the appearance of her blonde daughter, throwing things around the kitchen and escaping to an empty industrial landscape beyond. From there, the album moves into parody of macho R. & B. with *I Need a Man*, and a series of documents on the passage through madness or emotional break out through to some sort of reconciliation in the figure of children, bearers of the future.

Clearly the notion of the concept album has already been given visual treatment, especially in the feature film world of *Tommy* and *The Wall*. Far less usual is a woman directing a female star through a scenario which, while limited by the video format to fairly broad strokes, can none the less address the conditions of viewing to which it is destined. From the rather familiar 'tune in, turn on and drop out' thesis of its opening, the tape as a whole develops a range of complicating factors, especially in further versions of the mother–daughter relation and the interplay between the blonde and brunette personae of Lennox. In particular, this play between the two visions of the protagonist seems to establish the ground for an understanding of the limits to the unitary personality (while still staying within a binary opposition between 'good'/repressed and 'bad'/wild characters familiar, again, from the horror film among others). Formally, the optimistic completion of the tape in a future

symbolised by the children is only one part of its organisation. Each of the segments can, presumably, be marketed separately in other formats, video juke-boxes and broadcast for example. Yet the viewer who has been through the whole tape will read into the smaller samples the complexities which the whole can give it (just as the faithful fan can add in a wealth of reference not available to the casual viewer).

It impresses me that this tape can build in a complex mode of address in this way, allowing for the many ways in which it will undoubtedly be read, while still retaining at heart a commitment to a feminist position, in particular as that revolves around the mother–daughter relation, to the exclusion therefore of a certain kind of male expropriation. Again, the play with Lennox's star persona through its repositioning in the context of the housewife and tart personae gets beyond the sheer production of ego-ideals and, while retaining a place for admiration of Lennox's skills as performer, opens a range of critiques around the fan position by showing what those skills do not include: crucially, in the fan/star dialectic, the relation of mothers and daughters in the tape. While this emphatically does not escape the marketing needs of the production of stars, it does offer a wider range of accentuations of the star than is usual.

This issue of accent is important for the understanding of struggle over the meanings of tapes. If we imagine first a word being spoken, the accent – inflection, tone of voice, accent, dialect, accompanying gestures, etc. – determines how we understand it. If someone uses a word because it has been suggested that this is the word to use here (for example, I will argue below (pp. 160–2) that the independent sector in the UK has learnt to stop saying 'community arts' and begun to say 'cultural industries'), there is likewise a trade in 'accent'. Words do not reflect existence, they comment on it too, within the social networks of communication in which they exist (Volosinov 1986: 23). These networks are riven by all the inequalities of society as a whole: it is a delusion to believe that communication is magically free of the imbalance of wealth and power characteristic of our period in history. Words are the site of struggle between various groups in society, with dominant discourses 'obscuring' the possibility that words can mean differently, hiding the fact, even the idea, of struggle, change and heterogeneity as much as possible. In dominant discourses, as we shall see in the next chapter, each successive signifier is used, at least in part, to guarantee the fixity of

the preceding one (obviously an unending task). But the different accents within a linguistic community − accents of gender, class, race, geography and so on − maintain a kind of guerrilla war through irony, humour, parody and other kinds of word-play.

Likewise images are not free agents. They do not exist outside of the circulation of meanings either, and as we internalise them, for example in the form of ego-ideals or objects of desire, we participate in their social production. Many pop videos work with such possibilities, accentuating their narratives in playful ways, experimenting with angles, lenses and special effects. By and large they do not, however, break up the major grounding principles on which they are produced. A tape like the previously mentioned *The Chauffeur* may not show the star, but still performs the rituals of heterosexist fantasy. *Papa Don't Preach* is still an anti-abortion song. Howard Jones's scratch *Life in One Day* is still the discourse of individual creativity. Dire Straits's *Money for Nothing* remains bound to the MTV discourse it purports to disdain.

An impressive mixture of expensive computer graphics, treated concert footage and quotes from various other sources, *Money for Nothing* is a particularly interesting example, largely because it is so self-conscious (and also because its award-winning graphics make it suitably familiar). The tape opens with the computer-generated figure of a young man entranced by the MTV logo and theme tune ('I want my MTV') flying into the television set on which the band are playing. The elegantly treated concert footage appears on screens within the screen in a narrative carried through by the computer-generated caricatures of blue-collar workers, in whose persona Mark Knopfler, lead singer, opines that playing guitar on MTV is money for nothing. Within this scenario, the tape quotes not only MTV logos but also another video, *Sally* by the Ian Pearson Band. Clearly meant as a joke at the expense of moronic sexism on MTV, the quoted frames are no less sexist for being quoted: the prizes gathered by the Dire Straits tape clearly demonstrate that you can have your cake and eat it. The figure of the youth as victim of the medium which opens the tape replicates the most ill-informed prejudices about audience use of video (see Chapter 7) and indicates a serious lack of respect for their audience on the part of the tape's producers.

A far more fluid approach to the medium emerges in the videos for Talking Heads collected as *Storytelling Giant*. Of the ten tapes, all but two credit David Byrne, lyricist and lead singer, as variously

producer, director and/or with 'total video concept', as he is indeed credited as director for the compilation as a whole. The best of these tapes, especially *Road to Nowhere* and *Wild Wild Life* (which derives from Byrne's film *True Stories* (1986)) show a depth of affection for the North American culture which is at the same time subject to a bemused grin and an intimation of depths unspoken in the discourses of the dominant culture: ageing (again), self-image (again), biography and autobiography. Another title from the compilation, *Love for Sale*, uses found material from US commercials in a scratch mix, but in this case the on-the-beat editing and the very slickness of the image track tends to diminish the power-pop of the soundtrack, interrupting the music rather than commenting on it. But most seriously, given Byrne's importance to the production of *Storytelling Giant*, the compilation raises the question of authorship.

The notion of the *auteur*, raised in the 1950s by French intellectuals claiming respect for the cinema which authorial figures had provided for literature, has gone through many vicissitudes. It should be clear the *auteur* is not coextensive with a named, historical individual like David Byrne. Authorship pervades a body of work, becoming a quality of the work, rather than some essence inherent in the historical writer. But around Talking Heads, Byrne's authorial persona almost outruns the power of the tapes to make their own marks: like children too close to their parents, much of Byrne's offspring seems to cling to his apron-strings. The exception is *Road to Nowhere* where visual invention – of which there is a great deal – is subordinated for the most part to a more or less metaphysical consideration of the range and limits of the culture in which both song and tape take their places. In this tape, the relation to TV culture is explored with an honesty and integrity which is normally swept aside (as in the Howard Jones and Dire Straits examples): genuine pleasures cannot be enjoyed as kitsch – they must be 'native' in the sense that the user should not use a discursive position of power to enjoy without responsibility. To do so is both patronising and dishonest – a point to be expanded in the final chapter.

One does not have to make absolute judgements of value to insist that judgements need to be made from the standpoint of the fitness of a practice for a specific cultural community. If that community is a colonialist one, recruiting its pleasures from other cultures in a spirit of exploitation and irony, as when the *haute bourgeoisie* collect the quainter ravings of the poor, that is the same

abuse of power as visiting the demented in Bedlam for a Sunday treat. The high-culture abuse of popular television ensconced in *Money for Nothing* seems such a practice. Even more so the image of adolescence generated in the pop video discourse is colonised in a process in which the representation of adolescence is made to function for and on behalf of a quite different set of cultural parameters.

Video is a dialogic medium, reliant on accent, on multiple readings, on intertextuality, on the struggle over meaning as a social production. It is also a dialectical one, a medium that deals with loss and desire and the moment of becoming between them. It works dialectically, too, in the interface of image and self-image, between the social and the solipsistic. Pop video rolls between the dialogic and the dialectical as it attempts simultaneously to introduce the adolescent to the adult's world of loss even while it panders to what it *imagines* to be adolescent desire. That pandering comes in the form of representation, whose condition is the absence of real desire. What we get is precisely an imaginary desire, one built from the circuit of self-image in which adolescence, for the older social group who make the bulk of videos, emerges from memory and the past. This emerges in two ways. Often the (male) director projects fantasies of sexual prowess on to his stars, creating thus a fantasy of his own ('successful') desire to be desired. Alternatively, in the imagined past, the core issue of loss, the issue of sexual difference as the first piece of rule-governed learning imposed on the child, is rendered once more whole, perfect, like the aerobic body. All the threat and pain of sexual difference can be fantasised away into an innocent, primordial, undifferentiated sexuality such as that manufactured through the teeny-bop idols for young women (cf. Garratt and Steward 1984: 140ff.).

Yet even here what comes into circulation is not androgyny but its representation, a neurotic and fictive assault on memories of loss for the producers, an unthreatening mode of entry into heterosexuality for the young women, a permissible moment of dalliance for young men before their assimilation into the same old difference. The Michael Jackson of *Beat It, Thriller* and perhaps even more so of *Bad*, his blackness, his adulthood and his masculinity in question, lives out for a global audience the impossibility of remaining Peter Pan, and its irresistible temptation. His construction as erotic spectacle and impossible object of desire, while also potentially the werewolf of bad desire, plays through a

further inflection of the androgyne, the metaphysics of the white man's presence to self as it is played through its reliance on the maintenance of a Black male Other. The one thing which stops the seduction from completing itself, from the reduction of all pop video to narcissistic suburbanity, is the *difference* that video insists upon: we watch the little people on the screen as we might watch children play, or as children watch their toys – manipulating and seducing them, just as they would seduce us: moulding, to an ideal formed beyond as well as through the monitor, that which remains obstinately and obdurately alien.

Chapter 5

How to watch video art
My father will heal you with love

It is only a little over twenty years since Sony introduced the first publicly available portapaks, almost exactly twenty years since they became available in the UK. Yet within that period, the protean entity video has hurled itself outwards from any centre it might have possessed at origin to lose itself (its selves?) in a hundred simultaneously-pursued tracks. Sadly, much early videotape has already degenerated beyond any viable viewing quality. It is impossible to see video art's history, both because the evidence is fading, and because it was never a single history in any case. Readers who want some such guidance are referred to Stuart Marshall's excellent writings (1978; 1979; 1985), Gregory Battcock's 1978 collection, Anne-Marie Duguet's monograph (1979), Rob Perrée's *Into Video Art* (1988) and Kathy Huffman's *Video: A Retrospective* catalogue (1984). Most of the historiography, like most of the discourse on video, resides in catalogues to shows, in little magazines, many of them short-lived and hard to find, and in the memories of those who participated: a history as dispersed and dialogic as the form it monitors. For this discussion, I have tried where possible to restrict myself to work which is moderately easy to find, especially work which has been broadcast on Channel 4 in the UK through the series *Video, European Video, Time Code* and the two seasons of *Ghosts in the Machine*.

What follows is therefore not a methodical movement through a history, but an exploration of a set of problematics in the viewer relation to this phenomenon, video art. Crucially, artists' video is posed as video: whether it be broadcast or in a gallery, whether it joins in the defining contractual circulations of the art market, whether it sits on a domestic receiver, in the shop windows of rental shops or in British Council touring packages, this practice is

signalled as video – a practice and an experience marked off, especially in the UK experience, from other forms of art practice. Yet this broad generalisation is a product not so much of artists' as of curators' practices. Certainly, few artists treat the medium as a purely transparent species of communication, and are interested in the intrinsic and extrinsic properties which it has. But then many documentarists' choices of specific strategies are every bit as informed by 'aesthetic' considerations as the construction of a multi-monitor installation: intrinsic properties inform the selection of video as a recording medium, playback and other 'extrinsic' qualities define it as a distribution medium. Likewise, in art as well as documentary practice in the independent sector, there are a multitude of strategies to be deployed, sometimes several within the same tape. I've chosen then to focus more on the viewer relation to the work rather than textual practices. But at the same time, some kind of textual analysis is unavoidable, if only because of the irreducible materiality of the image and the soundtrack.

Video sits in an uncomfortable relation with television. The two media are so easy to confuse one with the other, since television relies extensively on video technology, and since video, despite being carried on some of the same machinery as broadcast, none the less contains television, just as TV learnt to contain the feature film, variety shows, radio games and the art of conversation. Video contains television in the sense that, among the other media it can carry, television is the closest relative. But video goes further still: it even attempts to contain the viewing relation within it, in a gambit which exists to pre-empt the power relation between set (power) and viewer (subject). Nam June Paik's installation *TV Buddha* is a fine example of this: a camera is trained on a statue of the Buddha who sits contemplating the image of himself on a monitor linked in to the camera. The closed loop puns across the contemplative mode of Zen and the 'couch potato' image of the TV consumer: passivity as eastern path to wisdom or as western path to addiction. William Atherton's *The Television Live in Glasgow* is a tape documenting a performance in which the TV set acts as stand-up comedian, complaining about the working hours and raising questions about how it is treated by viewers. There are less obvious containment strategies such as the autobiographical/confessional strand in videomaking identified by Rosalind Krauss in 1976 and most usefully accessible in the *Genlock* touring package curated by Jez Welsh for London Video Arts, spotlighting the special relation of

makers to tapes, but at the same time exploring the relation, through that peculiar intimacy of small-scale production, of intimacy with the viewer. As cinema expropriated previous forms like theatre and photography, and as photography had borrowed its frames from the oil painting, so video expropriates the formal properties of the media that went before, including television. At the same time it includes not just the text, but the viewer's relation to it.

Like most media, video was not born as software. Though there is some disagreement over the role of military demands on the development of closed circuit surveillance technologies, video appears to have developed as an adjunct to the recording industry through the Bing Crosby laboratories, and in the closely-linked TV industry itself as simply a cost-effective way of dealing with the technical problems of broadcasting (cf. Armes 1988; Keen 1987). But as soon as it became available to the amateur market, and therefore to users without allegiance to hegemonic forms of media production, software began to form a key area of interest for a whole network of politically and aesthetically motivated people, so much so that the key magazine of the period was titled *Radical Software*. But within those uses lay implicit a notion of beating television at its own game, destabilising the power the screen was assumed to have over viewers, breaking down the centre– periphery relation of broadcasting, and thus focusing tightly on the relation between producer and viewer. In artists' video, this seems to mean an ambiguous position around the term 'community'.

First, it means limited, often very limited, audiences. There is a kind of work made for a circle of friends and peers, who can be expected to recognise the paradigms involved, to recognise the quotations, admire the technique and engage in the debates. Research is a perfectly legitimate practice in a new medium – even in an old one, for that matter – but the circulation of video art as a whole was for some time, and in part is still, in a close-knit community within the televisual culture, even within the video culture: a dialect with few speakers. None the less, as a dialect in the process of formation virtually *ex nihilo*, there is a fascination in the emergent and more public forms it begins to take on. Again, as indicated above (p. 81), there is no single dominant mode of this dialect. A tape I made in 1988 met with guarded approval from its Canadian commissioners: 'The interesting thing about tapes from people who aren't tape makers is that they don't play by any of the

rules.' Without there being in any sense a body of correct video practice from which to dissent, this comment from the producers indicates a sense of a shared expectation of video art. My piece worked perfectly well in its own formal terms, but it was clear that it did not come from a shared perspective of tasks and solutions. Though I had made a tape, I had yet to become a tapemaker.

On the other hand, it is still slightly unclear what is meant by a videomaker. We tend to think of a photographer as someone who prints their own photographs, or makes a living from photography, or exhibits and publishes somewhere moderately prestigious. But a tapemaker is more than someone who has made a tape, just as a photographer is more than a person who takes photographs. Though the dialect is not formed, it is clearly distinct both from television and from amateur video. My position in the 'community' is the somewhat tangential one of an occasional pundit, someone who knows about the area and who knows the work of the *actual* tapemakers. Which makes me, I suppose, a *virtual* tapemaker. Perhaps a working definition of artists' video might be virtual television. On the other hand, this community is international, and although scattered and dependent on often shaky means of dissemination and communication, is able to gather from time to time, and to share out ideas, tapes and the associated practices.

The relative paucity of use of dialogue in tapes might make up one of the paradigms of video practice precisely for this reason (which would be one reason why mine looked so unlike a video). One reason why television is such a difficult subject to write about is that viewing practices associated with specific programmes are so closely linked with the specificities of a local culture: TV studies are an intensely national activity, far more difficult to export than television programmes. Video moves through a related problematic, but by minimising the importance of dialogue and script, it tends to displace the 'voice of God' role of voice-over in TV, the dominance of soundtrack discussed in Chapter 3 and of course to elide some of the problems of translation that dog the internationalisation of small-budget film and TV productions.

Music, on the other hand, is a common factor, both pre-recorded and specially-generated. That, in many respects, is why this chapter follows the chapter on music video. I had initially wanted to begin the chapter with the example of Cabaret Voltaire's *Sensoria/Do Right*, and their video work more generally, as an indicator of the transitional phase between pop video and the art sector inhabited

by groups like Projects UK and others plying their trade in the independent record scene. What emerged from watching the tape several times over, as well as watching other tapes adjacent to it on the *Gasoline in your Eye* compilation, was a dialectic there between the opacity and transparency of the medium, between tape as document of a specific performance, including the direct eye-contact with the singer's on-screen persona which seems to guarantee the viewer a space in the tape, and tape as mediator of the performance for the viewer. In doing so, however, it merely sets the ground for the tape's real work, which I read as a meditation on the world of the senses.

A sensorium is the seat of sensory perception in the brain. Sensoria are then many seats. Cabaret Voltaire's tape *Sensoria* uses editing, dramatic and unusual camera movement, a variety of performances and the song itself (including found sound) to diffuse any centralising consciousness, but it is not this itself which interests me, nor the address to the politics of the dance, which affords the tape its most memorable visual images. It is the concluding image of the healer, a figure somewhere between *The Wicker Man* and the preacher of *Wise Blood* who dominates the second half of the tape, with his knee in the startlingly curved back of his customer, both of them with their lips drawn back in pain and concentration, shockingly physical, while behind them the daughter holds a placard reading 'My Father will heal you with Love'. The flavour of love as something dangerous, drastic, ugly, sinister, impossible, grave, a gateway to manipulation and hell-fire, which disengages itself from this scenario isn't easy to render in words. Its situation in, specifically, a pop video places the tape in a special relation with the viewer which, I believe, steps beyond the delivery of heterosexual ideologies of romance. Beyond even the critique of banal sexism set up in the Clinton tape discussed on p. 65ff., *Sensoria* inveigles the viewer into finding in the tape a new set of relations with genre videos in the music sector. The tape doesn't ask to be deciphered, because it is not ciphered in the first instance: it engages in the impossibility of encoding love, that impossible negotiation over hearts, that nexus of body, mind and soul for which there is no other symbol.

What I want to draw from this brief description is that the more elaborated levels of meaning in the tape rely in the first instance on an interplay between what you can see in the tape (text) and what the camera had in front of it (pretext). Without treating the images in any flamboyant way in post-production, the finished tape still

insists equally and simultaneously on the action in front of the camera (termed 'pro-filmic' in cinema theory: pretext seems more fit for video) and on the material quality of the tape itself. Such a dialectic runs through most of the videos that I will be describing here like a ground bass. At the same time, there enters here also a new factor in the analysis, as we bring the camera into the equation: the randomness that so often inhabits visual systems, no matter how hard we try to organise them into coherence, wholeness, perfection.

This dialectic of pretext and text disrupts the potential (illusion of) wholeness offered by the realist cinema. The Imaginary uses wholeness, as a fantastic annealing of the pain, guilt and anxiety inflicted on the growing subject as it comes to terms with loss and separation in the process of discovering sexual difference and the taboos associated with it. In the previous chapter I argued that this analysis is good for pop video: here I want to suggest that video art quizzes that completion. The yearnings for wholeness, closure and order are the aesthetic sublimation of the same impulse in us which produces that characteristic fascination with the perfect body of the star. The camera has great difficulty supplying such wholeness. Photography has no trouble: perspective and framing can provide a link through to an established visual language as old as the Renaissance if not older. But, and this is an important fact to remember, the unit of the moving image technologies is not the frame. Movement means precisely that the unit, the minimum analysable quantity, is not the single frame but three frames – the one before, the one now and the one to follow.

Video, like film, deals in time as its fourth dimension, extension in time, forward *and* backward: a structured element as important to the videomaker as the third dimension to a sculptor. Likewise for video, space within the screen – including the production of depth through, for example, use of off-screen sound and deep-focus – is complemented by the use of the monitor as itself an element in the tape, so that the phrase 'single-monitor piece', while denoting the simplest kind of installation, none the less indicates that the work is, in potential, an installation with sculptural qualities. To call a tape a 'single-monitor' tape is to acknowledge that it is made for exhibition in a specific way: in 1987 artists protested at the Independent Video Festival at Bracknell because their work was being shown on video projectors, not the monitors for which it had been designed. This had to do both with a loss of definition inherent

in the magnification of the image for projection, but also, crucially, with the breakdown of the sculptural analogy between the monitor as a free-standing light source and the possibilities of three-dimensional space, something cinema (and the approach to the cinematic of video projection) cannot aspire to.

This certainly seems true as I sit here writing, the art tapes playing on the monitor in my living room gathering the space around them as a sculpture does, inflecting the play of light, the spatial dimensions of the room. This may well be an effect of the notorious ability of flickering images to attract the attention of the wandering eye, but then bright colours and sheer scale have the same sculptural effect and we recognise them as legitimate sculptural devices. Movement is recognisably sculptural in the work of Calder, as machine movement is in Tinguely. The tape *Vertical Landscapes*, broadcast in the UK as part of the *Ghosts in the Machine II* season by Channel 4, has a startling version of this: the constant movement of images upwards across the screen leaves the viewer's eyes after the tape's conclusion compensating for the loss of that motion by giving the illusion that the whole room, the monitor in particular, is moving downwards.

This is a particularly clear example because it relies on an optical effect to complete the work of the tape. For once the loquacious medium of TV seems to be waiting for a reply, to be acknowledging its own incompleteness, its inability to reach a conclusion in the constant, endless process of addition. Likewise it indicates a persistent quality of artists' video, even those pieces which most closely follow an aesthetic of wholeness: their incompletion. In the case of *Vertical Landscapes*, the temptation is to place the completion outside the tape, in the eyes of the viewer, and expect to close the loop in this way. This could potentially suffice for this piece, but my own feeling is that this is leaping to a conclusion as an aesthetic solution to an intellectual problem: the incompleteness doesn't go away because we displace it from the tape to the viewer. The viewer, too, remains incomplete: what was this experience for? Have I changed? Have I had fun? And the tape remains open for re-viewing, with a different set of attentions and concerns emerging perhaps.

Repetition has emerged several times in this book: as the absence of an original in video viewing, in the form of heavy rotation on MTV and similar pop video channels, as a function of difference .... Re-viewing is, in this context, neither an essence in the medium, nor a product of centre-to-periphery programming,

and thus neither simply a dislodging of unitary consciousness, nor merely a mechanism for diffusing excitation in the system. Repetition as an aesthetic device can become extremely anxiety inducing as well, as we will see below (pp. 94–6). But the possibility of repetition of a specific experience offered by video, a repetition which cannot, of course, be the same each time, has to do with the imaginary relation of viewer and tape, a relation built out of, first, the viewer's drive towards completion and, second, the need of the tape, as a sign in social circulation, to move through encounters with subjects. Both partners, and the society in which they meet, come into this specific mode of existence through and in this relationship: both are and remain radically incomplete, but through their interaction offer glimpses of what completion might be like.

However, the possibility of repetition is only a possibility: it relies on something beyond the relationship as such to spark it off; a catalyst which, from the standpoint of the viewer/tape relation, is entirely contingent, arbitrary, random. Visual language in the electronic media walks very close to the chaos that reigns beyond the boundaries of language. What occurs in front of the camera is so susceptible to change, to organisation, to restatement and to reuse that the notion of coherence comes into question. Much video art plays directly on this quality: Ingo Gunther's *Rotorama*, for example, a kaleidoscopic, brilliantly-coloured tape using video's ability to replay and rework to unveil the random breakdown that shadows television's apparent completion. Where TV solves the incompletion problem with endless flow, and MTV with micro-rotation, video throws the problem back out again: no easy solutions, many risks. The relation of solipsism and sociality emerges again here, in the sense that only social consensus builds a language, but genuine individualism means abandoning the common ground of language, whether verbal, visual or aural. The soundtrack of Gunther's tape, for example, oscillates between music – the socially-defined language of sound – and noise, the eructations of the non-human, the alinguistic. Even more significantly, found elements of music on the soundtrack move, through the sheer density of their layering, towards the condition of noise. As if the individual removed from the production/reproduction cycle of social language by the monodirectionality of broadcasting is presented with social sound at the limits of meaning, ready to dissolve back into the prelinguistic. Solipsism emerges as an effect of

over-much sociality when the individual subject is urged, through the tape, to take on a position of solipsism. The effect in this tape is not so much critical as randomising.

Such randomising factors however obey, in all appearances, the laws of chaos, or more spectacularly of probability, in that the emergence of a kind of emotional charge and the ghosts of meanings from the whirling, fragmented sounds and images of, for example, the Gunther tape move towards a patterning which, while it remains other to the hierarchically-organised discourses of television, emerges with formal properties from which the viewer still makes meaning. Even though that meaning may be fragmentary, and perhaps occluded by the baroque extravagances of the tape, it is there to be made. And it is important to stress that such spontaneous patterning is a quality of the electronic image, not exclusively of the spectator making gestalts from the random flights of photons. Visual language, like verbal, has a way of re-asserting its rights over its marginalia. It is, at times, as if artists' video is clearing the ground for the next imperial move of the televisual: the expropriation of 'artistic' uses of advanced effects, increasingly common on both sides of the Atlantic and in the Pacific basin. Art work emerges into the zone of commodity capital as a promising mode of R. and D. for the facilities houses, advertising directors, creatives and technicians throughout the industry. One reason for the emergence of video art as a dialect (veering towards the condition of a grouping of idiolects) is surely its reaction against such co-option.

Repetition has another effect, briefly indicated above (p. 93), of producing anxiety. Advertisers (or more properly speaking, media buyers) use repetition as a way of getting campaigns to stick in our minds: some artists' uses of repetition reveal the paranoia lurking beneath this recycling of ads. When scratch artists force their on-screen figures to repeat an action over and over, it gives the sensation that some irrational, or malevolent, force has seized them, forcing them to rehearse the rituals we associate with the insane – the repetitive gestures of Sam Fuller's *Shock Corridor*, for example, or of Barry Levinson's *Rainman*. These figures are out of control, outside the world of discourse which alone makes us human. But their similarity to us makes them indices (where an index is a signifier which indicates or points towards a specific signified which is also capable of taking on a role in narrative, e.g. a picture of a gun signifies a gun, but is also an index of the narrative role of guns, to

go off) of an inner life which we expect to be a 'natural' corollary of any picture of a human being. Grab-frames, the repetition of a frame or group of frames to give the impression of a repeated gesture, is one of the most common of mid-1980s video techniques and one which seems to drive on-screen characters to the level of puppets in a particularly disturbing way.

Scratch tapes don't form a particularly coherent grouping. Early Duvet Brothers and the work of Gorilla Tapes seemed quite close kin with the earliest work to reach reviewers, animal rights scratch mixes of 1982 and 1983 produced by a group calling themselves Nocturnal Emissions. But George Barber's work in tapes like *Yes Frank No Smoke* is already very different, and some of the work included on Barber's two *Greatest Hits of Scratch Video* compilations had very little in common except a useful marketing ploy. *Yes Frank* is a geography, both funny and disturbing, of sexual anxiety mapped out through a set of treated and repeated quotations from American feature films. Although the first impression of scratch is of its magpie relation to TV, not only for images but also, as Catherine Elwes has pointed out in an influential critique (1985), in its editing techniques (and there are thus problems of copyright), this tape particularly evokes both humorous and disturbing responses in the several audiences I have watched it with. One sequence may illustrate what I mean. Barber quotes a scene in which Roy Schneider is made to stutter 'Y-y-y-y-yes Frank, y-y-y-y-yes Frank' in a way that makes him appear the butt of a joke going on among the other characters sitting behind his back. When I finally caught up with the source of the quote, it is Schneider who is in control of the situation, the audience identifying with him against the men behind, who are not party to the star's facial expressions.

Such a shift from identification to ridicule is an extraordinary achievement, one that shows very clearly the unfinished nature of the video image. What is even more impressive is the play between the image as fitted into the existing work and the memory it seems to drag with it from its initial position in some other piece of work, film or broadcast. In *Yes Frank*, even without recognising the source, it is quite possible to read off the general significance of, say, the footage drawn from *The Blue Lagoon*, a 1980s remake of a classic tale in which two marooned infants invent the nuclear family from scratch. In Barber's tape, the manufacture of innocence in the feature film is played back through its deconstruction as a source of fear and guilt. Yet the prettiness of the images, their initial lure, remains as an

adjunct: the two conflicting sets of meanings coexist in an uneasy dialectic. Yet again, the structural nature of incompleteness emerges, here as an impossibility of pinning down *the* meaning of a given textual movement in the tape.

Sexual anxiety, as deployed through *Yes Frank* and *Sensoria*, is a widespread interest among videomakers, perhaps a reflection of the impact of feminism on video as on so many other forms of social and art practice (though the relative youth of people working in tape may increase its impact, as may the public/private dialectics of the medium itself). The masturbatory possibilities of video have scarcely missed the eyes of entrepreneurs and moral crusaders, or of the general public. The inflection of this aspect of the culture in video art is most typically the confessional tape mentioned above (p. 87). But above all, it is the inherent incompletion of the medium that opens it up for this kind of exploration. This is perhaps clearest in the shifting approaches to narrative which have characterised video production in the 1980s, as in the work of North American feminist Max Almy. Almy's *Perfect Leader* is a hilarious pastiche of the selection of figureheads for the ruling class: portraying, through a combination of high-tech effects and mathematically-precise timing, the stages of preparing a perfect leader. Criticised by some for its slickness of presentation, it in fact uses that slickness as part of its attack on the mediated construction of leadership (cf. Almy 1984; Mann 1984). Like other works of hers, *Perfect Leader* emerges from narrative traditions (building robots, for example) into new spaces for telling.

Anne Wilson and Marty St James are responsible for a number of tapes and installations devolving on mundane glamour: holidays, hotels, canal trips . . . . The tape *True Life Romance* replays, as much of their work does, elements from romantic novels, sometimes transliterated to the screen, sometimes choreographed into a balletic montage of images timed across the beat of theatrically stylised dialogue derived from the style of Harlequin and Mills & Boon. Rather in the mood of Barber's work, their approaches foreground both the triviality of cliché and its depth – truisms, after all, become truisms because they are true often enough for enough people. At the same time, the shreds and tatters of a story are there, while the story itself is not: parts of the telling, parts of the plot, jostle one another in a new discourse which is not primarily organised around the telling of the tale. What seems to be occurring is a shift in the syntax of storytelling, even a shift from syntax

towards paradigmatic organisation, rather like the 'ideogramatic method' of Ezra Pound's *Cantos*.

Linguists use the term syntagmatic to indicate not only the ordering of sentences according to the rules of grammar, but also to describe the 'horizontal' axis of language, the ordering of words and phrases in time. The various ways in which, in spoken language, sounds combine to form words, words combine to form sentences, and sentences combine into larger discursive entities are rule-governed, relying on a system of 'correct' and 'incorrect' combinatorics so that /hot/, /hat/, /hit/ and /hut/ are all correct, as is /het/, with the minor drawback that it doesn't mean anything in common English. On the other hand, /hxt/ is an incorrect combination. Similarly, work instigated as early as the Brothers Grimm indicates that narratives are governed by rules every bit as strict as those governing word-formation. When the rules are broken, meaning becomes impossible: if, for example, events occur not only out of order but without recognisable causal relations, or if characters fail to maintain sufficient unity throughout the story. English readers find this a problem with the names in Russian novels, a big enough problem to destroy their pleasure. More seriously, many readers still find the demands of Joyce's *Ulysses*, let alone *Finnegans Wake*, far too obscure: the fracturing of traditional narrative rules, the dissolution of characters into interweaving interior and exterior monologues, the mixture of dialects all contribute to an interference with familiar modes of meaning-production.

Normally, we think of combinations as the rules by which things combine with one another, or even as the logical, natural motion from one thing to the next. Saussurean linguistics stresses that in order for these rules to operate, there has to be a regimen of absolute discontinuity between the signifiers – verbal, aural, visual or whatever – which are being combined. There must be a way in which they can be perceived as discrete. This discontinuity between discrete signifying elements is a manifestation of difference, the ground base of language without which rule-governed systems cannot operate. Systematic difference of this kind is marked in the relation between edges or limiting boundaries: gaps marked, for example, by the spaces between printed words or by edits in video. But there is also a difference internal to the sign and logically prior to the differences between signs – the difference between signifier and signified. Saussure offered a formula for the sign as

$$\frac{s}{S}$$

where the signifier relates to the signified across a bar. Contemporary linguistic analysis asks us to see that bar as a crucial part of the formula: there is a line drawn between the material signifier and the 'mental image' of the signified which needs to be taken literally. This is the space between the material of communication (sounds, images...) and both the speaker's intention and the listener's comprehension. Signifiers and their meanings are not firmly anchored to one another.

Signification, especially in video, is marked by the *internal* difference of signs, their individual incompletion: as Derrida observes, 'The order of the signified is never contemporary, is at best the subtly discrepant inverse or parallel – discrepant by the time of a breath – from the order of the signifier' (Derrida 1976: 18). Derrida's point is that there is a difference, if only one of time, between signifier and signified, so that the two elements of the sign cannot be seen as unified. Each is incomplete without the other, and they are constantly attracted to one another, but can never be completely and finally reconciled with one another. This internal structural quality means that 'spacing' between semantic elements needs to be conceived of within as well as between the elementary particles of meaning.

It is in these terms that we can begin to understand the necessity for rules of combination in the generation of meaning. It is impossible to conceive of a language made up exclusively of words in isolation from each other. No single word or sound or image is complete in itself: therefore it must seek completion in combining with other signs. Just as certain elements in chemistry are unstable enough to have to combine with others to form molecules, so meaning is possible *because* individual sememes – the basic building blocks of meaning – are incomplete. As the speakers of language – and as subjects spoken by it – we are therefore forced into pursuing meaning down the axes of combination in language: to the endless pursuit of completion along the axes of the syntagm and the paradigm.

In a slightly different context, Rosalind E. Krauss (1986: 106) argues that Dadaist photomontage foregrounds the white space on which visual elements are aggregated: the whiteness which separates the images is also the ground on which they can combine.

This dividing space is the condition of the syntax which links images to one another in a meaningful whole. This white space between visual signifiers is 'the fluid matrix within which each representation of reality is secured in isolation, held within a condition of exteriority, of syntax, of spacing'. But to hold each smaller photo in such a relation of exteriority is to undermine the claim of photography to be the record of presence. The gaps in Dadaist montage make us aware that photography records that which is always already absent, that photographs record loss and incompletion. In such a context, spacing ceases to be the condition of organisation and becomes almost its rationale, the rules of a new syntax preceding the signifiers to be combined.

Video, by contrast, has at least three tools at its disposal for quizzing the givenness of its images and their relations to each other. It can foreground its own syntax by emphasising the role of the edit (as in scratch video) or, for example, the nature of the apparatus (as in the dissection of the scanned image in Mona Hatoum's *So Much I Have To Say*). It can emphasise the conditions of its syntactic operations (Paik's early *Variations of Johnny Carson vs Charlotte Moorman*). And, quite familiarly now, it can document the conditions of breakdown of the syntagmatic axis (the Gunther tape *Rotorama* mentioned on p. 93, or Jeremy Welsh's *I.O.D.* with its exhortation to 'Imagine Other Destinies'). But it is equally significant that within the practice of video art, and especially noticeably in the area of narrative experimentation, the uses of the vertical axis, the paradigmatic, begin to overtake the issues of syntagmatic organisation.

One mode of syntagmatic organisation might be /article//noun/ /verb//article//noun/. By contrast, paradigmatic organisation is the vertical ordering connecting the actual noun used in a particular sentence with all the other nouns which might replace it. In narrative terms, this means that certain events or characters might be able to substitute for each other: a story can be told in western dress or as science fiction by shifting the elements of the story along appropriate paradigmatic axes. But there is a sense, identified by Robert C. Allen (1985) in daytime soap operas in the US, in which a shift can be identified from syntagmatic organisation of narrative to paradigmatic. This Allen identifies as a shift from interest in the flow of events to an interest in the ways in which characters might react to a much-attentuated series of occurrences. Allen argues that this

shift is apparent in the shift from plot-dominated to talk-dominated soaps, where the interest moves from what happens next to what the characters will make of events.

The trials of narration in the contemporary video are more than the set-dressing which a lot of pop video employs to spice up thin ideas, running hackneyed plot through in snippets or reverse order to liven up an otherwise undistinguished conception. At its most successful, the shift from syntagmatic to paradigmatic, or between one register and the other, creates genuine complexity. The Robert Cahen tape *Juste le temps* demonstrates some of these qualities. Heavily treated images of a train journey devolve upon shots of a female passenger, whose fragmented body and unaccountable gestures create an atmosphere of tense desire and mystery into which the viewer immediately begins to hurl new fragments of narrative, unavoidably attempting to fill in the constitutional absence at the heart of the tape. Alternatively, the tape can be read as a series of micronarratives, each too short to do more than impress a motion, a gesture, the passage of light across a compartment on the retina. Cahen's title seems to pun from Godard's dictum, 'Ce n'est pas une image juste, c'est juste une image' (This isn't a just [correct] image, it's just an image) to suggest that the subject of the tape is the interplay of time and perception. The term narrative image is used to denote the images used, for example, in posters advertising films, where the poster image sets up a narrative tension which can only be resolved by going to see the film (cf. Haralovich 1982). Magazine advertising frequently uses a similar strategy: the implied narrative can only be completed through purchase of the advertised item. Cahen's tape punctuates such narrative images with ghostly landscapes created between tape-delay and the sort of intermittent vision you get from a train window. What is at stake is not occurrences, or the succession of occurrences, but their reverberations, the paradigms they evoke and deny as the time just carries on, disordered, incomplete.

In *The Interpretation of Dreams* (1976), Freud describes the two fundamental processes of unconscious life, condensation and displacement. Condensation combines several meanings into a single signifier; displacement replaces an anxiety-provoking signifier with another, less dangerous one. Lacan observed in 'L'instance de la lettre dans l'inconscient' (1966: 249ff.) that these terms match very closely with linguistic concepts: condensation with selection and paradigm; displacement with combination and

syntagm. These in turn can be read as the poetic formations of metaphor, condensing terms together, and metonymy, having one thing stand in for another, or more particularly, a part stand in for the whole. Lacan takes this process a step further by suggesting that in metaphor we see the relation of the subject to language, while metonymy reveals the relation of language to objects.

In metaphor, what is at stake is the difference between the person who speaks and the 'I' by which a speaker represents themselves in words. In order to speak, we have to enter language, and in doing so must experience a division between conscious (and therefore linguistic) self and any other elements of psychic life that that excludes. Speech acts always require a speaker, but their representation of the speaker in words is, as a representation, always built on an absence, the absence of a full human entity from the act of speaking. The word 'I' stands in for the speaker, but in doing so represents him/her. Any representation rests on the difference outlined above between signifier and signified: there is no necessary connection anchoring them together, and neither is complete. The enormous complexity of the human psyche cannot be contained in the word 'I', which therefore is said to denote the absence of the subject, not its presence.

Much, if not all, speech takes the form of a thesis, in which we can understand, at the beginning of each utterance, the phrase 'I say that . . .'. But as we have seen, the 'I' that speaks and the 'I' it speaks of are both incomplete. Therefore speaking requires a further signifier to qualify the first, to hurry in to complete it and therefore maintain the representation by keeping it in process. But this leads only to another incompletion, and on to the next signifier. In this way, Lacan can talk about each signifier as a metaphor of the subject, representing the subject back to him/herself mediated by another signifier. Thus the paradigmatic axis functions in language to underwrite the relation between speakers and the words they use, continuously stitching away between self and language through a process of substitutions: the subject searching endlessly for its (impossible) full place in language.

Metonymy meanwhile concerns the impossibility of language ever containing the object as it is in and for itself. Every reference to objects is partial – as in the classical metonyms such as 'the crown' standing in for the legal form of the state. Every object is perceived from a specific point of view: no human symbol system will exhaust its plenitude. Therefore the process of attempting to grasp the

object in words (or any other symbol system) is doomed to become an endless procession of partial descriptions and abandoned circumnavigations. Thus, again, the object appears to the subject as the other side of language, the underpinning around which language is built, but which remains separate from it. This metonymic, syntagmatic dimension of language is ultimately the most ambitious aspect of it, attempting to map the entire universe in the geography of human meanings. It is in this context that we can, perhaps, begin to understand some of the shifts which are occurring in art practice generally and in video art in particular.

The reference of this syntagmatic axis is to an impossible plenitude of language, language coextensive with the world, a map, in Borges's parable, the same size as the kingdom it portrays. For apologists of postmodernism, this is the project of high modernism: the making of total systems of meaning, a totalising and totalitarian advance which attempts to homogenise the world in the dominance of the signifier. What they seem to me to be missing, apart from a misunderstanding of differences within the bogie of modernism they have created, is a sense of the centrality of defeat to much of the modernist enterprise. If a concern for the signifier rather than the signifed (medium rather than content) is a defining instance, as Rosalind Krauss (1986) argues more convincingly than most, the early work of Nam June Paik falls neatly within the definition since it is clearly engaging with the properties of video as such. But to remain at this undifferentiated level seems wildly remiss: even in the earliest tapes, Paik is already engaging in a dialectic between the artist as individual and the television as mass medium – a dialectic which already decentres him as subject since he can never hope to be as full, as constant as television, already a 'postmodern' inflection. Paik's work is, in many senses, *about* television, and in some instances is an addition to it: it is also work, and as such an addition to the world. It would be a wild over-generalisation that read this off as a supplement which usurps the world to which it is added, or which deprives that world of reality in some magical exchange.

The glory of the modernist enterprise is the address, not to fullness but to its representation, a yearning for fullness in the relation between human artefacts and the world they inhabit. Such an impulse lies most clearly behind the documentary film-makers of the 1930s and 1940s, but it is incorrect to limit the uses of an intrinsic quality of language to a specific historical period, or to miss the vital interplay between the metaphor and metonymy. In

Graham Young's *Accidents in the Home* series, domestic furniture and appliances of astonishing banality become the actors in microdramas of extraordinarily rich associations. *Accidents no 9: Indoor Games*, like its fellows, deals in the obtuseness of artefacts, how the things we make take on their own lives apart from our purposes. But also deeply self-conscious of itself as video, the tape doubles over the elaborately staged events, treating the images, isolating moments from the flow of activity, engaging off-screen space by small visual cues. The doubling up of events with images produces here its own distortions, as if merely making pictures of designed objects makes them into actors in their own inhuman dramas — inhuman because they do not require human intervention once set in motion, as in the twin indoor golf gadgets sharing a ball in *Putter* or the tumble from the sofa in the absence of human agents in *Holiday Insurance*.

Indoor Games is particularly interesting because it is completely silent, though screenings I've attended produced a lot of spontaneous sound from the audience. It is precisely a silence *into which* . . . , a lacuna inviting an auditory response. Many tapemakers are also engaged in making (or borrowing, remaking) their soundtracks. Especially in the case of the spoken voice, this has begun to take on a special place in the discourses about tape. In terms of music, there is a kudos to 'originating' your own music, which ties in closely with the same discourses: a sense of the authentic, tied in with a sense of the authorial, a discourse of, to use a term with an enlighteningly paradigmatic relation to authorship, the authoritative.

Authoritative discourses underpin the genuineness of the work through reading it as either an expression or, in a less loaded modulation, a product of an author. The presence of the author either on screen or as a voice on the soundtrack, or least physically as signatory of the maximum number of elements of the tape (music, lighting, script, camera, editing . . .) signals to the producers' peers that the tape has status as a videotape: an authored, authentic, authoritative tape, not an amateur gamble like the one I presented to the Canadians. In these terms there is a serious risk that the kind of *auteurism* which marred cinema studies for so long is returning to haunt video, just as we thought video was to lead out from the era of origins and authors.

The problem is compounded by the institutions of the art market as it stands — where the artist is a necessary figure in attracting

grant-aid and buyers into the sector. Similarly, video is generally a small-scale production, compared to the usual output of television programmes or feature films, even low-budget films: an authorial handle seems more appropriate to the scale of art production. On the other hand, there are others involved directly — teachers, technicians, maintenance engineers, performers, friends and colleagues who have looked over the script or popped into the edit suite — just as there are in other media: I write this book alone, but it will be read by several people before going to press, and each of them will have ideas about how to improve it. Their names appear traditionally in the acknowledgements. But there are many others involved: the peer group, my friends, the potential audience for my book, relatives who may read it because it is 'my' book, not really knowing much about video and its culture. This social audience we have always with us, and it makes the issue of authorship, once we get beyond the lawyer's office, open to all sorts of questions.

Video has additional problems, though it shares them with the mode of production of this book. Where is the original? I compose directly on to a word processor: the 'original', if there is such a thing, is a set of polarisations in a magnetic medium more or less completely inaccessible to human intervention save through the kind of mechanism which replicates the text as soon as it reads it. Video likewise: though everyone preserves a master and a few sub-masters, few people would dream of using them for viewings. Like the negative of a photograph, they are less the original than they are a process through which we go in order to get a show-tape. Again, like my word processor, the physical thing, the U-matic cassette with the tab taken out, is a magnetic medium without useful characteristics until placed in the kind of machine which exists, among other things, precisely for making copies.

But worst of all, in the authoritative discourse is the attempt to reduce the meaning to what can be subsumed within the name of the author. To mark a piece as being 'Bill Viola' or 'Cecilia Condit' or 'Jaap Drupstein' is to reduce it to a horizon which is itself in any case an absence: the 'real' entities Viola, Condit and Drupstein are simply unavailable. Even those artists I count among my friends, to whom I speak about their work and the work of others, are removed from the work they have completed, by the time of a breath, if only that, but far more rigorously by their four-dimensionality, the way they cannot be repeated. There is a qualitative difference: the two are not interchangeable.

What we see is light, not things: photons spattering over surfaces in space into the retinal purple, a flurry of electrons and neurochemicals in the meccano of the brain. This is not vision but what carries it, just as magnetic tape is the vehicle of video, not its essence. The video apparatus is a whole elaboration, and it is in its every form, even the most secretive, deeply imbued with the social. To focus on the author delimits the possibilities of the work, defusing the address to the viewer with the intimation that this is only someone's point of view, there, there, it's not real. It is. The materiality of video is the guarantee of its part in the social world, not the fact of its birth at some lost moment in history.

This is not to argue against art history as a potential tool in deepening and broadening understanding of video work: I am greatly in favour of the study of history − it gives us an understanding of change. But I do want to argue that the attempt to anchor meaning in the moment of textual conception is inadequate. The presence of the artist to camera or microphone is a gambit, one of many, one with its own specific flavour, but none the less a stylistic device, not a guarantee of truth, wholeness, presence. The artist's voice is a signifier, just as much as the words she speaks, as is the case in Zoe Redman's *Passion Ration*, in which the message of the soundtrack is as much to do with the tone and gender of the voice (and the fact that it is the tapemaker's own) as it is a function of the script itself. Like any act of representation, the voice creates spaces and gaps. I argued above (p. 99) that signification rests on the exteriority of signifiers from one another. There is also a sense in which the distinction between signifier and signified, the material marker and the mental image associated with it, is so profound that the sign needs to be read as 'exterior' to itself, or perhaps in a more graspable metaphor, as hollow. If the signifier is a shell, hard, fixed, there, then the signified needs to be understood as fluid, not so much formless as omniform, moving in and out of the spaces made for it in time-based meaning structures like videos. The relation between signifier and signified is then one of isomorphism, of sharing the same form, but there is no absolute control exerted by the one over the other. And both, it cannot be asserted often enough, are products of the social, in this instance of the social structures of language, music and vision.

To copy is then a positive term, not a negative one: it is a question of process over origin, of the ongoing nature of work brought about by its incompletion, internal and external, over the anchoring of

meaning to a tired Romantic myth of the artist. The way in which work – in the sense of intellectual and craft labour as process in LeWitt, André, Buren and Kelly among others – has emerged as a key concept in the art of the last two decades should emphasise the core of this argument: that video is a process which doesn't finish because its makers abandon it. The partial objects and shards of stories which make such a familiar part of the video landscape are the condensations and displacements of the audio-visual world, a dialectic in which the one thing that isn't given to understanding is the meaning of what's going on – that has to be searched for, played with, gambled on, lost, partially unearthed, misrecognised or thrown away.

Video is an apparatus, in which the physical machinery and the psychic relations it has with those around it are not just metaphors of one another but to all intents and purposes are models of each other: start one moving and you start the other. As Thierry Kuntzel notes,

> In 1925, Freud saw in the 'mystic writing-pad' [the *'wunderblock'*] an almost exact representation of the psychical apparatus, in that it resolved a problem of writing which had hitherto been insoluble: the constant ability of the receptive surface to receive, the permanence of the traces in the wax of the writing pad. But two functions were missing: speed – simultaneous inscription and deletion – and the possibility of making the traces which had disappeared reappear. Does video not constitute the perfect model, the writing pad being no more than an approximation?
>
> (cited in Bellour 1983: 33–4)

Video is a process also of forgetting, the active process of forgetting, which is never without meaning, and which may demand a great deal of commitment and hard labour. There is a special mode of memory for the things we thought we had forgotten, the name of the boy in the next row in class in 1971, the name of the lead singer with The Yardbirds, the names of bones in your foot or of streets in a town we no longer visit. But where television is designed to forget on an industrial scale, video is condemned to remember, not everything, but at least where it put everything when it put it away behind it. Video remembers the process, the hard work of forgetting.

Thus video, to refine the point, has the potential to be less a medium of forgetting and more a medium through which is

recorded what has already been lost, the memory of absences which once motivated desire, or which can still promote anxious, guilty or – modified – nostalgic emotions now. These are qualities that emerge startlingly clearly in artists' video, for example in Catherine Elwes's works about pregnancy, birth and child-rearing, though there they appear also with the possibility for quite stunningly liberating moments too. If this seems pessimistic, that is because of two terms in play: first, the impossibility of a lasting paradise under the terms of capitalism, and, second, because, under capital, it has proved impossible to think of desire positively. Each affirmation of desire as productive and affirmative posits first an Edenic state prior to contemporary social order in which desire functioned 'naturally'. Yet we know that desire is completely and inextricably interwoven with the social formation of the subject, with language, the unconscious and the Symbolic: there is no 'pure' desire to return to. Blaming the policing of desire in the state or some other mode of original sin for our alienated state (alienated, implicitly, from Eden) therefore posits a mode of socio-political alienation which deprives desire of its positive role by placing its full reality in a mythologised past. Thus the reification of 'natural' desire perverts it finally, as Lyotard argues, through such theories into the plaything of a totalitarian politics which imposes willy-nilly an (illusory) wholeness on the social body.

Chapter 6

An other and its others

Video art: the term itself seems to harbour a contradiction. Not only the age of mechanical reproduction, but the age of electronics lie between us and the primitive aura of the western art tradition. And film and television critics have had their part in a history in which the terms of art discourse – creation, genius, author – have been systematically emptied of their relevance to film and broadcast analysis (but cf. Marshall 1978; 1979; 1985; Sweeney 1985). Video art is a practice which engages in wholly other spaces, the world of gallery distribution, of sculptural installations, of performance art. An analysis firmly based in materialist principles has trouble with the resistant avant-gardisme and art-based idealism of the term 'video art'. The play through cybernetics and ecologies, the unlikely mixes of zen and McLuhan in tapemakers' accounts of themselves (cf. Bellour and Duguet (eds) 1988b; Schneider and Korot (eds) 1976) are no simpler to negotiate.

Video art: curious that so fundamentally technology-defined an area of work should emerge into the world of art, even while it defines itself in terms of a relation to television: Paik's 'Art for 25 Million People/Bonjour Mr Orwell' show, the earlier (1969) New York exhibition 'TV as a Creative Medium', a book title like *Transmission: Theory and Practice for a New Television Aesthetics* (D'Agostino (ed.) 1985) testify to the relation to broadcast. Yet Paik's *Family of Robot*, showing in London's Hayward Gallery in the winter of 1988, is as far removed from broadcast as can be imagined, even while broadcasting donates some of the raw material processed in the multiple screens. A small observation: Paik's work addresses TV as a whole – the apparatus as well as the texts – as we might express an interest in cinema more than in films. And a more serious one: the routes through which video art has emerged as

initially not-TV, then as a medium exploring itself in its own right,
and into the third term of its existence in the 1980s, negating the
two previous ones and introducing a far closer relation with tools
other than the camera – a study of these trajectories might offer a
chance to understand something of the local problem, why is there
so little work on video art among film and television theorists, and
the larger one: what challenges can the practice of electronic art
forms pose to the orthodoxies of media theory?

The art establishment in the UK has in general been slow to react
to the emergence of the new form, despite brave attempts from the
Arts Council and, latterly, the British Film Institute. Yet video is still
seen as a poor sister of film, as here, for example, in Isaac Julien and
Kobena Mercer's introduction to a recent issue of *Screen*:

> Data compiled by June Givanni elsewhere indicates some of the
> characteristics that constitute black British film as a 'minor'
> cinema: the prevalence of material of short duration, shot on
> video, and in the documentary genre, indicates a pattern of
> underfunding, or rather, taking the variety of the work into
> consideration, a considerable cultural achievement that has been
> won against the odds of meagre resourcing.
>
> (Julien and Mercer 1988, referring to Givanni 1988b)

A constant cultural referent emerges here as the easy way in which
low-budget work can be automatically read off from the use of
electronic cameras. Video is neither cheaper to produce than film
(higher editing costs cover the relative cheapness of stock) nor is it
necessarily chosen as a medium for purely fiscal reasons. Yet the
hegemonic pretensions of 'film culture' to incorporate video, like
that other, art-originated reading of the form which sees it only in a
relation with television, pushes video out to a marginal position
with regard to art and to film and to broadcasting.

That video has often been an option for women, young people,
Black and South Asian Britons has increased its distance from the
heartlands of 'the culture' in the UK (noticeably more parochial and
isolated in this sphere than any other European or North American
country). Institutionally and discursively, broadcasting's other,
whether the video art analysed here or the community and trades
union off-air sector discussed in the next chapter, even the corporate
video area, is the lowly and despised partner in the light of whose
poverty the wealth of film or the power of broadcasting may be
made to shine. While ostensibly well-informed as to the emergent

dominance of the electronic media, there is a tendency among critics to dismiss it on any one of a number of grounds: David Byrne and Stephen R. Johnson's tape, *Road to Nowhere*, for Talking Heads is too commercial; Despite TV's East End anarchist account of the Wapping dispute, *Despite the Sun*, is too amateurish; Isaac Julien's own directorial debut, Sankofa's *Who Killed Colin Roach?*, now appears not as a video but as evidence – of underfunding. Corporate video is not television, video is not film, tape is not broadcast, and in the pages of the national press, video art bounces around between the art critic, the film reviewer and the TV columnist.

Two exhibitions in the autumn and winter of 1988 in London have broken the capital's usual reluctance to give major gallery space to video art: Bill Viola at the Riverside Studios and Nam June Paik at the Hayward Gallery. The Viola show featured a retrospective of single-monitor pieces and the installation *Reasons for Knocking at an Empty House*, and was held at a small, locally-financed non-commercial space. The Paik exhibition was an expensive show made up of the seven members of *Family of Robot* plus three related works, *Passage*, *Monument* and *Connection*, six video chairs, eight other installations, a selection of laser and video-generated still images and a retrospective of sixteen single-monitor pieces from *Global Groove* (1973) to *Digital Zen* (1988). The Hayward is part of the prestigious arts complex on the South Bank, which includes the National Theatre, the National Film Theatre, a cluster of concert halls and the newly-opened Museum of the Moving Image where Paik also has a work, *Satellite Baby*, on permanent display. Yet this belated flurry of respectable awareness of the medium and its potential rests four-square on the most recognisable categories of traditional art discourses: the name of the artist. I want here to enquire, through the Viola and Paik shows, about the status of 'art' in film/TV theory.

Bill Viola Colonist

When the old Americans made their movies – Douglas Fairbanks as Zorro for example – there was still the innocence of those for whom the colonial process was incomplete: the delicious irony of fighting for the liberation of Los Angeles from the Spanish viceroy. The final stage of colonialism is withdrawal – from the standpoint of the colonist, although it may be analysed as neo-colonialism from the standpoint of the colonised. The dialectic of return is incomplete

in North America. It is for this reason that the issue of the relation to colonised peoples is returned to so often in the cultural domain: because it is unfinished business in the hurtling day-to-day realities of American life. This in turn relates to the return, in fiction, to the Spanish and to the pioneers – not the early settlers, in whom too clearly the weight of history emerges in the tragic divisions of their souls between the savagery of the land and the utopian obsession of rationalism. Not them but their fictional counterparts, the cowboys, with their longing to bring reason to the land, that relation not to people but to the very landscapes in which they have their being.

The relation that emerges in the landscape segments of *I Do Not Know What It Is I Am Like*, the 90-minute cornerstone of the Viola show, is doubly confounded by an English writer's immersion in another imaginary relation to the colonial lands, a relation in which those primary colours are always tinted with absence. There is an impossible regret which emerges in the contemplation of the natural in the English breast. In mine, it is commingled with a second sense of loss relating to my parents' origins in Ireland: a country of legend, impossible to return to, a country perhaps, from a cynical standpoint, from which mercenaries go forth to build or to defend the *imperium* of others. In *I Do Not Know*, what is in play is not nostalgia. Viola, I suspect, sees himself as something like a prospector, someone whose touch on the country is light, whose forays into the land are entirely justified by their distance from everyday living. On the other hand, those disappearances from the everyday have to be brought back into the everyday, like minerals from a prospecting trip: that is their price. Some part of him merely needs to know that the landscape is there. Yet belief requires some repeatable experience: a tape. But then that is what I want to extract from the tape, in part: an entrée into another consciousness, in this instance a consciousness *of* – of landscape, for example.

The sadness of video is its obeisance to mechanical time. The joy of *I Do Not Know* is its effort towards eliminating that sense of time through a mode of perception that is neither intellectual nor yet emotional, a belief in the perfectibility of contemplation. At the same time, the tape is edited. Edits do not announce themselves, the cutting is more like that of Frederick Wiseman than anyone else: a documentary cut that appeals to our expectations of the documentary, that it be impartial, even natural. What returns us to the material of video is the soundtrack. An initial gambit with music simultaneously demonstrates the professional skill of the artist and

performs a specific gesture towards the splendid artificiality of the shot (the camera moves below the water-level in a lake, likewise the mike, so that the music shifts from the sound-track to the 'profilmic', to reality in the world of the tape).

The prospector listens in order to atune his ear to the sounds of this natural world. But now the ear is electronic, and the sound is not of distant winds soughing in the trees but the rasp of air moving over the mike. Ironically, the foregrounding of the mike, of the means of production, also foregrounds the presence of the mike in that real world. It pushes the soundtrack into the realm of the camera-eye, the physical sensation of being there – on the prairie, with bison. Likewise with the scenes of decay: how close do you wish to get to death? How much of an account of death does this physical process of bison or fish decaying into the earth give? What relation can these animal deaths have to living human consciousness – or so it seems to ask. Yet the power of this contemplative mode of viewing is that it allows the question in the first place. With *Chott El-Djerid*, a slightly earlier tape, the motion of the image and the merciful absence of the irritating *zazzzzzzhhhiinnnnngngngngngngngngggggg* which makes up Hollywood's account of the desert's sounds, none the less returns us constantly to the concerns of the west, with the surfaces that so entrance us, the painter-lines of the video screen. Yet even there, the power of that contemplative gaze outlasts the edits.

The figure of the owl presents a different set of issues in *I Do Not Know*: the alienness of that bird's gaze into the lens, the rigidity with which the bird maintains its birdness, the unrelenting watch of a bird whose eyes are attuned to hunting – the position of the spectator is that of a mouse before the gaze of its predator. Looking is not here like the triangle of looks in the descriptions familiar from Laura Mulvey's work (1975; 1981). Looking entails no human emotion yet. The question that emerges is finally ethical, and it is this elasticity between the contemplative and the ethical which most moved me in watching Viola's tape. The question is one of becoming, the already achieved issue of becoming, before a camera which precedes but finally cannot, could not, dominate the playback. The eye of the owl poses a question – and to enter into dialogue, as any question must, is to enter into and accept a contract, or to accept your presence for another. Finally this exchange of looks demands that the viewer accept the presence, not

of the tape, but of the owl, or rather, in the end, the unreturned and unreturnable gaze of the owl.

Raymond Bellour (1985: 119) concludes an interview with Viola conducted in 1984 and early 1985 with a short postscript: 'Since the interview, Bill Viola wrote to me, "I have just received a grant from the American Film Institute to do a new tape about animals. I'm trying to become artist in residence at the San Diego Zoo".' *I Do Not Know* might be that tape – certainly there are shots of animals – especially the birds – in zoos and a credit to San Diego. Would an artist in residence in a zoo have to stay in a cage? Viola does not. But he does confront there an historical passage from the peasantry to capitalist culture, from the anthropomorphism of a culture close to animals and measuring itself against and through them, to a culture in which they are enslaved, brutalised, rendered spectacular. As John Berger notes, in the exchange of looks between people,

> the *existence* of language allows that at least one of them, if not both mutually, is confirmed by the other. Language allows men [*sic*] to reckon with each other as with themselves .... No animal confirms man, either positively or negatively ... its lack of common language, its silence, guarantees its distance, its distinctness, its exclusion, from and of man.
>
> (Berger 1980: 3–4)

The zoo, Berger argues, emerges in part as evidence of colonial power, like the great museums, in the age of imperial capitalism. Yet in zoos the marginalisation of animals is completed: they can no longer be the centre of the spectator's gaze: what we look at is the monumental moment of their disappearance from human culture.

Viola can be the presenter of the colonised because of this missing dialectic. If the coloniser is forced into representation (cf. Bhabha 1985) the issue is: what is the relation of the colonised to the land? Presentation? Viola presents the land. The fact that the presentation is mediated is itself presented, not represented. I argued in Chapter 2 that video's relation with silence is privileged – video can *be* silent where film can only represent silence. Here also silence is the ground from which the tape can attract vision, but also that from which the soundtrack emerges. What in a film would be 'wild track' is here sync. sound, but it is also proof that the equipment was once *here*, the bonus which improves the communication of an impression of reality. Viola goes for the reality principle – a Bazin of the video – save that the route to the real is via the technology. Yet

it is not the artist but the viewer who supplies the reality effect. In effect what happens is that the viewer is invited to reconstruct the artist's experience of the taping as their own experience.

At the same time, there are many other routes through Viola's *oeuvre*. The experience of watching the 1979 tape *Chott El-Djerid (A Portrait in Light and Heat)* rolls between one of illusionism – here is the Sahara, here is frozen Saskatchewan – and another of sheer painterliness that Clement Greenberg would have liked, while Viola's own account is of 'a synthesis between the inside (technology) and the outside (the mirage of the landscape)' (Elwes 1988: 4). The overwhelming otherness of the mirage-veiled landscape leads also in possible further directions: elsewhere Viola suggests

> a transformation of the physical into the psychological . . . . If one believes that hallucinations are the manifestation of some chemical or biological imbalance in the brain, then mirages and desert heat distortions can be considered hallucinations of the landscape. It was like physically being inside someone else's dream.
>
> (London 1988: 37)

Question: in the last sentence quoted, is the 'it' the tape or the experience of making it (as the tense of the verb suggests)? And in either case, who is or was the someone into whose dream an access becomes possible? Is this too a colonial relation?

Viola's relation to Japan in several of the tapes, his proximity (shared with Gary Hill and indeed many other West Coast artists, like poet Gary Snider or pop guru Alan Watts) to Japanese Buddhism, emerges, for example, in the sequence of time-lapse photography in *Hatsu Yume (First Dream)*. Here the permanence of a rock is pointed up by the fleeting passage of ghostly tourists around, beside, in front of it: a presence of another order, a presence which has as purpose to point up the relative lack of presence of human subjects. Yet there is still the need for a human mind – and its technologies – to register the relation and the scale at which it is effective – a scale in which a rock is both important and unimportant. Yet, again, it cannot be without impact that the humans by whom the permanence of the rock is measured are not just simply people, they are Japanese.

The soundtrack to *Anthem* (1983), perhaps Viola's best-known tape in Britain, is a scale of notes generated by modulating 'a single

piercing scream emitted by an eleven-year-old girl' (London 1988: 51) who is also East Asian. *Anthem*, like *I Do Not Know*, is immense in its reverberations: an artwork which describes (as a geometer describes a circle) the trajectories of technologies – architecture, industry, leisure, surgery – towards the common edge of perception, death (more coyly 'the separation of the body and spirit' (ibid.)). What is so fascinating is the constant return, not only in Viola's work but across a range of video practice, of spirituality as a touchstone. Returning with a rhythmic insistence like the ocean: what repressed of the postmodern is taking on these religious guises in order to be reborn?

The experience, to come back at it another way, of Viola's work is an inscription in the field of the visible. The necessity of being seen, as a condition of seeing, resolves the dilemmas of the colonial moment in viewing, though even so the juxtaposition of the distanced observer in *I Do Not Know*, catching the images of animals on a minute video screen, with the 'real' experience of the fire-walkers elsewhere in the tape (see interview with Elwes, Elwes 1988) remains an uncomfortable one. This is not simply because the assumption of the transparency of the medium to one experience and its inability to communicate the other is unsuitably self-contradictory for this kind of analysis, but because the tourist's gaze keeps coming back to haunt us as we watch. Yet much of the work involves a self-scrutiny, under the eye of the bird, which is specifically in the realm of the visual. In *I Do Not Know*, the tragedy is of the incompleteness of the relation – a visual terrain which, because of the irreversible historical gap between us now and the animals, is riven in two, and in which the human eye is now alone and therefore itself incomplete: in Berger's terms, there is no common language (Berger 1980: 26).

Such a theme becomes explicit in *Reverse TV*, a series of portraits of viewers seen from the perspective of the TV set. One recent review suggests that the piece 'reflects the numbed position of the TV audience by offering the monitor as a mirror to the viewer's own passive image' (McLean 1988: 19). I watched something very different: the soundtrack again leading, by placing the portrayed viewers in the context of their own living rooms, emphasised the space of their living, especially the double portraits. The pace of the viewing, the silence and stillness of the viewers, had an impact like the early photographic portraits described by Benjamin in his 'A Small History of Photography' (1979), those which, requiring a

lengthy, motionless sitting seem to produce an air of introspection, gravity, momentary transcendence. At the same time, what emerges in terms of the Berger analysis quoted above is that it is the TV itself which has become the condition of language, of a new visual terrain in which mutual recognition, or at least the recognition of one of the parties by the other, is alone possible.

To be at home: the *Reverse TV* portraits are not negative. This is not to suggest that they are positive. The relation, to return to an earlier example, seems to me to circulate in the grammar of the title *I Do Not Know What It Is I Am Like*: the non-identity of the two 'I's, knowledge in question not of what 'I' am but precisely what 'I' am *like*, the relation of these two questions through a third term, the 'it', itself in question: 'What It'. Reverse portraits allow for a narcissistic gaze, an introspective relation to these others: is this what it is that I am like, caught looking in the gallery at these still, quiet images of people comfortably settled by their sets? The transcendence emerges from the realisation that the question requires no answer. It is the myth of fingerprints: there are so many individuals, individuality doesn't count – except to the individual.

And it is here – 'where all ladders start' – that the issue of the artist returns, shadowed by the question of spirituality, which is held in abeyance in this analysis and art practice alike.

Nam June Paik Korean

Motorola, Carlson, RCA Victor, Philco, Andrea, Capehart, Crosley, Sentinel: the 'antique' cabinets (the term is the catalogue's) of long-defunct black and white sets, the sets of infant Americans now ready to take on the mystery of the set: is it TV that we watch? Or is that which has disappeared with the Ecovision and the Baird televisor some irrefragable element of myself (because it is important to be wary of the word 'we') – a childhood? Paik's 'childlike' playfulness, on which his reviewers discourse at length (reviewers because, in Meaghan Morris's neat distinction between reviewer and critic (1988: 118–19), the reviewer cannot reveal the end and is therefore debarred from discussing structure: in Paik's work, there is no end to reveal) is as apparent in his sculptural use of the bric-à-brac of the nursery – in this instance the old TV relegated to the children's room, hanging on there as a working element long after the demise of these dinosaurs in the 1960s and 1970s living rooms of North America – as it is in the simple visual puns of the *Family of Robot*.

There is the childhood of his audience. But there is also the adult in the audience, who enjoys the child's play of Paik's exhibits. Paik as child is easy to assimilate: he is, after all, Oriental. The colonial relation re-emerges: a Korean, disengaged from the experience of war and US imperialism by an innocence which defuses likewise the imperial intention and allows it to relax into indulgence. This is significantly worked through in the poster for the Hayward show, in which the robot grandfather is surrounded by a border of nursery pink, and inset into the composition is a photographic image of Paik's own grandfather – gentleman or priest? – in traditional Korean costume, posed formally for the portrait photographer; a photo that seems old, prior to the invasions of the mid-twentieth century, the innocent spectacle of the anthropological curiosity.

Yet Paik's work itself seems to legitimate the colonial gaze. Does he not share the iconography of 1960s and 1970s bohemia: Cage, Ginsberg, Beuys, Cunningham? Is he not, with his ceaseless recuperation and reworking of cliché, a colonialist himself? Are not the incessantly flipping and tumbling postcard images of cities in the triumphal arch of *Connection* not the very model of a global colonialism? Like the translucent, inch-long bodies of the tropical fish through which the skittering flow of scratched electronic imagery is to be perceived in *Fish-TV*, Paik seems to make us up out of the colours of television. The bodies of the fish resound with the garish colours of the TV screen, itself imitating their unsuitably flashy dress-sense, caught in a loop. But the circuit is not entirely closed, however, because the tape is of a fixed duration and must stop to rewind, and because the fishes, within their glass prisons, are free to move and some of them, their bodies darkening on the sand at the bottom of the tank, to die. The relation is complex.

For a start, even shocked by the death of fish as part of an artwork, by the emergence of something eternally unrepeatable (as art becomes repeatable in the mechanical or electronic ages?) and irreversible (as drama is reversible: as fictions may be unmade as well as made) – even brought to a limit point (after all it's only a fish), I am complicit in its end. Enjoyment has its own consequences. On the other hand, not enjoying has the same consequences. Some kinds of freedom are seriously circumscribed. This is true, too, of the 'free' play of Paik's tapes, rolling in the same installation: recurrent images of Beuys and his hat, of naked women, of picture-postcard indices of specified towns, cities, tourist spots. Paik plays with tourism as a fund of images, but it is still a fund (a bank, a hoard, a

treasure, an economy): trapped in a monetary circulation, caught in the stickiness of the medium it trades in – neo-colonialist rather than neo-TV (cf. Eco 1984: 18–27).

The global gesture of some of Paik's work – the *Satellite Chair*, for example – is enabled to make the move only by the reduction of difference to its ciphers – postcard imagery which homogenises and reorders as framed and recognisable. The apocalyptic announcement of the end seems to be coming from the nursery, where the infant is surrounded by toys each one of which is so deeply impregnated with his imperial investments of self as to have lost their single identities and to take on, not some whirling simulacral status, but the lineaments of an overwhelming self. And, in turn, the motivation for that would seem to be an uncertainty (becoming an aching void) at the heart of the artist. This is not a monstrous ego – the term is patently wrong for Paik's public persona: it is precisely not ego but some moment prior to ego formation, in which the whirling images are engineered to take on the shapes of a more primordial desire – to lie and be at the centre of the universe. *Satellite Baby*, at the centre of the network of satellite news installed at the Museum of the Moving Image, is not an uncle or a granny but the infant, Freud's 'His Majesty The Baby'.

In 1973, Paik runs a brain scan on John Cage to provide a full-screen image. Also a document of an event, yet even this art without cameras is profoundly humanist. So too is the document of Cage performing his famous 3 minutes and 51 seconds of silence at Harvard Square, its instructions reminiscent of the Yoko Ono of the 'Grapefruit' period: 'see your eyes with your eyes'. The impact of LSD on the Black Mountain avant-garde seems to have been profoundly influenced by the Aldous Huxley of *The Doors of Perception*, whose Blakean title echoes a revived Romanticism – 'If the doors of perception were cleansed every thing would appear to man as it is, infinite' (Blake (1790–3) 1966: 154). In this Romantic reworking, the innocent vision of the child is a through route to the godhead of humanity. In *TV Bra*, a record of an early experiment in chromakey, Charlotte Moorman is shown in *rehearsal* of a cello performance, topless and with a 'bra' made of chromablue, a colour which, because of its wavelength, appears 'transparent' to video equipment, and through which, therefore, other images can be played back. The ritualised performance which she is preparing seems like a purification and a breaking out from the constraints of the everyday. Yet Paik's insistent manipulation of both the props

and the performer move it into the grounds, not of purification but of degradation. In the late 1960s and early 1970s, Paik's work takes place firmly within the boundaries of the North American avant-garde.

'I am a poor man from a poor country so I have to be entertaining every second' Paik tells his interviewer in *Nam June Paik: Edited for Television* (1975): what is and is not art is perhaps an imperial gesture as it relates to the producer, but that cannot alleviate the burden on the viewer. In the work of Beuys and, to a lesser but still significant extent in Cage's work in the late 1960s and early 1970s, the liberation of the artist in everyone is part of a broad political project to destabilise the circumscription of art by defining discourses and practices, like the commodity status of artefacts and the gallery system of the artisan–craftworker mode of production. Humanising the technology through direct work on the electron scan is Paik's vital contribution to the culture at its earliest stages, and perhaps an indicator of the still to be realised future of electronic arts – hardware, not software poses the apparent teleological constraints on communication. Placing various magnets on the cabinet to disrupt the signal in the cathode ray tube, tinkering with the scan-gun to produce a work like *Point of Light*, minimising the technology through the inspired pun of *Candle-TV*: Paik's realisation that the art world cannot recognise work on the image-generating machinery as art leads him to more 'external' and, crucially, *visible* strategies. What is worrying is the way in which this is read back as the genius of an infant, someone whose grasp of language (the English language in its imperial phase) is notoriously strange, *infans*.

This is a poor television, the television of the poor man from a poor country. Like a child, he must entertain. In *Suite 212*, one segment replays the domestic and directionless chatter of passers-by in Washington Square. The work is Fluxus-inspired: what would a people's TV look like? Frank Abbott's *Magic Hour* (UK, 1986) gives a different perspective on the same issue: amateurism, exhibitionism/voyeurism, the factors which

> the policing of taste, artistry and professionalism usually filter out .... If we had more participatory forms of television, then they would be more awkward, more unfinished, crude and tense – a search for language in what people already do, what you call amateur or holiday cultures.
>
> (Cubitt 1986b: 131)

But Abbott is still worried at the political upshot – that control over distribution networks will determine the extraction of programming from producers, that a popular programme-making environment in the 1980s becomes immediately, and in the nature of contemporary capital, a deregulated one. Paik's populist humanism is all too easily reduced to the exploitative level of Ugly George, the New York cable bandit who made his mark by persuading women passing by to strip for his portapak. This is not Paik's fault, but it is part of the rhetoric in which he is celebrated. Paik's humanising gesture, for example in the strikingly beautiful video chairs, is too easily shifted from a subversive play to one which homogenises and thereby makes the global *imperium* possible.

Postmodern *Imperium*

Homi Bhabha (1984: 125–33) argues the relation of speech and writing in the formation of colonial discourse. Colonialism and empire use the written records of government, while the plenitude of speech is reserved for the parliament at the heart of the imperial metropolis. The difference is precisely one of deferral, a Derridean *différance* in which the formal properties of communication are exploited as the means to power. The same message may be made: the specificity of the rulers is that they are apprised of decisions straight away (and may perhaps therefore enter into dialogue with them), while the ruled are always told too late. Time, the time of communication, is a means to power.

A vivid example of this emerges in the decision in October 1988 by the British government to institute a ban on broadcast interviews with 'terrorist' groups, legislation mainly used to silence Sinn Fein and the IRA. A similar ban has operated for ten years in the Republic of Ireland, giving rise to a curious legal problem: can a reporter legitimately refer to a speech, if she doesn't actually quote the words? Can a broadcast journalist give an account of the content of a speech? The answer appears to be a resounding yes, according to the, then, Home Secretary Douglas Hurd, speaking (*sic*) in parliament. The purpose of the legislation is to remove from the IRA and Sinn Fein the right of speech, seen as unmediated in the form of broadcasting. This fits well with the current state of judicial practice in the six counties, where Diplock courts can arraign, try and condemn suspected IRA activists without benefit of a jury, supposedly the backbone of the British democratic system.

The move from speech to writing is then a profoundly colonial one. It concerns the relation of time to power, and of the control over the means of dissemination. This is where Baudrillard's whirligig model of history is so tremendously inadequate. Like some prophet of monetarism drunk on the 'freedom' of the free market, he hurls his imagery into colossal, all-engulfing and synchronous vortices in which everything and every consciousness is affected simultaneously. Yet this is manifestly not the case. Like the Tory wealth which supposedly trickles down – yet takes a seeming age to do so – Baudrillard's precession of simulacra hurtle differentially for different people. The universe, as the scientists now say, is lumpy: there are patches where matter and energy have aggregated, and others where there should be stuff, but is not. In the circulation of discourse, the intersection of power/knowledge and the production of meaning is so intense that it operates, precisely in temporal flows, to institute a regime of meanings, hierarchies of readings, layers of access. The radical 'equality' of the cultural market in Baudrillard is as untrue as the meritocratic rationalisations of monetarists. Both will ultimately create an immiserated underclass: poor and information-poor. At the same time, what psychoanalytic perspectives might we apply to a man who wishes to deny the physicality of origination? The absence of genitalia as marks of sexual difference in *Family of Robot* allows Paik to be both sexual and yet ungendered and infantile, an effect deepened by the silence of the family. Since the notion of family rests four-square on the procreative act, the absence of the figures of its possibility suggest a utopian or neurotic fantasy of the act, a fear of (sexual) origin which produces in turn a phantasm of generation without origin, of creation *ex nihilo*, the fantasy of continuous being or, finally, Baudrillard's hyperreal.

In these circumstances Paik's movements around a poor TV, or his other strategies in multiply-recycled images take on a seriousness which needs a serious address. However, their success within the limited ambit of legitimate art circles in the UK and North America raises a further issue – what is this quality which, in Viola's *I Do Not Know* and the Video-Chairs, strikes home with a powerful emotive reach, beauty, challenge: since something in this work clearly does speak strongly, though in unfamiliar tones? Media theory, as it were a body of knowledge, has not addressed video as such. The terminology of postmodernism prescribes without definition or description. There is still the necessity to use the term, unhappily, guiltily – art.

Two statements by the editors of the recent special issue of *Communications* (Bellour and Duguet (eds) 1988b) offer some sort of glimpse into the difficulty of this unhappy consciousness. Raymond Bellour: 'There is vertigo in the video image, in its principle, in its very being. In the thousands of points which present the weave of the image, how can you fail to recognise the swarming of ideas' (Bellour 1988: 327). Anne-Marie Duguet: 'The time for a heated defense of video has passed. No question any more of searching for its essence starting from elementary technical considerations, no more lost battles over the definition of a terrain that is necessarily uncertain' (Duguet 1988: 221). Duguet's warning is repeated throughout the issue, but so is Bellour's drift into definitional idealism. The problem that seems to emerge is one concerning the discourses of video: discourses, in this issue, of what video is, far more than of what it does.

The worst offender in this regard is Fredric Jameson. In 'La Lecture sans l'interpretation' (Jameson 1988: 105–24), Jameson is in imperial mode, bringing in the English literary figure of the text as the central point of his analysis. This allows him to use one tape and two references (other than to his own work). Of the references, one is a collection containing only one essay on video (Turim 1983 in Kaplan (ed.) 1983), while the other devotes 120 of its 300 pages to reprinting well-known essays by Benjamin, Brecht, Althusser, Enzensberger and Baudrillard (Hanhardt (ed.) 1986). On the basis of these two references, he allows himself to observe that the recurrent theme of video theory is the absence, delay, repression or even the impossibility of a theorisation of video (Jameson 1988: 106). Carefully preparing the ground, Jameson argues for an 'autonomous theory' of video, freed, in particular, from the procedures of film theory. However, he then deals systematically with video as text. In speaking of video time as *durée*, for example, he can be explicit about the effectivity of texts: 'this is precisely machine time, to which these machines that are our spectatorly bodies must adapt themselves, whether we like it or not' (ibid.: 107).

This textual strategy is backed up by a major failing of analysis: confusion of broadcast and video, by means of which he can state, quite incorrectly, that Williams's early concept of continuous flow is the only commonly accepted framework for analysis (even the essays in the Kaplan collection he quotes in the same paragraph could have informed him differently). This allows in turn for video to join the undifferentiated textuality of Baudrillard's hyperreal,

removing all the qualities that make it distinct and which have found such recognition among practitioners. For example, video is for Jameson 'in a certain sense "anonymous" in the good sense of the word (as in mediaeval production, for example)' (ibid.: 107), while artist's use of video as a mode of self-exploration and confession is one of its most dramatic qualities, and one deployed by artists with startling regularity at least since the early 1970s (cf. Bellour 1988). This combination of literary strategies with the confusion of television and video allows more radical — and cumulative — failures of analysis.

Jameson, patronisingly, comments that 'The most profound content [of experimental video] can be described as being that of Ennui': the culture of boredom which is almost unavoidable as the conclusion of the hyperreal is ascribed to all video art (Jameson 1988: 107). 'It is not the least original aspect of video to have abolished the most traditional and oldest category of the "work"' (ibid.): had he investigated the lines back from video into performance art, this wild over-generalisation might have been avoided. Even in the field of literature, the 'open work' is a far from unheard term (cf. Eco 1962; 1981). 'What characterises the video process in particular is the constant rotation of elements, so that they change place at every instant' (Jameson 1988: 116): yet the long take is an important usage among artists, especially feminists, disturbed by the machismo of the fast edit in broadcasting. 'Whatever could be considered a good or even great video text would be bad or defective every time that an interpretation revealed itself as possible, every time the text permitted such spaces for thematisation' (ibid.: 117): ruling the production of meanings may serve the interests of the academy, but it does not speak to the makers and viewers of work. 'One would like to defend the proposition that the most profound "subject" of all video art, and even of all postmodernism, is very precisely the reproductive technology itself' (ibid.: 119). This last statement, itself remarkably close to Greenbergian modernism, is mercifully covered by the realisation that 'if all video texts designated simply the process of production/reproduction, then they would all have to own up to being "the same" in a particularly sterile manner' (ibid.: 119), yet there it is, the unmistakable finale of his own logic. Finally he can reach the apogee of the argument, after a two paragraph run-down on the history of the sign since the dawn of capitalism:

> There remains to us only this pure and arbitrary play of signifiers
> which we call postmodernism... the logic of postmodernism
> which I have tried to portray in its strongest, most original and
> most authentic form in the youthful art of experimental video.
>
> (Jameson 1988: 120)

The metaphors of strength and weakness which weave in and out of
Jameson's text act like the return of the repressed of postmodernism: empire, totalitarianism and the feminine. Imperialist
because, in common with other apologists for the postmodern,
Jameson imposes the US academy's elitist and reactionary rewriting
of 'French Theory' (cf. his friendly reference to the Quisling Paul de
Man (ibid.: 121)) on a whole domain of practice whose specificity he
has not investigated. The conditions and practices of artists and
viewers alike, the activity of work in the making and viewing of
video material, are emptied of their materiality. At the same time he
implies that 'the omnipresence of the media' (ibid.: 105) in 'the new
media society' (ibid.: 109; my emphasis) are truly global effects of
historical change: everywhere, in a single society. This imperial
rhetoric obliterates as no longer real that majority of the world's
population who are not saturated with media: the developing
nations, the homeless of the industrial world, those excluded from
the media by disability . . . . The imperial gesture of postmodernism
is complicit in the homogenising ideologies of the postmodern.

By the same token these arguments are totalitarian, insisting on
the impossibility of global systems of thought – including the most
important popular political movements of our era: ecological, anti-
apartheid and anti-nuclear – in favour of a disabling metaphysics of
the end of history, disguised in the myth that there can be no future
since history is already over: 'The year 2000 will not take place'
(Baudrillard 1986: 18). That this fatalism provides an alibi for
philosophy in the place of field research, and style in the place of
journalism should make us think of Benjamin's formula concerning
the aestheticisation of politics.

The Aesthetic Domain

There seems every possibility that the centralisation of cultural
practice which has characterised the 1980s will continue in the
1990s: the demolition of local democracy in the UK, centralisation
of cultural power in the hands of corporate capital, government
departments and their dependent quangos. In addition, with

further legislation on the statute books or in preparation on secrecy, censorship, freedom of speech and ownership of the means of communication, allied to a host of other repressive legislation, the machinery of a totalitarian state is almost completely in place. Most seriously, the Left has become increasingly aware that the Thatcher faction, if not completely an achieved hegemony, has, in an increasingly current phrase, 'captured the moral high ground'. Europe risks, in the 1990s, the fate of Reagan's United States – a violent right-wing consolidation couched in the rhetoric of religious fervour.

The possibility of mobilising the apparatus of the Thatcher governments' legislation in the spirit of outraged proprieties, in an enforceable hegemony based on 'incontrovertible' moral and – crucially – spiritual values (cf. Saïd 1988) is a terrible prospect. Outcry at time of writing over the British government's handling of the war with the IRA will most likely lead to EC legal procedures in 'terrorist' cases being increasingly standardised on a continental scale. The leadership of the Labour Party are competing here, as in censorship, secrecy, the Malvinas war and the legality of political and extra-parliamentary campaigns, to be more authoritatively repressive than the Tories. The Left has lost the high ground, largely through the wilful acquiescence of its national leadership in the suppression of every spontaneous movement of utopian sympathies – the Wapping dispute, the miners, the seamen, the Greater London Council and metropolitan boroughs. But there is another contributing factor: the failure of the Left, in moving away from the pastoral nostalgia of William Morris, to make up for the engagement of the socialists of the first years of this century in debates on the aesthetic, understanding the word as a secular form of that dimension of human aspiration which would otherwise be termed spiritual.

Religiosity will be a danger because the intellectual Left has still never lost its puritanism and because it has remained, variously, colonialist, knowing, coy and patronising about popular pleasures. Popular culture at various moments and in a variety of practices verges upon the sublime: the Right, it is to be feared, will eliminate such profoundly humane pleasures, or appropriate them for the moneyed elite and the cultural forms that carry their stamp of approval. What is required is a way to grapple, not with the textuality but with the practices and experiences which at present we must still speak of as if in a foreign language or as if confronted

with the limit point between the animal and human worlds. Lacan observes on this subject that

> It appears – and this phenomenon can only be a subject of astonishment for us – how greatly the symbolic process as such is inoperant in the animal world. A difference of intelligence, adaptability and complexity of the two systems cannot be the sole criterion on which we can permit ourselves to designate this absence. That man [sic] should be held in symbolic processes in a way to which no animal can accede in a parallel manner cannot be resolved in terms of psychology, but implies that we must have to begin with a complete, strict knowledge of what this symbolic process means.
>
> (Lacan 1986: 57–8)

The problem of the spiritual and the aesthetic, joined in Lacan's exploration of the psychoanalytic ethic, devolves therefore on the issue of the provenance of the symbolic, and specifically on the issue of sublimation.

Sublimation involves a complex interplay in which desire is cycled through the vagaries of a relation between intra- and interpsychic dynamics, moving between the subject and the Symbolic. Sublimation takes the banal object of desire and makes it Other: makes it, to be precise, impossible, absurd. Lacan uses the example of courtly love, in which the beloved is moved beyond object-choice, which always derives from the imaginary relation to (an ideal of) oneself, the realm of that unnameable Thing (*Das Ding*) which lies at the heart of this volume of the *Seminar*. The Thing pre-dates and precedes good and evil, the pleasure principle and the reality principle and their dialectic, and indeed is constitutive of them. It is an Other that lurks at the centre of those ambiguous and ancient others – the mother's body for example – as a destructuring absence whose reality underpins the *peu de réalité* of the subject. Its proper mode might be explored, not as belief – the refuge of the moral Right – but as unbelief, a constant questioning driven by the common, formative absence in human experience: a resistance to truth (ibid.: 155–7).

In positing the Thing as a central Freudian category from the *Entwurf* to *Beyond the Pleasure Principle*, Lacan analyses not only the problem of ethics but the problem of evil after the death of God. Marking the cruelty of *jouissance* in a variety of historical texts, he moves towards a domain on which Freud himself was deeply reserved:

The real barrier which halts the subject before the unnameable field of radical desire in as much as it is the field of absolute destruction, of destruction beyond putrefaction, is properly speaking the aesthetic phenomenon in as much as it is identifiable with the experience of the beautiful – the beautiful in its blazing glory, that beautiful of which it is said that it is the splendour of truth. This is evidently because truth is not so pretty to look at that the beautiful is, if not its splendour, at least its covering.

(Lacan 1986: 256)

Something like such a secular account of the further reaches of human experience, the capability for joy and for holocaust, some attention to the sublime (as, perhaps, the sublimated) may be the only barrier between us and the fatalism and brutality of the developing hegemony.

Baudrillardiste futurology, governed by the phantasmic plenitude of the totalising, central Code, is, as Peter Wollen suggests, symptomatic of 'a loss of faith in human reason and a revolt against "modernity" considered as the elevation of instrumental reason to absolute status' (Wollen 1988: 33). Wollen goes on to suggest that the 'philosophical abyss' which has opened up between the formal logics that inform computerisation and the anti-rational stance of 'post-metaphysical' philosophy is responsible for an impasse in the development of an aesthetic appropriate to contemporary conditions. He suggests two paths: theories respectively of heterogeneity and intertextuality. Similar positions are emerging in a range of disciplines, especially in the form of reference to the work of Bakhtin and his circle and the new currency of terms like heteroglossia, dialogism and carnival. As Robert Stam points out (1988: 117), 'The last few years have witnessed, in fact, a kind of posthumous wrestle over the soul of Bakhtin' between Marxists and liberal Christians. The risk is that, in wrestling Bakhtin away from the Christian humanism of the status quo, his genuine contributions to the aesthetic dimensions of revolutionary praxis might be jettisoned as well. To such a dialogic programme, the germ perhaps of an ecological approach, I would only add that inequality and power are still the fundamental dystopian structures that will militate against the realisation of the aesthetic domain in practical terms.

Chapter 7

Out of sight

The previous two chapters have in many ways left out of consideration the possibility of video's representation of reality, preferring instead to talk about its relations with it. I do not intend some idealist mystique here: video is perfectly real. It enters into perfectly real (if really imperfect) relations with the rest of the world. And yes, there is a relation between the video image – at least those images made with cameras – and the world surrounding. Again, the paucity of the vocabulary prompts me to opt for a term that's less than satisfactory, at once too ordinary and too overweening, too narrow and too unfashionable: the word politics.

When Aristotle characterised humanity as the social animal, the actual term he used was 'politikon zoon', where in ancient Greece the word political derived directly from 'polis', the city. It is this usage of the word I have in mind when describing video as political. I've already argued that there is no video without sociality. Yet clearly there are domains of video which take politics more seriously, more explicitly or more centrally than others.

The alternative would have been to talk about community video (closest to the sense of 'polis'), campaign video, committed video. Each of which terms have their own histories and pratfalls. The term community was alwaysused within a specific kind of funding practice among art agencies in the late 1970s and early 1980s, but even at the height of its popularity, the word was already leaky. Rather than a sound container in which all members of the geographical community could be poured, the bucket proved to have major holes in it: different races, ages, sexes, classes with little in common but the same bus-stops. In many ways, for practitioners at least, a more useful and imaginative term than those, such as 'cultural industries' and 'enterprise culture' that have followed in the

UK and increasingly in Europe and the English-speaking world, it is none the less so historically marked as to be unusable. Campaign video is probably more narrow still than political video. A great deal of the work, the practices and the futures, are not bound to specific issues and cannot be usefully defined through the notion of a campaign, though many tapemakers are consciously engaged in a multitude of campaigns, and some are involved in political work of this tightly-defined kind regardless of their intentions. Commitment is still the term of existential engagement: its use would describe accurately only a small area of work and distort the actualities of much video practice in the 1980s.

The political is, for the purposes of definition, first and foremost a relation and only secondarily a relation *between*: it is more important that it is understood as a relation than that the terms of the relation be understood as individuals, classes, genders. Let us say, initially, that political culture entails a question of reading. Where cinema deals in a total and overwhelming experience, video has the option of using its tangential relation with its audio-visual predecessor to reveal, in its own terms, the film that lies within the film. Any reader does something like this, deciphering, searching for the secret meaning hidden beneath the surface of the text. An artist like Jeremy Welsh, the British maker of *I.O.D.* cited on p. 99, would argue that there is no secret, that the surfaces are self-sufficient, that the effect of depth is merely an effect, like perspective in a two-dimensional field. But the hermeneutics of interpretation suggest, not that there is a single overriding ur-text that, like a ghostly map of the final thing, originates the text we read. Rather the material form of the text, the phenomenon that we encounter as readers, generates its ur-texts (plural) after the event. Julia Kristeva's proposal for 'sémanalyse' (1969) posits an immanent pheno-text, that which presents itself to the reader in the most immediate way, and a geno-text, which is the deep structure underlying it and which 'sémanalysis', by analogy with psychoanalysis, tries to uncover. However, video hermeneutics suggest that the pheno-text predates the geno-text and multiplies it in the act of reading. Who put the 'ur' in 'surface'?

Politically, though, the reading has to emerge into a public domain where it too can become subject to the process of making meanings. This is what happens in *Calling the Shots* by Mark Wilcox, which uses actors and quotations to deconstruct a scene from the classic Douglas Sirk melodrama *Imitation of Life*. It is no accident that

Wilcox uses a film whose importance to the canon of film studies is so great: this is a reading to place in a history of readings. And it is a marker of the umbilical relation between the definition of political in play here and its narrower usage that this tape, unlike those quoted in the last chapter, has never been broadcast and cannot be distributed with any degree of ease (though it is part of the *Elusive Sign* package toured by the Arts Council and the British Council). Wilcox's interest is in a detailed analysis of the modes of melodrama: lighting, dialogue, camera angles, framing, as Mike O'Prey argues in the catalogue to *The Elusive Sign* (Curtis 1987: 50). It is also a tape which, ostensibly about the making of femininity in the Hollywood film, makes a series of statements about masculinity which move in intensity from the poignant to the fearful.

The previous chapter relied largely on examples of tapes which have been broadcast in the UK: this one will have to quote from less easily available videos. This may seem at first like the revenge of the marginal. On the contrary, video culture as such has no centre, and therefore no peripheries. This is not to say that there are no power relations – the next chapter will deal with them, in terms of struggles for democracy. But within the regime of the monitor, there is no hierarchy: Wilcox is not indebted to Sirk in any uncomplicated way – there is an economy at work in which neither text remains unaltered by its shadow. *Calling the Shots* will not stop the tears from falling during *Imitation*: the tears will not spoil the wit (and underlying fears) of *Calling*. This is the trade of the politikon zoon, a 'community' art in the sense that stealing images from Sirk's film doesn't diminish what Sirk still has. Sirk, unusually, got legal rights to the cutting of his work (though distributors had all other rights), as rumour had it, after a British television company broadcast a truncated version of one film: democracy of the image only up to a point. Yet the technology is such that it reduplicates, and in so doing creates the conditions for multiple readings, multiple forgettings. In this sense, it is broadcasting which is peripheral, and the amateur – in the optimal sense of one who works out of love – who recentres the field of meaning at the local level.

The 'post-political' drift of much contemporary cultural criticism is seriously hampered by its need – as in Foucault's work or, more frequently, in work deriving from it – to read all power as negative, just as the reading of all desire as positive walks towards the totalitarian. What is at stake is the mutual nature of struggle: pacifism, clean hands and an empty heart are not answers to the

exercise of domination. Peter Dews quotes Foucault's remark that 'Confinement, prisons, dungeons, even tortures engaged in a mute dialogue between reason and unreason – the dialogue of struggle. With the advent of the asylum, however, this dialogue itself was now disengaged; silence was absolute' and observes

> Thus although the concept of reciprocity does play an implicitly critical role in Foucault's work, this is not a non-coercive reciprocity which could be made the goal of political struggle. Rather it is a reciprocity of struggle which has now been replaced by an enforced tranquility; its effect is to make the social order of the present appear even more hopelessly unilateral and oppressive.
>
> (Dews 1987: 199)

So Foucault looks backwards, to an era before the age of revolutions, the industrial revolution and the bourgeois state, in order to find a social order which is less oppressive than the regimes governing madness, illness, sexuality and knowledge which he identifies in his major 'archaeological' studies as the characteristic organisations of our epoch. Thus the madman in an earlier period could speak to the sane of the fragility of reason: but inside the asylum, with its regimen of power and expertise, the madman is always to be spoken about. The 'gentle efficacy of total surveillance' (Foucault 1977: 239) replaces the robust dialectics of an earlier age.

Catherine Elwes's tape *With Child* works through the more fragile dialectic of personal politics, particularly the strangeness which adults acquire around childbirth. The artist, pregnant, rehearses the activities and expressions of the child, while the child's toys, notoriously two stuffed monkeys, take on the adult roles of sexual activity. Here the relations around the *auteur* become more complex than in examples cited in the previous chapter. But the spacing remains: Elwes uses the fact of her own pregnancy to represent herself pregnant, the effects of pregnancy, the poetics of perinatal trauma, and her own presence on screen is a representation of her presence. It is therefore itself an absence: a picture of something is always a picture, not the something. A picture of Elwes marks her absence from the picture plane. Yet there remains an uncertainty about the relations of the two. In particular, pregnancy and childbirth are given a prominent position in ideologies of women's oppression. The 'beauty', 'mystery', 'naturalness' of childbirth guarantee the absolute difference of the woman, tie her to the

biology of her sex as the essence which she is preordained to fulfil.

In this sense, the image of the pregnant woman moves through a series of phases within patriarchal regimes of image-making. If every signifier is 'hollow', as I argued above (p. 105), and women are, in Laura Mulvey's terms, signifiers who connote 'To-be-looked-at-ness', then they are surely the hollowest of all signifiers, waiting to be filled with the male look, to be impregnated, completed, made perfect. But the logic of that look is vitiated in the figure of the pregnant woman, who is already full, already complete, in the words of the ideology of sexual difference, 'in a way no man can be'. Men ostensibly envy women their childbearing. Yet the practices and meanings around pregnancy, especially on the part of (non-professional) men, are full of connotations of fragility and, if we search the lockers of the horror film, with terrors of monstrous births. Elwes's tape seems to pull on many of these facets of pregnancy, the cultural meanings, the social status, to such an extent that the suggestion that this is only a 'personal' piece would appear naive if not actually ideologically limiting itself.

But we are dealing with a genuine personal position here around the issue of pregnancy and the positioning of women as the objects of the discourse of pregnancy rather than as its subjects – people to be spoken about, for example in medical or artistic discourses, rather than subjects who speak for themselves. *With Child* is speech from a place, the place of the pregnant woman, where speech is not expected. At the same time, though, it is speech covered and constrained – but not determined – by the nature of the discourses which cluster around so heavily symbolic an event, pregnant, as they say, with meaning. The process of personal politics is tied inescapably to the politics of language, that most interpersonal of events. The speaker, in the nature of social communication, must be prepared at some point and in some way to relinquish control over the making of meaning to the person spoken to, and be ready to become in turn the addressee, or in any case to leave that moment of the process be. Personal politics is never completed (and misnamed as personal): where there is personal politics, it is always already social, as the word political itself suggests. And as a social form, it cannot be completed.

Personal politics is, though, a route through the interface of the social and the individual, that difficult interface which I have tried exploring above through issues of language and psychoanalysis. Elwes's work operates at a threshold where relations of power are

thrown into question, in a way that would not be possible if the exercise of patriarchal power were absolute. More than that, by playing, in the instance of *With Child*, with the iconography of pregnancy, she again recentres the discourse of sexuality around the issue of femininity in a motion which is socially illegitimate. Because after all the image of a pregnant woman is no simple signifier in a visual language but a picture which, in motion, attracts narratives around it. Here is a condition which is unstable: a condition that cannot be maintained, a plenitude that reaches its fullest just at the moment of highest drama at which it must come to an end.

As I write (8.8.88) Fergie, Duchess of York, has been announced as being in labour. The date has been ratified as 'momentous'. A nation holds its breath. That is the mainstream representation of pregnancy: the route royal to the bearing of heirs. That is pregnancy as signifier in a chain of signifiers. Significantly, the duchess has been hidden from prying eyes in her interesting condition, as she 'nears her time', as the circumlocutions fly outwards from the point of parturition. Birth is a fearful entity, and its mechanisms, even now, wreathed in ritual, myth and mysterious gobbledegook. Elwes's tape does something rather different with the image – it removes it from 'language' (literally in the sense that the soundtrack eschews words, more generally from organisations of discourse, aural and visual, that are centrally or hierarchically controlled). At the same time, freed of the limiting role of the voice-over, it attacks the image from inside, from its hollowness, all the more dramatically because of that dialectic of the full and the vacuous sketched out above.

Just as disturbing, in a more general analysis, is the fact that the tape has in some way ceased to be hers, despite her intensely personal engagement with it. Similarly, in some of Elwes's later tapes, her child appears to have become not just a separate person, but someone somehow belonging to a different social or discursive organisation. Again, the rules of social/political interaction, here at the micro-level at which we might hope to understand them, refuse to be held in check by the macro-structures within which they occur. Clearly men are beneficiaries of a system which gives them power, influence, wealth and other opportunities at the expense of women. Yet, though this is true of whole societies analysed at the global level, we do not live in whole societies, but in increasingly atomised cells within them, and at that level politics of a different sort goes on.

Elwes's tape, in any case, almost certainly means something very different from the above analysis when watched by women, or mothers, or expectant mothers: an instance of the leakiness of patriarchal meaning structures, in which one of the central groups of signifiers – women as signifiers of (male) desire and power – are also capable of signification.

For instance, video adds itself to domestic media like hi-fi, telephones, television and the home computer. With a few simple adjuncts, the leisure apparatuses become complex telecommunications devices capable of turning the home into an office. Major research undertaken by Greater London and Sheffield City Councils in the early 1980s pointed to the likelihood that buildings like the National Westminster Tower, a bank building dominating the financial district in London, were the last of the dinosaurs. In the interests of lowering the cost of overheads, capital would accelerate its flow out from the inner-cities, re-equipping workers' homes with modems and hard-wired links to in-house mainframes so that heating costs, cleaning, catering overheads and so on would be covered by the worker and the domestic infrastructure. The same strategy, it was noted, was used in the sweated trades, putting out piecework in garment and assemblage industries to homeworkers, almost exclusively women with child care duties, almost exclusively badly paid, and with the added bonus of being removed from all other colleagues and therefore from trades unionism. Video emerges, with the entertainment technologies listed above, in the home, that is in women's workspaces, whether that is outworking or domestic labour. The function of the video as electronic child-minder is supplemented by its role as site for fantasy during working hours, like the radio in a factory. What is peripheral here: the TV message from the metropolitan centres or the experience of work with the TV on in the background?

We know that timeshifting impacts on the way that meanings are generated in the viewing arena. But how does shifting the content of videotape alter what can be done with it? If capital begins to use video for training, health and safety, quality control in the outworking market, what price an alternative flow, from the grassroots inwards? And what might happen to work circulating in the big market of broadcasting? Is TV's very mode of delivery tyrannical and aggressive, swallowing up everything and reducing it to the same regurgitated pap? I want to return to these issues, but for the moment, let's think how they might relate to the figure of the

author. TV's ideology of presence and endless flow make the institution the author, not its shift-workers. There are the special programmes we turn on because they are Denis Potter or David Attenborough, but by and large we turn on the television: a machine for producing programmes, an institution, not a collection of individually recognised or recognisable *auteurs*.

Does timeshifting alter the homogenising process? Or is there a sense in which it no longer matters, from the point of view of the institution, whether we watch or not, so long as the set is on, the adverts keep being paid for and the moral guardians appeased? From the point of view of the BBC or ABC or any other ingredient of TV's anonymous alphabet soup, people only exist to be audiences. They need to be cajoled, their desires stimulated, their juices set flowing but their existence is a combination of the mechanical, the statistical and the bodily. TV has created the terms of its own incompetence to communicate at large with any *one*, while maintaining its position as *mass* communicator.

It is in such interstices that the television set begins to assume its autonomy. There is only the assumption that television works to guide us into allowing it to do so. Once the assumption breaks down, as it does through the rival illusion that the remote control gives us power over broadcasting, there is no end to the fragmentation, a fragmentation that does not need even to be 'hands-on'. Traditional (pre-video) television criticism has made a monument of the institutions and the texts of the small screen, as Foucault describes the role of history in *The Archaeology of Knowledge* (1972: 7). With video, the nature of the institution changes, since we can no longer presume the efficacy of its organisation. The video deck is discontinuous from the seamlessness of TV plenitude. What begins to emerge is a 'monstrous' politics which can 'embrace partial, contradictory, permanently unclosed, constructions of personal and collective selves' which one commentator, Donna Harraway, believes can still remain effective, faithful and socialist-feminist (Harraway 1985: 75). Or: what has changed is the relation to the institution, so that it becomes possible to think of the institution as from a distance and to begin to instigate discourses which do not presume its centrality.

The Max Almy tape *Perfect Leader* is an exemplary working through of these theses, a serious funk track laid down under an image montage in which the male actor is dressed and directed in a series of options around the notion of the perfect politician within a

visual matrix reminiscent of a computer-aided design centre. From the Mussoliniesque to the suave, from the religiose to the sophisticated, political change is presented as stylistic, mapping the results of market research on to the selling of a candidate, style never having changed the inner organs of the beast. Deconstruction here, as in the work of the philosopher Derrida whence it has come into currency, is not a synonym for fragmentation or reassembling dissociated bits into a new and perhaps self-reflexive format. It is an issue of uncovering the nature of binary oppositions – male/female, Black/white, art/science, speech/writing – which Derrida understands as the philosophical underpinnings of all western discourse and ultimately of western power. How does the tape deconstruct the category of leadership?

Here the question is around the way in which a man – and Almy is very much a feminist tapemaker – finds the wherewithal to become a leader. Our natural tendency is to expect that a certain array of 'gifts', 'charisma', 'personal qualities', 'leadership' and a list of other vapid clichés ('something undefinable . . . ') make a man a leader. Power-broking, however, has little to do with that: the selection of uncharismatic candidates in the very public decision-making of the US primary campaigns of 1988 show that many other determinants are in play. The deconstructionist moves in two stages. First, she reverses the expected workings: what if the making of a president were more important than the president himself? But then there comes another movement, one which emerges as comedy in the Almy tape: what if the dyad we have operated on in stage one is itself a blind for a more complex nexus of differences? What if the cosy relation of dominant/oppressed is not just open to reversal, but is actually an inaccurate description of relations? What if there are more than two sexes? What if sexual difference is more than men/women? What if political power does involve a personal politics, in the sense of personalities, individual psychic make-up? What happens then, when Almy's creation goes over the top as a fascist dictator? The machine produces a machine out of a man, but the flesh and the technology interact to form an entity which may not, like video itself, be quite in hand: a cyborg, occupying the liminal phase between the human and the machine, intelligence and information, the individual and the social (cf. Harraway 1985).

When I raised the issue of the 'apparatus' in Chapter 4, it was as a match between the machinery of the video deck and the psychic formations which we bring to bear upon it. I am arguing here that

the apparatus is in some form and in certain instances a cyborg itself, a creature part human, part machine, in which the defining boundaries and directions of flow are far less clear than we like to imagine. Almy's perfect leader is a case in point: a media-made machine, built out of a human being, whether we read that as the actor or as the character. Or: we do not see the leader figure from a point of view 'natural' to ourselves but from one constructed for us in the camera-angle, lensing, lighting, editing. We see the leader being organised at the same time as we are organised in such a way that we can see him being organised. In a theatre you have a natural perspective: you may sit where your eyeline matches that of the protagonists on stage, or you may be looking down from above or up from below. In every instance, however, your perspective on the action is the 'natural' one in the sense that it depends on where your seat is. In electronic media, perspectives are organised in the complex interplay of machine and viewer, not in the relationship between your chair and the monitor. There is a time-based perspective at play here too: the ability of screen and viewer to switch between perspectives, within and between segments of action. If the cinematic apparatus is designed in such a way that it produces the reality effect as a major function of its procedures, how does the video apparatus operate?

One line of thought leads through to an understanding of video as dream, the kind of working through which is associated with pop video analysis (cf. Burns 1988, for example), and which might be particularly apposite for computer-generated images, especially algorithmic images (images produced mathematically rather than with paint systems), which allow for perspectives not initially or necessarily premised on the human eye. Another looks to a more explicitly political relation. Tapes and projects like *Despite TV*, *Framed Youth*, *The Miners' Campaign Tapes* and *Ceiber* have served in many ways to focus attention on the documentary forms of video, but also to negotiate the notion of video as process, engaging geographical communities or communities of interest in the making of the work as part and parcel of the work itself, a practice with interesting parallels in certain contemporary artists' practice. Formally, the reliance of these documentaries on the combination of soundtrack and image leads to an analysis in which sound plays a more obviously important role. The Karen Alexander/Albany tape *MsTaken Identities*, for example, remains in mind not only because of its development as a girls' project in a

working-class inner-city area, but because of the lyrics to the a cappella song about waiting at the clinic as much as for the accompanying action. Despite its divergence from TV documentary, this tape shares TV's reliance on sound for its message. What distinguishes it from standard TV fare is the play between sound and image, rather than the familiar subordination of the latter to the former.

What is different about video documentary, as opposed to its Griersonian cousins, is that the reality effect (Barthes 1973) is not an available item in the repertoire. When we see an obviously video image on broadcast TV, on-screen anchor men and women hint at manipulation: the hostage making a statement to camera or hand-held shots of gun-battles are questioned for their possibly misleading effects far more intensely than footage bought in from the usual agencies. Yet the more degraded the image, the more likely it is to be a document, made by those most closely involved with the event, those without the resources of News International or Reuters behind them – the embattled poor. It is unsurprising that television news feels compelled to cast aspersions on the products of Nicaraguan television. This links in with the totalitarian inclinations of TV. If you stop to argue with the announcer – 'Bloody lies, how dare they? . . . ' – you miss what she's saying next, get shooshed by your viewing partners, are unable to respond coherently because you haven't heard the full story. The catch is that you never will hear the full story, because TV doesn't stop telling it, through its cycles of repetition and fading memories. Only with timeshift does the opportunity arise to do real work on the TV image, as taping allows the elements of narration to emerge from the mythology of total meaning into a space in which struggle returns to the construction of sense.

Struggle is the heart of documentary video practice, from the struggle to find cash and equipment, the struggle to gain and share skills, the institutional struggles around funding and access, legal battles like the clearance of music rights in the case of *Framed Youth* (mainly due to its subtitle and subject-matter: *Revenge of the Teenage Perverts* by the Teenage Lesbian and Gay Video Group), struggles for distribution, for broadcast airtime (sought because it is the quickest and most effective distribution medium, denied because of engineering standards used to maintain the professional oligarchy of the networks). But it also remains in the difficulty of preparing a

video within a news/current affairs area, without sinking into the patriarchal, patronising and ossified formal and ideological strategies of broadcast forms, and without access to the same equipment or levels of staffing.

For some, the choice of low-band equipment is an aesthetic/political one, an aid to demystifying the process of production, approximating community and campaign work to the available technologies of the high-street rental market. Such is the approach of Despite TV, the group responsible for the magazine tapes of the same name which cover the community of the East End. Their tape on the dispute at Wapping over Rupert Murdoch's print plant, *Despite the Sun*, equals and excels most of the broadcast material, because they know the area better, and because they are in struggle, taping police attempts to stop both themselves and a BBC crew from taping, while the BBC failed to cover the story at all. According to some sources, it was Murdoch's handling of the Wapping dispute which persuaded financiers to back his purchase of 20th Century Fox: in the light of this connection between local issues and multinational media operations, the choice of low-budget video techniques seems to be a political–aesthetic choice of great consequence. But the effect of the tape itself is not to document as such. What one comes away with is a vision of comet-tails and flares and saturated colour, the effects of night-shooting with VHS cameras, of sound that has to be strained after to be heard, and some startling images of massed ranks of police and lorries storming through the picket lines. The effect is not one of clear explanation, rational reportage, balance. It is of urgency, even desperation, of confusion and the constant threat – and frequent actuality – of violence.

In short, while it had an urgent message, the tape functioned not as a persuader but as a blast against the prevailing coverage, as a voice in a dialogue with other voices. Video, unlike TV, doesn't presume either the ignorance of the viewer or the uniqueness of its signal: video assumes your partisan assumptions, your plural access to media, your own decentred relation to it and its to you, in the sense that there is, as argued above (p. 37), no centre to video culture, rather the massed dialogues of disparate viewers with their sets and with each other. Other tapes, such as the award-winning *The Miners' Campaign Tapes*, argue their cases every bit as passionately as *Despite the Sun*. Again, unlike broadcast, *The Miners' Campaign Tapes* boasted their origination as part of the

support movement for the National Union of Mineworkers, in the co-operation of workshops across the country, amassing material and raising funds to edit and distribute to NUM shops and Miners' Support Groups. Their function was to raise awareness and support, to help the fight continue through demonstrations of solidarity, to encourage donations to the fighting funds, to help give some sort of coherence to the movement.

But again it must be asserted that these were documents, not news. They did not purport to tell the 'story' – did not, that is, construct the struggle as a marketable narrative – and did not seek to impose consensus. These are voices raised in anger, seeking not to describe reality but to change it. They do not pretend to objectivity. At the same time, it can be said that they strive to create an identity, in a way which has become a commonplace of the discourse around community and campaign video, and which relates it directly to a broader field of video practice in which the issue of identity is at stake, including some varieties of artists' video.

The machinery of *auteurism* clearly breaks down at the junction with process video, where the purpose of the work involved is not to end with a product but to provide a mode of access and engagement in cultural practice for as many people as possible. However people in the workshop sector, locally and nationally, are able to recognise particular workers as key figures in the culture. A particular project has the flavour of this or that enthusiast or *animateur*. The recognition factor is, on the other hand, also stacked around particular modes of organisation, patterns of work and senses of community which may run across different groups, or be the fault-lines within individual workshops or projects. In addition, key 'individuals' may be key because they are in effect institutions: the manager of a facilities house (a centre for post-production and equipment hire), a key worker in distributors like London Video Arts or Electronic Arts Intermix, festival directors, strategically-placed journalists, entrepreneurs and promoters . . . .

Yet there is at stake in the play of video and its progenitors a politics of identity. On the one hand, the radical movements with which video has grown up, gay liberation, the women's movement, the politics of race, demand that the identity of the *auteur* be signalled as Black, a woman, gay. There is a struggle here for access to the media, and since media institutions are not wont to give up power, its seizure in the form of low-budget work is to be celebrated as the beginning of that struggle. However, the construction of

identity on the basis of work, for example, 'by and for women' has tended to use 'by' as the determining term, since many feminists are happy to reach mixed audiences. The set of uses of a given work are qualifiers, not determinants.

In the Black sector, this emerges even more in an assertive dialectic around the presence and absence of the tapemaker to the tape, notably in Isaac Julien and Sankofa's *Who Killed Colin Roach?*, *Territories* and *This is Not an AIDS Ad*, in all three of which the director appears. In *Colin Roach*, this is almost incidental, not greatly marked, an instance of the tapemaker as a member of the community, in it, sharing its struggle. *Territories*, in Kobena Mercer's words, 'seeks to address images of desire into which black people could imagine themselves ... it is addressing a question which is raised by the event of carnival itself, that is, the plurality of sexual identities, of opportunities and possibilities of sexual expression' (Mercer 1988b: 22). In this process, the director's on-screen image plays a central but decentring role. *This is Not an AIDS Ad* is the clearest expression of gay love, a celebration in the face of the terrorism of UK AIDS advertising: the maker's sexuality an essential element of the meaning of the tape. In each piece, the presence of the tape to the community is an unsettling of the position of the author, a putting into question.

We have then, on the one hand, the assertion of Black tapemaking as a cultural practice. On the other, the politics of identity, already disturbed in the decentring of subjectivity and the 'death of the author' in contemporary cultural practice generally, is compounded with the politics of 'The Invisible Man', Ralph Ellison's startling metaphor for the invisibility of Black people to the dominant culture, their construction as Other, as the repressed part of a binary opposition, functioning to underwrite the normalcy of the white, heterosexual man. I am aware of treading on dangerous ground, of expropriating the cultural work of cultural Others into my own discourse. Yet it must be argued: individuals, even groups, do not make their work in conditions of their own choosing. The apparatus is still inscribed with its historically-acquired properties, and radical attempts to destabilise those expected qualities can provoke the most outraged responses or, worse still, boredom. The refusal of expected pleasures breeds all sorts of divisiveness, as was the case with the film *Handsworth Songs*, subject of acrimonious exchanges in the *Guardian* on its release (reprinted in Mercer 1988a; cf. Auguiste 1988; Fusco 1988; Gilroy and Pines 1988). Film, of course, still

occupies a more central space than tape in the literary culture.

But what remains problematic in the instance of authorship is the fading of the author from the work. Film studies speaks of the way in which a representation must represent something – such as a personality – in its formal absence. The image and the sound must be other than the voice and visual presence of the actor, let's say. Thus the towering images of the stars on their 30-foot-high screens give us the illusion of being in the close physical space of our idols (cf. Barthes 1980). TV already fails to do that: its largest close-ups are only slightly bigger than your head. It has its own structures of fascination. In video, something else is in play: the way in which figures fade from the screen. In daily life, people are always on the brink of becoming, constantly in process without ever actually *being*, in the sense of existing as finally achieved, complete and unchanging entities. Film offers the illusion of being: that is why it can offer such strong models for identification – its people are always far more present than we feel ourselves to be. But in video, the images of characters are always fading away. In life people constantly approach completion; in film they appear to exist completely; in video, it is as if they have existed completely just a moment before, but that that moment has gone, and they are losing being. Likewise the presence of the author to the work is a constant fading. The difference is not absolute, it is a changing relation: as the image is forever fading, never complete on the scan, the author fades constantly out of it.

In this sad dialectic of the electron scan, Barthes's *aperçu* in *Camera Lucida* invites us to imagine the emotional stress made manifest in the issue of identity: he argues there that the shifters 'here' and 'now' are disjointed by photography, so that what is here is what was then. For Barthes, suffering the loss of his beloved mother, the right to accept the documentary value of the photograph was an essential human one: to believe that she had existed, that a photograph of her held some relation to that dear and lost presence. The confessional of the video absolves its poets through a different but related quality, the supersession of images and the incompletion of each one. Though the video image and the magnetic sound are physical homologues of the events before the camera and mike – like Barthes's photographic document – they are different from it, at first only a little, during the moment of taping, but progressively more and more so as time goes on. The author fades globally from the tape, and in each viewing s/he re-emerges, almost, in moments,

in the interstices between images, like a ghost in the unseen control track. In video, the creative process may still give rise to metaphors of birth, but the viewing is far more like watching a small death.

The politics of cultural identity, in which so much video is engaged, is caught in its own dialectic: people making meaning, but not in conditions of their own choosing. But still making meaning: their own meaning, despite the circumstances. The importance of asserting your existence inside a culture which forever recognises you only as different is itself a celebration of difference, but within the terms of an homogenising and debilitating technology: the electron scan. The homologue to this in the video apparatus is the constant becoming of the viewer, addressed in the fading as a becoming. In the dialectic of identity, as the on-screen image fades, it enables the viewer to become. This on-screen fading calls the viewer into a relation, not of identification but of replacing what progressively absents itself from the image. This close relation with the screen performs the function in video viewing that identification does in cinema, but it is quite different, more a question of perspectives, and of an invitation to become in that space which is being vacated. This is the power of the flickering image: though, paradoxically, based on mutual recognition of difference, it is an invitation to become the same; to become Black, a woman, working class, gay . . . at the moment of their video fading. To become, not to be: video viewing marks a yearning towards a state of otherness as incomplete and unfulfillable as the fading of the author. Not, in the words of a well-known graffito, ' "I" is an other' (*je est un autre*) but ' "I" becomes an other – one which is no longer there'. In this same dialectic, it is not only oppressed communities that are other but each of us, irredeemably other than the dominant culture in which we might take our places.

The fading of the subject is itself a product of – or perhaps is reproduced in – a practice which has become central to political videomaking, the built-in obsolescence of the tape. It is a function of dominance to become monumental, to boast permanence, whether it be the playwright who is for all time, or the imperial architecture of City Fathers, from the Parthenon to the Rockefeller Plaza. Power always masks its transience in the hardest materials it can find, in the maximum opacity: the chrome and gleaming black of the limousines of the powerful or the mirror shades of cops. TV seems all transparency, but builds its monument in the incessant present it constructs, and in the trace that it lays down, so that we remember

how long ago we had the mumps because *The Lone Ranger* was on, or that it was a Thursday because it was *Top of the Pops*. TV is still, like language, totalitarian.

But video announces its own defection from the present: not 'hello, welcome, good evening all you viewers at home'. Tapes like *The Miners' Campaign Tapes* are made for a specific moment, and though they remain to document that moment of struggle, the only continuing value they have is in relating that moment to the onward struggle. Their existence in the present is as a pledge for the future, marked as the disappearing of the past. As such, they have begun to mark the fallibility of broadcast, to undercut the presence there – but only begun. The monuments of the transnationals are still in the process of building, and they will fill us with awe. Timeshift is dormant in photography: a memento, an appeal to reverent memory, as it was with the death mask, with medieval relics and with the Shroud of Turin. Such commending to the thoughts and prayers of the living guaranteed both that the object of our memories had indeed existed but also that s/he was remembered. In turn this served to alleviate the anxious fear of departure, that we will not ourselves be recalled, that there is the moment beyond which we are not and nothing will ever happen to us again. Video's success is due in part to its ability to mobilise our final fear of – and perhaps our longing for – death. The monumental denies death by masking it in the permanence of official memory: the archive, the monument, the museum, tradition, history (their history). Video insists on death, the democratic principle itself along with madness, birth, sex. Death itself is a moment of fading and becoming in the interstices of language and perception. This is the dialectic in which video finds its relation to identity: as much embroiled in death as it is in life, in the entropy of Freud's nirvana principle as in the organisational force of the libido.

This concentration of theory around video and its relation to death will not endear me to sectors of the video culture. Certainly an era in which theoretical practice was a practical calling seems to have passed, at least temporarily, with the passing of Left institutions. That is, however, exactly why I write: to find some grounds for optimism despite the current weakness of radical politics. At the same time, the awareness of death, in its own right and as a metaphor for all that oppresses us, is a vital part of any materialist culture. No life is as worth living as one that recognises its own brevity, the brevity and fragility of all lives, and the silence

that comes after. There is only one stab at living: to mess up your own life is shameful; to mess with other people's is beyond shame or reparation (and as to tinkering with the safety of the species . . .). There is no better reason for political action than wanting a decent life now. Video's relation to the fading of the subject, to death and to silence, makes it closer than other media to the state of the secular, unstable and atomised subject of contemporary capital.

The World Within Us by Terry Flaxton has some of this in its soundtrack, an actor reading the words of a character played by another actor, words written by another author: 'Before the image and after is nothingness like the memory of the womb or thoughts after death . . . discovered I return from a fleeting memory and have again to present a brave face.' Yet this 'image' is a literary one: in video the nothingness lies at the interstices between images, in the very motion of moving pictures. Between the image you have just lost and the image that has not yet become lies the nothingness: between the moment of Flaxton's character's return from memory and his having to present a face is not a presence but an absence, a call to action. In the literary voice-over, the nameless character invokes finally 'my severe right, my inviolable right, to be released from this fascination with the surface of things' as the introit to the last release. The weight and poetry of this particular tape is that it is so deeply fascinated with the surfaces, not even of things, but of their replication in the craft of video. This fascination with surface, expressed through 3D computer effects, lighting and props and meticulous set design, has to lay open again, in the context of a meditative tape on the death of an author, the question of the core vacuum in video's presence to itself.

Saturated in its own existence, television hurls itself after the tang of the unrelievedly real, the first-hand experience: a bogus empiricism. TV uses the fact that we experience it as present to attempt to overcome our doubt in its pretexts – to make us believe that the events in front of the camera are also present, to overwhelm our doubts by constant renewal of the barrage of presence. Ultimately, TV's refusal of doubt, its self-sufficiency, are given the lie by tape: to understand the present is to understand that it is a crossroads, a site of change, a site for action, a site at which final things are also possible, such as death, in which events no longer occur, a dead culture in which the clichés operate spontaneously. The price of this closeness to change and associated risk is that the tape will be out of date. TV is not out of date – it is always

replenished with more of the same. Tape is open to decay because it insists upon difference, and difference takes time.

Instant playback and the possibility of copying are two of the medium's qualities which, in particular, differentiate it from television. Video is a supplement to television's presence, one which, in adding to it in an apparently subordinate way (as writing is added to speech), alters it completely, undercutting the sameness of TV, its identity with itself, by showing up the internal differences of television. Tape's use tends towards comment on television – and other media – simply by being recorded, by emphasising the timeshift between event and instant playback. If you can rewind and watch the events you've just been involved in, there is no doubt about the difference between the playback and the event. The monumental presence of TV's perpetual present is chipped away from under it by instant playback's constant foregrounding of time, just as, in the opening sequence of Wim Wenders's *Alice in the Cities*, the mismatch between polaroids and the world of the film is used to emphasise not just the gap between representation and reality in spatial terms, but in temporal ones too. TV promises simultaneity between an event and its viewing: video denies that possibility. Things change. That is the *sine qua non* of political action.

Another of video's great qualities is that you can edit on it. Post-production is the broader term, covering not only editing but the wider range of effects, from subtitling to £1,000-a-day effects generators like those used for title sequences and pop videos. Editing again is a relation of difference, one which video re-introduces into broadcast TV in such a way that distinctions between the two begin to crumble: the supplement overtaking and profoundly altering its principal in the shared culture of video, broadcasting and computer graphics. Yet as far as viewing is concerned, these are only textual effects: the major unsettling is about whether a given set of images are live or taped, taken from a camera or generated elsewhere. There will be little doubt when the subject-matter is something like that of *Get It Shown*, one of the scores of tapes that expressed the anger of the miners' campaign and its policing. While broadcasters shied away from shots of police brutality, and almost always filmed from behind police lines (giving thus a police perspective on events), this tape spoke unashamedly from the standpoint of the miners. At the same time, its title – *Get It Shown* – indicates the scale of the problem and the necessity for a free-standing video culture: the need to circulate work

autonomously, or at least with integrity: uncut.

I remember once watching a tape called *Romford Calling*, a good-humoured tale of frustrated ambition and lunchtime drinking, at the Bracknell Festival. The makers filled in the section of the festival form marked 'Purpose of Tape' with the words 'This is the only video ever made in Romford.' Romford is precisely the kind of suburbanised area in which video's possibilities are the gateway to a wider cultural development. Some of the routes along which that might grow are already in place: the remnants of the library service – probably the only valuable legacy of Victorian Britain – maintain a video lending scheme, despite the prevailing climate, which has proved invaluable in distributing tapes on a local and national scale (as well as some involvement, in Sheffield and Tower Hamlets for example, in production and access). The education service is, in some instances, an invaluable resource base for equipment and screenings. The commercial lending libraries are not able to invest in developing markets for 'minority' interests. Government policies in favour of 'free market' economics effectively facilitate the emergence of centralised commercial forces in the media and the homogenisation of the market by exclusion of new, challenging or radical work.

Political video productions benefit from the proximity, occasionally even the identity, of producers and end-users in the community. What is striking, however, is how isolated each 'community' is from every other, a function of suburbanism, and how thin the networks are, even those developed for *The Miners' Campaign Tapes*, of which 7,000 copies were distributed. The 1986 joint workshop production, *In The National Interest*, capitalised on the network as it existed then, but with little of the success of its predecessor. Broadcasting is, instead, attempting to contain this kind of work through the aegis of Channel 4, in which one-off screenings of controversial materials afford tapemakers a much-needed source of revenue and an immediate mode of distribution. This has to be paid for, however, with censorship, 'balancing' programmes offering right-of-reply to the wealthy and powerful and the loss of impact that video can have when used as video, not just part of TV's seamless presentation of itself.

While every chance to get video work out into the homes of the UK is to be applauded, the limitations of broadcasting need to be taken on board seriously, not just by tapemakers but by viewers. Timeshifted viewing restores to video practice something of its

radical critique of the undifferentiated, timeless presence of television's flow. The greatest challenge to the video culture is to devise modes of distribution that can circumvent or supplement more radically the centralised mode of television broadcasting. The age of the mass audience is over: there is no point in feeling nostalgic for the heyday of cinema delivery, of houses packed for Griersonian documentaries. Ways of reaching the domestic audience with challenging, dangerous tapes will need to be developed, and with them new ways of using the electronic media.

Chapter 8

Powerplay

There is at least one other way of approaching the question of community video. I wrote the following paragraphs in 1987, for a very specific audience.

There are over 150 video workshops throughout the United Kingdom (see the April issue of *Independent Media* in any year for a current listing). There are also many schools, colleges, libraries, youth clubs and community centres which offer some sort of access and training to specific groups. At one extreme, political, process video fades into the work of small independent production houses making tapes for local government, trades unions or industrial clients and for broadcast; at another into the amateur sector, now flourishing in this country, and elsewhere into the art market, community arts, the promotional strategy of a whole campaign. At the same time, this is a profoundly domestic technology, and this contradiction is one reason why video has become so heavily policed in the UK and, differently, abroad.

The ideology of professionalism is deeply entrenched in British moving-image media: the idea of letting a user group free with recording equipment almost unthinkable. Community video is in part a product of the felt need for a mode of expression which takes on the lineaments of the most popular of media while shifting the balance of production towards the end-users. What is striking about these examples is that the production of local news and current affairs is so widespread and in many cases so fascinating, yet there is little opportunity to reach audiences across the country. Where a specific issue or campaign might be expected to have an audience reach beyond the immediate locality, there exist precious few modes of distribution.

Distribution of video work is largely accomplished through small specialist houses – Albany Video, London Video Arts, Team Video, Concorde, Cinema of Women, the Other Cinema and Circles Feminist Distributors. The subject of several important reports, among which the *Videoactive Report* by Jon Dovey and Jo Dungey (IFVPA, London, 1984) was the most influential, the problem remains central to community video in the UK. Recent developments, such as the Institute of Contemporary Arts' *Good Video Guide* aimed at library service purchasing of community and artists' video, and the British Film Institute's appointment of a Video Production Officer, are significant attempts at helping the sector to organise itself, but have yet to fulfil their potential. Perhaps what is needed is a syndicated network of news and campaign coverage drawing on work produced in the UK and EEC countries trading programme items for magazine-format packaging and distribution, either on broadcast, cable or cassette. Sadly the exigencies of carrying out the daily tasks of maintaining basic provision are themselves so demanding, poorly paid, under-resourced and minimally staffed that developing new modes of networking is an unlikely priority for the immediate future. And within the enterprise culture, distribution networks which, because of their concentration on oppositional practices are never going to attract commercial sponsors, would need permanent funding: that is simply unavailable in the UK, and will remain so under any foreseeable change of government.

There is a further problem at this juncture concerning the specification of video formats for particular projects. The levels of both skills and equipment available to particular groups may be constrained by a number of economic factors, but to a great extent, aesthetic and social choices are also being made. The decision of community video group 'Despite TV' from London's East End to work with VHS equipment is more than an effect of poverty, it is a deliberate statement of an aesthetic. The crudity of the image production is part and parcel of the urgency of the tapes' impact, and a signal that equipment within the reach of ordinary pockets (VHS camcorders can be hired for under £20 a weekend) is capable of producing significant work. The importance of this for working against the centre-out model of contemporary broadcasting is crucial for political uses of video. On the other hand, a tape such as the recent history of their own

work made by Chapter Workshop from Cardiff, South Wales,
demonstrates an abiding belief in a progress model of technical
provision: in a telling slip, the voice-over speaks of an 'increase in
production values', rather than an improvement or any other
kind of shift. Certainly, that tape's comparison of black-and-
white reel-to-reel footage with the broadcast quality productions
of the mid-80s is a telling reminder of the development of video
technology at the lower end of the market. Still, there appears to
be an assumption, yet to be worked through, that improved
production values are essentially to be desired. Against this, it
could be argued that using amateur standard equipment can be
the starting point for a richer and broader culture than the elite
mystique of professionalism.

On the other hand, there are the pressures of working with and
maintaining low-band equipment, the paucity of budgets for
production other than for broadcast or broadcast-quality
distribution, the lure of professionalism, the pressure of peers and
most of all the political conviction that community audiences
should have the same – or better – quality of production as the
undifferentiated, atomised 'mass' audiences of the broadcasters.
Unfortunately, such a trend must simultaneously make
production more expensive and more restricted than the low-
band equivalents. A rich video culture needs both, yet it is
unclear whether there is any kind of consistency within or
between regions in the allocation of funds to the various levels of
provision, or whether, in some instances, programmes are made
in high-band for reasons other than social and aesthetic ones,
such as the need to convince potential clients that a group is able
to handle broadcast-quality equipment.

However, because there is an increasing demand for high-
quality independent product (and for independently-trained
Black people and women to compensate for the failures of the
broadcast establishment to train or provide employment for
these members of the community) many major new
developments are largely bound in with the prioritisation of
training provision, especially in centres outside London,
traditionally the major centre of media production in the British
Isles. The North East Media Development Council and
associated Training Centre in Newcastle-upon-Tyne has been an
exemplary centre for this kind of provision, a training-led
combination of existing workshops in the area, developed in

conjunction with the Association of Cinematograph and Television Technicians (ACTT), the major trades union in the broadcasting and film industries, and the European Community. This has created a local climate for the development of media work, including archiving the region and newsreel production on a regular subscription basis. The City of Birmingham is in the process of developing a similar policy for the West Midlands: Sheffield, Nottingham and Cardiff have similar plans. Partnerships between industry, local government, grant-aided workers and outside agencies such as the EEC are the hallmark of these projects, and a focus on economic development and therefore on training skilled locally-based personnel, the core of their practice.

Initial training is now widely available. A serious problem has arisen over the last few years concerning the development of courses at advanced levels, furthering the generic skills of beginners courses, adding specialist knowledge and more deeply and broadly based skills. Several issues are at stake here. Should funders prioritise the needs of disprivileged members of the community, or should there be a constant rider that training should always be to the benefit of the independent sector specifically? What of people trying to enter – and to intervene in – the broadcast production industries? And while no one doubts the acquired skills of trainers, who is to train them in the latest technologies, and in the very different skills of teaching as a vocation in itself? In addition, many workshops find themselves bound willy nilly into training provision, regardless of their own motivation and programmes of work, partly from a sense of duty, partly from the necessity of obtaining available funding. This can lead to increasing frustration as available time and energy are absorbed by a repetitive series of low-level workshops, with little or no opportunity to acquire new skills or to exercise to the full those already available.

The large scale training-led developments are characterised by the equal and opposite need for a certain number of 'prestige' productions: Trade and Amber workshops on Tyneside and the Birmingham Film and Video Workshop in the West Midlands lead the local industrial development with productions – often in partnership with the BFI and C4 – which act as shop-windows for the projects as a whole (while of course also fulfilling other social and aesthetic parameters). A tape like Chapter's *Penrhiwceiber: The Greatest Improvisors in the World* illustrates the multiple uses

of a single project. A group of miners from a pit village trained at Chapter and made in the process two tapes, one a campaign tape opposing the closure of the local pit, the other a longer, more sustained portrait of the village over the period of that campaign, the Miners' Strike and the ultimate closure of the pit. What is so startling about this work is the way in which it covers so many functions: training, campaigning, archival documentary, an expression from and to a specific community, and its distribution as a tape to wider audiences. Tapes like the Birmingham *GirlZone* and *Out of Order* as well as film work from Newcastle serve related mixed functions.

For the community at large historical circumstances have produced a discursive formation in the UK in which concepts of class-struggle, let alone of mediation of that struggle through moving-image technologies, are all but defunct. There is still a risk, identified in 1985 by the late Pat Sweeney, that 'yesterday's video activist has become today's cultural entrepreneur' (1985). This in many ways leads back to the all but unanswerable question of the definition of 'community', a convenient label for fundraising in the early 80s, but at the end of the decade impossible to use unselfconsciously in the embattled inner cities. The vast majority of the individuals making up 'the community' (including most video activists) live within the popular culture of the day. We might dream of escape from it, and of the creation of an alternative culture, but this can only be done within the context of major defeats for the working class throughout the first world. In any case, the independent sector will have to work from motivations which embrace the pleasures of popular cultural forms, as well as those that, like Brecht's theatre, develop new pleasures – including the pleasures of intellectual challenge – from the process of attacking the old.

Today the term cultural industry, with its associated terminology from management discourses, is far more likely to be bandied about than the language of the older community arts movement. While much of the activism does remain, especially in areas like Scotland, Wales and London with their entrenched refusal of Thatcherism, the notion of a community has been progressively eroded, not only discursively, but in the implementation of social policy since 1979. 'Popular capitalism' has successfully atomised even further the already fragmented culture-consuming population. There is little point in regretting

such major social movements: the challenge to independent video practice is to create, within the historical conjuncture, its own agenda of work to be done. In many respects, this inverts the question I raised above, so that it reads now 'what kind of community is it possible – and do we wish – to create?' Which in turn raises the question of communication and networking. What are the best routes for extending awareness of media issues and sharing media skills? Which tapes should be pushed, and via which networks? What forms of networking can be developed, free of the centralising thrust of corporate capital and contemporary government in the UK? Should the sector train individuals, or should it be giving access to whole communities? Or what balance might be struck between the two? In what sense might access actually create community where there was none before?

The time is surely here to begin to link up across media, to devise new networks, and to disembarrass ourselves of the ancient nightmare of national barriers, respecting instead the rights of the myriad small communities that make up our continent.

The previous pages are edited highlights from a paper written for the Interuniversity Commission for Community Education at the end of 1987. The prevailing purpose was to be cheerful and expansive about the nature of the 'community video' sector in the UK. The fact that Black activists are tending to use film, that the sector is riven by political and personal differences, the importance and weakness of the little magazines and Left publishing generally were all either left unspoken or skated around. The effects of the demise of local government in the big cities, with their novel 'tradition' of grant-aiding cultural work, are virtually unmentioned. The shift of workers from the cultural to the commercial sector, the impact of educational policy changes on the expectations of school-leavers, the end of funding for representative bodies for the sector as a whole, and the likely provision for fully commercial local stations in forthcoming market-led legislation on broadcasting have become more urgent concerns subsequently. There has, moreover, been a growing accommodation with the notion of cultural industry policies, increasingly seen as the only possible strategy for survival into the 1990s. Without wishing to claim a conscious attempt to suppress the emergent culture of low-budget campaign and community video on the part of government, the very existence of

the sector in any recognisable form is in danger. What will be in question for the rest of this chapter will be the nature of a 'recognisable form', and whether what emerges may not supersede the ambitions of an earlier generation.

The United Kingdom has one of the highest concentrations of video recorders in the northern hemisphere: well over 90 per cent of homes have one or more TV sets, and of these almost 50 per cent have a video cassette recorder. At the same time, the UK has one of the lowest penetrations of telephones, and the market for domestic computers is bottoming out rather more swiftly than some observers had expected. The early demise of the Phillips LaserDisc, a play-only system without recording capability, seemed to point to a leaning towards interactive media: these other figures seem to point to a relatively low level of use which may be reflected in the actual – as opposed to the potential – use of video. Certainly there was no audible outcry over the banning from high-street shops of the Panasonic twin-deck home video editor on the grounds that it was 'manifestly' designed for laying off copies (though twin-deck audio cassette machines are now standard on most hi-fi systems). At the same time, audits of technological holdings in a variety of local government, education departments and government offices have unearthed a common history of technological innovation. An enthusiast organises the purchase of video equipment. It is used extensively while the activist is still in post. But when they leave, due to the lack of trained staff, motivation, or changed political circumstances and priorities, the equipment finds its way to a cupboard, where it stays unused. A variant is common in education: a particular worker or department takes on proprietorial rights over video equipment which becomes unavailable, or available only to favoured colleagues.

High-street shops now afford cheaper and more reliable rentals on video cameras than most small workshops can manage. But editing facilities are like hen's teeth, and it is on them and the availability of training and peer support that the strength of the workshop sector now rests. These local struggles over technology are a microcosm of wider social trends which move large masses of money and political muscle. In November 1987, for example, the war over digital audio tape, which promises magnetic recording equal to compact disc quality, had reached a pitch at which CBS, leaders of the US record industry, were about to license spoiler mechanisms which would make it impossible to record from their CDs. The last

time a company had built an effective spoiler system, Sony, world leaders in hardware manufacture, bought the rights to the invention. This time, it bought the company. Sony now own CBS records and appears to be launching a major diversification into software manufacture, the first transnational to do so, if we discount the uncomfortable partners in the Thorn-EMI combine prior to their divestment of the entertainment divisions during cash-flow crises of the mid-1980s. The phonogram industries organised by the International Federation of Phonogram and Videogram Industries (IFPI) are still in the vanguard of the global war between hardware and software manufacturers and the particular battlefield of commercial copying ('piracy'). In the autumn of 1988 they announced a major victory in Indonesia, thanks to the European Community's threat to withdraw favourable trading agreements unless the Indonesian government clamped down on video and audio cassette piracy. As Chesterman and Lipman (1988) narrate with such gusto, copyright is the quiet revolution in the internal dynamic of global capital.

The video rental shop and the rack of videos for hire in newsagents, grocers and off-licenses is a familiar sight in the urban environment in this country, the language of tape a commonplace of conversation: 'Have you seen . . .?' 'No but I've got it on tape.' Market researchers use the UK audience as a touchstone on the vexed issues of zipping and zapping – respectively using the fast-forward button to 'zip' through adverts, or the remote control to 'zap' channels, jumping from programme to progamme during advert breaks. And UK legislation and action against 'copyright theft' has been of major concern worldwide. Copyright is used, among other purposes, for a censorship worthy of truly authoritarian regimes as was the case with material from the government agency the Central Office of Information, which refused scratch artists Gorrilla Tapes permission to broadcast material deriving from their coverage of the Reagan–Thatcher summit of 1984 in one of their pieces (cf. Dovey 1986). It is also used by broadcast corporations and other rights holders, as is music copyright, to hinder the making of alternative work: for example, RCA refusing to allow a song by the Eurythmics to appear on the soundtrack of *Framed Youth*.

The fate of an image, a song, a phrase in a visual context – like 'Play it again, Sam' or 'Peel me a grape' – is in some respects like the fate of words. Only a handful of words are copyright – Kodak,

Xerox, Coca-Cola . . . – but otherwise the elements of a vocabulary are open for use and struggle over meaning as argued earlier in this book (p. 26). Legislation over copyright is a pre-emptive blow for evacuating the struggle out of the use of audio-visual material. As argued previously (p. 91), the unit of video is not the single frame but the succession of frames, including those that have gone before: a frame still is not a quotation from a video, it is a ghost of its passing, just as a photo is not a quotation from a life but a trace of its passage. In a society in which the visual is the major mode of communication, work *on* images must be, increasingly, criticism *in* and *with* images. The right to copy is justly becoming a matter of major concern.

The fixed capital of video may well be in the domain of the copyright owner, but the variable capital is the work done by the viewer, and it is work which, though unpaid and to some extent exceeding the general determination of commodity exchange, none the less exists in a form of economy. The work done by viewers to entice meaning into existence is not momentary in its effects. The mark of a thousand readings accrues to the well-read text, *Jane Eyre* or *Casablanca*, *Rawhide* or Ronald Reagan. And in the viewer, the trace of all those readings remains as a sedimentation in which the layers of past engagement inflect every new one, comparing, assessing, remembering, quoting. Those readings, in turn, do not flit through consciousness without trace, but precisely etch their paths in layer upon layer of memory, remembered and obscured: parts of ourselves.

It is because the moving image is so much part of our inner selves that the issue of control and its political form, censorship, have become central to debates about the moving image. Censorship I take to be the deliverance of control over media to a state agency, to be run at the will of the ruling faction in a social formation. I do not necessarily equate it with the action of, for example, Women Reclaim the Night marches, fire-bomb attacks on sex shops, or picket lines on cinemas (from anti-racist protests at Griffiths's *Birth of a Nation* to Christian anger at Scorsese's *The Last Temptation of Christ*). In such cases, there is a genuinely *popular* seizure of power, and though you might wish to argue over individual cases, it is at least possible to argue with a picket line, while a board of censors, however constituted, cannot be confronted in anything like the same way.

In the sense of state control over communication, the United Kingdom is one of the most heavily censored of advanced capitalist

nations: we scarcely notice the censor's certificate, 'so deeply has
the harness worn in' (Montague 1972). As the technologies of
domestic leisure have shifted from reception technology to
duplicating equipment, the problem of policing has shifted
dramatically: the policing of Whitehall photocopiers in the case of
leaks from disaffected civil servants — Ponting, Goodall, the
Westland affair — is merely a case in point. The war between
hardware and software manufacturers is then placed in a new
struggle between the ideology of the market-place and the state's
function in facilitating the reproduction of social coherence so as to
provide a stable market and a stable workforce. The contradictions
this produces are perhaps most evident in the provisions suggested
in the White Paper on copyright of 1987, in which laws pertaining
to the pirating of texts in the conditions of eighteenth-century
bookselling have been stretched beyond coherence in an effort to
contain the impact of machinery, such as video decks, computers,
photocopiers and audio cassettes, for which the old laws are
manifestly unusable. For example, the right of quotation exists for
printed materials, for example the right to use quite substantial
sections of a book in a review. The same right however does not
exist for moving image media: even stills belong outright to
copyright holders, and cannot be used even in education without
permission and, usually, payment. Despite extensive lobbying
during the last half of the 1980s, educational use of off-air video
recordings will still be policed via a clumsy and, it is to be expected,
largely unworkable system of competing licensing agents.
Companies will be expected to bid for the licences to suitable
programmes. The onus will then be on teachers to find out who
holds the licence, to join their scheme, and fill in forms and pay for
each programme recorded for classroom use. Programmes which no
one has bid for will be free, but licensed programmes will entail so
much paperwork, in such a notoriously difficult area to police, that
there is every chance that the laws will be flouted — or alternatively,
that teachers will lessen their use of electronic media, precisely at a
time when it is more and more important to develop media skills in
school and college students.

   Intervention in the circulation of software is the commonest
route to imposing this coherence in the cultural sphere (though, for
example, in Indian cinema, censorship is usually exercised in the
laboratory, during the processing of film). In the UK, cinema has
largely been censored on a consensual basis, through local

government licensing and the advisory role of the British Board of Film Censors, a gentleman's agreement which has served the national and the local state well in such areas as the representation of colonial policing methods and labour relations. In the United States, the Hayes Code successfully blended censorship with market research through established panels of suitably middle-of-the-road pressure groups engaged to monitor scripts in pre-production for possible offence to specific constituencies. TV likewise has a mixture of statutory and market-related curbs to guarantee the anodyne and homogeneous programme content required by, variously, advertisers and the paternalist allies of the ruling class.

The passage of the Video Recordings Act through parliament in 1984 illustrates this alliance rather well, being a Private Members Bill, brought before the House of Commons by an MP in his own name rather than as part of a government programme of legislation. But at the same time, the member in question, Graham Bright, was allowed to leave his post as a junior Home Office minister in order to bring in the bill, and to resume his post afterwards – an unusual procedure – and to have access to Home Office lawyers to help draft it. The parliamentary debates were a minefield of ill-informed and downright false arguments, factual errors and absurd assertions. Yet the record of debate is remarkable for the consistency with which MPs of every party supported the bill, with very few objectors. Despite the manifest incompetence of the drafting (which has produced a law in which the central act of the Christian myth may not be shown but pop videos of dubious sexual exploitation are exempt from certification), the bill became law with virtually no amendments of any stature. The risible 'research' on which the bill's supporters in the House, the press and in powerful right-wing lobbies based much of their argument is still in circulation (Barlow and Hill 1985; cf. critiques by Brown 1984; Cubitt 1984; Cubitt 1989; Petley 1984; Taylor 1987).

The first trial under the act involved pirated cassettes of Bombay musicals: an indicator that the links between copyright and censorship (and colonialism) are closer than one imagines. After a series of mutually contradictory legal actions, Palace Pictures have withdrawn *The Evil Dead*, a highly successful horror film, from video release and do not plan to purchase again in the 18R (restricted) zone of genre films. It is illegal to circulate, even to loan without remuneration, an uncertificated videotape. The law is that a tape

showing any of a shopping list of acts is to be banned, and that the only defence for trading in uncertificated tapes is that they fall into an exempted category such as sport or music. This removes from juries the test of obscenity, that a given artefact tends to deprave and corrupt, and gives both them and the censor into the hands of a judiciary bound only to observe the shopping list. This in turn may be read in terms of a wider movement to limit the powers of juries in areas such as common assault, many driving offences and fraud. It also relates importantly to the increasing centralisation of powers under the Thatcher regime, notably the advance of police powers under the Police and Criminal Evidence Act 1986, legislation drafted in response to inner-city uprisings since 1981 and the miners' campaign of 1986. Public order and public morality are twins in Tory policy-making.

The role of local control over local cultural activity is a constant nightmare in Tory rhetoric and legislation, such as the notorious Section 29 of the Local Government Act 1988, which prohibits the 'promotion' of homosexuality by local government bodies (including libraries and the education service). The Greater London Council, which was summarily destroyed as the local government body for London on the suitable date of 1 April 1986, had spent up to £2 million in the preceding year on film and video, much of it in access, distribution and training, and much of it dispensed through agencies staffed and controlled by women, lesbians and gay men, people with disabilities and Black people. 'Riot money', the cash found for deprived inner urban areas in the wake of the 1981 uprisings, added to the money made available for cultural use after the Law Lords' disallowance of the GLC's cheap public transport policy (cf. Carvell 1986), allowed local video practice not only to build up a basic infrastructure of machines and trained individuals, but to create a mood of expectancy and hope. By 1989, much of the equipment bought then was faltering and, worse, funds had virtually dried up and some local boroughs, facing bankruptcy, could no longer afford to prioritise cultural activity of any kind, let alone the capital-intensive work of video workshops. The abolition and penalising of local government has led to a state of crisis in local video production. In this climate, it is easy to see why the previously voluntary advice of the censors, used as the basis for local government licensing, should have attained national, statutory status, and why that move should be disguised by an ironic shift from the word 'Censorship' to the word 'Classification'

in the title of the British Board of Film Classification since it has taken on the censor's mantle.

The effect of these moves has been effectively to deregulate small-scale video production, removing it from local control, forcing it to 'compete' with far larger and very differently oriented companies, edging it towards standardised productions and, despite the rhetoric of 'reducing dependency', actually driving videomakers more and more into the arms of the two largest funders. (Why ask the dependent why he relies on your support: rather ask the patron.) The British Film Institute and Channel 4 have, in the absence of strong local power bases, inherited the central position in small-scale production. Increasingly developing joint policies, and increasingly subject themselves to internal and external pressures to conform to industry standards, structurally the two major funders occupy an increasingly dangerous central position. Despite the best efforts of many staff, the range and quantity of work being produced are rapidly diminishing. Internal power struggles at the BFI portend further centralisation of decision-making in terms of both production and criticism (cf. BFI 1989). Meanwhile, Channel 4's commissioning editor for the workshop sector is circulating a document which draws attention to the reluctance of other producers to develop work under the Workshop Declaration, the agreement drawn up between the major funders and the major trades union in film and television, ACTT, to allow for long-term, culturally oriented support for collective film/video practice (Fountain 1989: 7). In the interests of flexibility, at a time when other funders' levels of support are dropping, Channel 4 appears to be setting course for reducing the reliance of the sector on the continuity of funding which the declaration had offered. Again, the discussion document remarks 'In the new era of private enterprise support for culture, the workshop sector, as it currently defines itself, may seem less attractive to private sponsors than other art forms' (ibid.: 6). Like the BFI, Channel 4 cannot be central, but will be anyway.

The model underlying such recent developments is that of the 'new realism', the phrase encapsulating labour movement capitulation to Thatcherite economics. Within this new ideology, the buzz words are efficiency, management, even leadership: terms drawn from a (somewhat outmoded) conception of the operation of large economic units. In many areas of life, from education to health, and particularly in the arts, we are witnessing a programmatic de-

professionalisation of key workers, and their substitution with managers. Ironically, the 'free market economy' model which is being imposed is also and simultaneously one which, by weakening the professional position of teachers, doctors and cultural activists, increases the central power of government. The form taken in each of these spheres is that of the centralist, homogenising, monetarist state and its closest organisational ally and formal twin, the transnational corporation.

What disturbs me most is the immanence of the transnational at the local and domestic level both through their domination of the hard and software markets and more specifically the way in which their success, rather than being challenged by the guardians of audio-visual culture, is actually being emulated, with the arguments of accountancy taking priority over cultural concerns. As alternative modes of distribution are actively cut down – the library at the end of my street, for example, has been closed despite a long and arduous campaign to keep it open without council funding – the stranglehold of large corporations on the circulation of images becomes ever more watertight. The recent loss of grants to independent distributors in the UK is particularly disturbing in this instance, as is the closure of the Women's Film, Television and Video Network and the Society for Education in Film and Television, two of the four national representative bodies for work in the grant-aided sector.

The role of the transnational corporation (TNC) is one of the great themes of contemporary literature on global politics and the global economy. Chesterman and Lipman (1988) give a series of indications of the scale of operation of TNCs in the global video software market. Hardware, like video decks, are also assembled by TNCs at 'offshore' plants in the Third World, effectively deskilling populations which are maintained as cheap labour by authoritarian regimes, themselves designed to maintain stable home markets, currency and institutional infrastructures (Gordon 1988: 59) and kept in power by a combination of TNC cash and western government military aid. Until the advent of the chip-based camcorder, the very design of portapaks, highly susceptible to dust and humidity, effectively debarred them from use in equatorial climates.

The domestic UK video market is a less familiar subject for analysis of TNC involvement in the local economy. Early in 1988 the big five distributors commenced a strategy of joint advertising

for forthcoming blockbuster releases in the national press. In the case of one of their number, the explicit rationale was to keep other, smaller independent distributors from entering the market through cartelisation and upping the ante required to contact the public. The *Daily Mirror* for Friday, 21 October 1988 contains an 8-page 'Video Oscars' supplement featuring ads from three of the cartel, CBS-Fox, Vestron and Warners. Elsewhere in the same issue are ads for theatrical releases from Warner, Vestron and UIP. In this climate, the 'free' market is as effective a block to small company entryism as the most closed commodities ring.

Major companies copy and package their titles, hold rights to the geographical area and are responsible for advertising campaigns. But they sell local franchises to a middle tier of entrepreneurs with the capital necessary for large-scale purchasing and managing infrastructures for local delivery to individual store-owners. Thus a whole new level of profit-making is installed between copyright holders and end-users, such that the profit margins of the small retail rental outlet are further eroded. This in turn adds extra weight to the tradition in retailing towards self-exploitation, combining the use of evenings as leisure time (and so the time to rent videos) with the need to extend opening hours in order to maximise revenues. Newsagents, off-licences and amusement arcades doubling as rental outlets are, moreover, frequently run by immigrants with long traditions of mercantile self-sufficiency and intra-familial support (or exploitation, depending on your perspective). In these circumstances, the range of product, the rate of turnover and the rental charges are determined by such considerations as the difficulty of pursuing defaulting customers, the improbability of seeing product before it arrives (since there is no 'leisure' time to spend previewing in a cinema) and the re-introduction of block-booking by mid-range franchise holders.

Perhaps because this sharing out cuts too deeply into their own profits, distributors are increasingly moving into the sell-through market, encouraging the end-users to consider themselves collectors (a notable feature of North American advertising for several years). This might lead in other circumstances to the establishment of exchanges, on the lines of the early development of distribution networks in the first years of cinema exhibition. However, in this country the provisions of the Video Recordings Act make such mutual benefit associations virtually impossible. The insistence on certification makes it a crime to circulate, even to

swap, uncertificated videos. Certification costs money, and labels showing the classification need to be marked on the box, the cassette and in the vision track of the tape itself, aiding an increasing centralisation among the cartel. This is in turn fostered by the economic crises of the last fifteen years and the monetarist 'free trade' policies in force in much of Europe and North America. In such a context, the building of an effective alternative culture is hard to envisage.

If this is true in the UK, on a global scale the struggle seems completely pre-empted. Figures for VCRs are hard to come by, as they tend to be based on a count 'per household' which is such a fluid numerical indicator as to be virtually useless. But recent figures from War On Want show that Africa, Asia and Latin America had just 5.7 per cent of the world's computers in 1985; Africa as a whole had 125 people to every telephone and many countries were without the equipment to patch into the international network. In Europe meanwhile, the market for personal computers grew by 66 per cent, and the domestic market by 243 per cent in 1987. Within the European market, the UK had the lowest rate of growth, though this is accounted for by the earlier exposure to cheap processors such as the Amstrad brand range. Like the VCR market, the personal computer market is bottoming out, though 536,000 sales in 1987 is still a substantial turnover. By contrast, Senegal is expected to have a total of 5,500 personal computers in 1989. Video ownership figures can be assumed to parallel these tallies. Yet video's effectiveness as a distribution medium is extraordinary, and could radically effect the current lack of distribution networks for African films within Africa itself (cf. Armes 1985). The international market for pirated goods seems to double up the hegemony of the US and the UK as dominant exporters of pop music. Despite the success of Indian and Chinese cinema, with their vast internal markets, and the traditionally protectionist stance of Japan, US-produced feature films dominate world video markets. Video in the southern hemisphere, like virtually all imported technologies, is effectively used exclusively in the interests of the transnational corporations and their local client bourgeoisies.

Yet that video as a phenomenon has impacted on the televisual cultures of the areas where it has taken root cannot be denied: for example, the density of use in the Gulf States and Alaska, where the number of VCRs per household is between 80 and 90 per cent, is surely shifting the grounds on which moving-image media

circulate. On the other hand, the impact of video on the overall cultural life of these disparate areas is unlikely to be closely analogous. The explorations in this book are intensely local. The peculiar ecology of the British Isles's different broadcasting services is based still on scarcity models of terrestrial broadcasting. This facilitates the paternalistic operation of the duopoly (BBC and ITV) in the UK and a monopoly (RTE) in Ireland (which none the less, as befits the mixed economy of Irish broadcasting, must compete with signals from England, Scotland and Wales). These institutional determinants have created expectations about the nature of broadcast media – backed up by a moralising tradition in the English ruling class and the stranglehold of a reactionary Catholicism on cultural legislation in Dublin. Within these parameters it is possible to read the advent of the VCR as a popular media resource as a progressive moment in the struggle to defuse the metropolitan and oligarchical organisation of broadcasting.

On the other hand, the major use of the technology is in timeshifting existing programmes and for watching rented feature films. I have already discussed the issues around timeshifting (pp. 27–39): it needs only to be repeated that the programmes timeshifted may enter into a new relation with the viewer but they are still the same programmes. By the same token, the films watched on video are by and large the same films, bearing the same ideologies and coming from the same institutional sources, as the films on broadcast or in the cinema, except that there is a greater need for a fast change-over of titles, so that many films which might otherwise disappear without trace have important circulation in video formats. It scarcely needs to be pointed out that films on video lose enormously in size, sound reproduction, picture quality and aspect ratio (the shape of the image: no cinema shape matches the shape of the TV screen). The difficulties facing any small independent company wishing to enter the market-place with novel product, whether minority interest films or the kind of work discussed in the last three chapters, are very real and almost overwhelming.

Copyright, censorship, public funding and distribution form the grim antithesis to proselytising visions of the medium in action. There can be little doubt, viewing some of the tapes that do get made and circulate in some form through the culture, that there is a degree of urgency about this state of affairs. Most of the tapes I have used for examples in this book have been broadcast in this country.

Some have not and will not be shown. The aptly named *Get It Shown* is one of several tapes made in support of the miners during their campaign against pit closures. Its shocking footage of police brutality will remain with its viewers for a long time. Yet a question emerges: isn't it better to exchange wide dissemination through the broadcast media for a narrower but more controlled circulation through the *samizdat* circuits of the labour movement and its supporters? Can broadcasters be trusted not to interfere with messages antipathetic to the status quo? Connie Genaris's elegy to male love in *Jean Genet is Dead* makes more cogent and passionate sense than a thousand mini-series and government sponsored adverts on the tragedy of AIDS: could broadcasters be expected to cope with that? Very few if any broadcast crews shot from among the miners for news bulletins. Few if any TV directors and executives speak from their position as gay men. Nor does TV address striking miners or gays, who obstinately remain the other to broadcasting's 'we'. This indicates the need for a video culture, the need to circulate work autonomously or at the least uncut.

Distributors exist and carry out invaluable work, making artists', community and campaign video available to a wider audience. Many libraries and many teachers take part in an informal network for getting the work shown, fostering discussion, helping new makers, critics and activists. But it is not the weakness of the culture that aids the increasing hegemony of the vapid, the unchallenging, the negative, the oppressive, the cheap and the shallow, but rather the isolation of activists. If, as seems likely in the UK, representative organisations for sector workers are likely to disappear, at least temporarily, that isolation will increase, and render sector workers and their culture increasingly open to relations of dependency. In the nature of things, bureaucracies tend to amass influence, to draw things in to themselves. Such has been the experience of the cultural sector in the UK. Major cultural bodies like the Arts Council, the British Film Institute and Channel 4 are moving into the position, not of facilitating communication within the sector but of providing it. The combination of roles – source of finance, channel of communication – is a dangerous step into further dependency.

It is not a question of the 'public', a convenient fiction at best, not 'liking' other cultural forms. We are all schooled to recognise the modulations of dominant culture, but only some take a route through it of rejection or renegotiation. Class, gender and race collide with the vagaries of biography to drive some people

through life with an alternative purchase on reality, something which, in the video arena, devolves upon perception (of self, of others, and the relation between them) and communication (the mediated nature of perception and interpersonal relations). Video is about the status of the individual in the social: its figure is that of the commuter with a Sony hand-held, headphoned video-walkman. Video atomises even the domestic audience, so that individuals watch their timeshifted programmes without the controlling intervention of the family institution. Video aesthetics seems to point up the lack of (loss of?) an irreducible human experience of consciousness, to insist on the historical and the contingent, the mediated and vengeful immanence of the body, the fundamental loneliness of individuality. Yet the kind of aesthetic attack on dominant modes of knowing which contemporary video practice suggests is subject to an awesome repressive tolerance: few people even see the work – how many will be affected by it? We are allowed the aberration of video art because it is perceived as an aberration, a luxury item, an eccentricity. Yet, in potential at least, this address to the central icon of the reproductive cycle of capital, the TV set, is vastly important.

There is something disturbing about recognising, embedded in our own psyches, the media skills that are as familiar to us as breathing: our ability to zap channels and pick up, in less than a second, what kind of programme is on, who is in it, how long it has been on and whether we want to watch some or all of it, and to do this with four or more channels simultaneously while checking a newspaper and holding a telephone conversation. We relate our experiences in anecdotes drawing constantly on cultural form, and nothing is so difficult in learning a new language as picking up references to everyday popular cultural entities, pop stars, TV presenters, politicians, places . . . . At certain moments, with certain tapes, the extraordinary intimacy between TV set and viewer comes home as a nightmare: psyche colonised by the TV. But this is also the condition for critique. The struggle over meaning is intra- as well as interpsychic, and if part of the game-plan involves the use of legislative machinery in an attempt to control the rules of play, we should attempt to understand how that might tie in with psychic formations. That is, the sphere in which the making of meanings meets the policing of meanings.

The interplay of psychic and social, and between the pragmatics of conversation and the structures of rule, create enormous

problems for analysis. The dominant culture dominates not only because it has achieved power, but because the bulk of the population colludes in its own oppression. It is frighteningly fashionable to enthuse over advertising, kitsch, golden turkeys, etc., as if the struggle for cultural form was over. The attempt to build an alternative is in the hands, it often feels, of fewer and fewer people, maybe talking only to themselves (as in Saïd's sinister anecdote about the 2,000 scholars who write 2,000 books, each with a print run of 2,000 (Saïd 1983)). It is not the weakness of the culture but the isolation of its proponents which aids the increasing hegemony of the vapid, the unchallenging, the negative, the oppressive and the shallow. The passion is drained out of an era that swapped emotion for cool. A handful of dedicated exhibitors, educators, journalists and enthusiasts working with producers have maintained and will maintain a culture here. But there remain these question marks over the future. The next chapter will attempt to analyse in more general terms which possibilities emerge from this matrix of the personal and the political, the technological and the cultural, the global and the local for the emergence of a democratic video culture.

Chapter 9

Lost generations

No one said it was going to be easy. Certain themes are persistent in the self-analysis of video activists: access, work-practices, end-users. The spirit of critique (and self-criticism) which at times can seem so introspective and even petty marks the sector off as different, not only from others but from itself. But this endless self-questioning is also functional – it makes us constantly conscious that *we* must make the culture in which we wish to live, according to *all* the strategies that we can employ. This is not a quest in the classical sense: there is no definite end in sight. It is not teleological, guided by an historical goal, but eschatological, governed by the principle of hope. It is science as defined by Lacan, the practice of disbelief. To disbelieve is to test every proposition against multiple, conflicting, even contradictory cases, and ultimately to challenge ideals of knowledge which we hold. Such a practice subjects the nature and notion of knowledge to change through social practice, in this instance the social practice of video, and writing about video. The task of such a materialist practice is not to prove but to disprove. Video practice, with its transparent manipulations of image and sound and its particular temporal relations, is forced to take change into account, as other media may but are not forced to.

Enmeshed in the Symbolic, video is also imbricated in the production of history and cannot claim eternity like other media, not least because of the phenomena of lost generations, as the material moves from master to submaster, to broadcast, to timeshift, where it begins to degenerate with every play. Moreover, video must test the probity, the fragility, the reality of its sources and itself at every turn, for example in Gary Hill's *Why do Things Get in a Muddle*, whose radically disturbing account of entropy relies less on Gregory Bateson's texts than on the technique of getting the

performers to recite their lines backwards prior to reversing them into 'normal' speech. This is not simply a matter of techniques which other media may but also may not employ: it is a question of the ways in which video, whether as art, as campaign material or as timeshift, partakes of the processes of becoming, not as a matter of choice, but as a function of its specific historical and material conditions. This becomes an ethical position, defining itself against any refusal to question, any wilful ignorance which exceeds the powers of imposed stupidity. Acceptance of the comfortable banalities is acquiescence in the evils worked everyday in the name of our comfort. Video, as a practice which excludes the metaphysics of Being underlying broadcasting's eternal presence, denies that cosy, finally sadistic apathy.

This has to do with seizing the practice of radical critique as our own. For this book, that has been at the risk of an equally radical confusion. The intensity of self-questioning (as distinct from self-reflection) in the independent sector raises methodical doubt to the level of cultural *raison-d'être*. Moreover, confusion may not be all bad: the 'logic' of cultural capitalism is all too clear, too neat, too rational. To think for ourselves is the first duty. The mediation of 'public opinion' carried out by dominant media produces the homogeneity on which the status quo depends. Alternative media must escape the statistical norms of polls and pundits to arrive at a democracy of the image.

The core function of television is the resolution of conflict between the giver of laws and the ill-fitting, rebellious subjects that cannot be totally suborned to its narcissistic Imaginary. Narcissistic because power, like the narcissism of the infant child, recognises no limits, no rules: those arrive only with the Oedipus complex, with its first act of legislation, the prohibition against incest, on which sexual difference, according to psychoanalysis, is premised. Imaginary because it is embroiled entirely in self-image, excluding the Symbolic world of language and communication which, however ruled and regulated, is always a matter of other people. In its classical phase, when most closely related to Christianity, science attempted to reveal and to conquer nature: Mother Nature. In the period in which we live this Oedipal rape is resituated in another set of projects designed to rebuild a pre-Oedipal phase of wholeness. Total immersion in the mother's body through the absorbative properties of the video monitor (cf. Skirrow 1986); reformulation of the maternal body through the imagination of the ecosphere as

totality; recovery of infantile conditions through legislation like the
Education Reform Act, which seeks to restore the classroom
conditions of our rulers' childhood (and, in a more round about way,
via broadcasting deregulation, imaged on the model of the impact
of commercial and US army stations on the BBC of our governors'
youth). The mode of survival after the great western systems have
failed – religion, science, the humanism possible before Auschwitz –
must be an artifice. For the rulers, that artifice must be one which
offers to absolve, to wipe out difference, to collapse the Symbolic
into the Imaginary. Broadcasting homogenises, and through its
Imaginary community proposes an absolution by producing a
series of perpetual Others in order to produce a register of the Same.
Guerrilla media plunge into a universe of boundaries and their
transgression, of difference and heterogeneity. The refusal to be the
Same, and the insistence on (decentred) individuality form the
second necessary condition of democratic media.

The term 'art' is one which is treated gingerly on the Left. My
preferred definition has been that art is that field of practices which
is retailed through galleries – an instrumental and in many ways
dismissive description, one which follows the lines of film theory as
it cast off the literary notions of author, creativity and genius. Yet it
is to art, to the aesthetic domain, that a secular age turns for the
production of profound meanings which might help us understand
our status in the universe and our relations to ourselves and others.
The secret of religion is that it recognises that these yearnings for 'a
tune beyond us, yet ourselves' (Stevens 1955: 165) are properly
popular, and form an important element of the field of popular
pleasures. The intellectual Left has still to lose its puritanism. It has
remained variously colonialist, knowing, coy and patronising about
popular pleasures. It is essential to recognise in ourselves and others
the actually existing terms of pleasure, and to seek out that
passionate involvement which is now almost entirely left to the
dominant media.

Lacan as analyst of masculinity contends that what artists share as
a problematic is the *'manque à être'*, the paucity of being in the
world which bedevils the Lacanian – male – subject. We – men – are
constantly hailed by ego ideals of ability, of assurance, of fullness to
ourselves. But the obdurate reality of our beings is always and in
various ways less than those ideals. The experience of lack which is
the core of Lacan's psychoanalysis is the heartland, again in Lacan's
analysis, of spirituality: the yearning for fulfilment, the proximity of

annihilation. The roots of a passionate culture thrive, not in a comfortable mulch of pious wishes, but at the foot of that other tree on which Christ's despair speaks for the human condition: 'My God, My God, why hast Thou forsaken Me?'

We have survived: survived the Death of God, the end of science, the decline of the west, even ecological disaster. Carnival today, perhaps to this extent different from the medieval carnivals described by Bakhtin, is a kind of *danse macabre* which, once a year, tries to reclaim a sense of place from the anonymity of the streets. It is a celebration of where we are now, a celebration of survival, a bid for making these spaces we inhabit Home. This is where video is posed its awesome task – to reverse that trend, to make Home the site of carnival. The fear and loathing that once surrounded the nomad witnessed by the prayers of the Gaelic monks for protection from the Vikings is with us still in the rhetoric of Thatcher, who in a 1978 speech on immigration announced that 'The British character has done so much for democracy, for law, and done so much throughout the world that if there is any fear that it might be swamped, people are going to react.' (This speech gave the Metropolitan Police the name for 'Operation Swamp', the massive presence in Brixton which sparked the uprisings of 1981.) In the modern period, this becomes allied with the cult of the anonymous, wandering, amorphous 'man of the crowd' from Poe to Launder and Gilliat's *Millions Like Us*, and undergoes a further transformation in the age of suburbia, the private car and the domestic leisure centre. In the dialectic of displacement, the displaced serve the function of validating Others, proving our rootedness by calling for us to act as hosts. In this exchange, the powerful get more power. Surrounding the airports with immigration controls and customs regulations, binding our movements and the potential of the electronic image to surveillance by closed-circuit television: they still do not trust us to fly. The holiday-maker sneaking in an extra bottle or a gram of hash has a tactic of refusal, but as de Certeau argues, tactics are for the weak: the strong have strategies, and strategies depend upon the occupation of a place – be it geographical, institutional or discursive – a place which 'permits one to capitalise on acquired advantages, to prepare for future expansions, and to give ... an independence in relation to the variability of circumstances. It is a mastery of time by the founding of an autonomous place' (de Certeau 1980).

Although the postmodern suburb is not locatable within geographical space (since one suburb is much the same as every

other), it is tied to other communities of interest through the car, the
telephone, the (carefully selected) dinner guests and institutional
sites such as schools and supermarkets. For a segment of society,
these communities of interest constitute the local. For others living
in the inner-city, the Third World of the suburban psyche,
geographical territory is the major marker of cultural identity. The
postmodern thesis of the mediasphere fails to recognise the
localisation of power within the hurtling images. It extends the
totalitarian grip of capital by the same token – insistent on the
ontological nature of the phenomena it describes, giving
hyperreality a metaphysical status as the end beyond which we may
not move spatially or even historically. Such fatalism is an alibi for
style in the place of journalism, allegory in the place of analysis and
observation in the place of action. It is a strategy of pessimism from
a position of power: promising, in the work of Baudrillard, Deleuze
and Guattari and, even more so, among their North American
avatars, the fullness of 'consumer society' to itself, the availability of
satisfactions, the fulfilment of desire and so, as desire is the motor of
history, the end of history and the beginning of time as a pure,
uninflected extension of the western present. Alternative media, by
contrast, must be specific to their time and place, must recognise the
parameters of their specificity, and build their strategies on that.

Negation appears to me the most useful tool we have in hand for
understanding historical processes in an epoch in which history is
largely ignored or abandoned as unusable in a sinister and simplistic
discourse of 'That was then, this is now.' The celebrants as well as
the Cassandras of the postmodern operate in a shifting terrain of
verb tenses which work through simple, ugly and constraining
binaries – 'In the past ... but now', 'nowadays ... in the future' –
without either specifying the thresholds at which these momentous
changes are to take (or have taken) place, or how the two thresholds
relate to each other. At the same time, the modern is held to cover a
period as extended as Foucault's Classical Age, starting in the
sixteenth century, or as curtailed and amorphous as 'the twentieth
century' or 'pre-war'. The return of chronology, and an
unquestioning transfer of the epistemological break from the
discursive to the material universe, goes hand in hand with the
abandonment of the world beyond western Europe and North
America, possibly adding Australia and Japan.

Television, I argued in Chapter 2, proposes itself as the eternal
present, while video makes that proposal leaky and finally

untenable. But in that case, we have to argue a position dangerously close to the weird chronologies of postmodernism: after video, no more presence. Yet that does not mean that we have no alternative but to accommodate ourselves to ahistoricism and the abolition of the local. The alternative to presence is not the simulacral, but process and becoming, the micro and the macro of historical struggle. The role of negation is to refuse the givenness of the world that presents itself to us, mediately and immediately: to recognise the specificity of what is now becoming, here, in its relations to more global historical change. What I would propose is a kind of ecological model. The most successful political alternative of the 1980s and 1990s, one which offers a *grand récit* despite Lyotard's strictures, ecology provides more than an ethics of shopping, though that is in itself a remarkable achievement.

'The Butterfly Effect' is the term given by meteorologists to the idea that even the minuscule drafts created by the fluttering of a butterfly's wings have eventual effects in the closed system of the weather: just as nothing is forgotten in the Freudian unconscious, so the atmosphere retains every breath, every draft, every local condition as a part of its macrosystemic permutations. It is an effect illuminated with great elegance in Steve Hawley's tape *The Extent of Three Bells*, in which the comet-tails produced on video equipment by the movement of candle flames across a darkened room is choreographed with the music of traditional bell-ringing. The dialogics systematised by Todorov out of Bakhtin and Volosinov suggest a parallel cultural model: not a word, not a sign that is lost in the global movements of the cultural formation. Utterances may be mislaid, repressed or denied, but their effects cannot be lost, destroyed or, ultimately, forgiven.

I remember a science fiction story, misplaced in the library of memories, in which, despite fears of changing history, a machine is sent back from contemporary New York to observe the origins of life on this planet. As the machine returns, the triumphant demonstrator waves a long purple tentacle over his head: 'There, you see', it says, 'Nothing has changed!' Our memories are ourselves, and we have charge of creating memories. But the process of remembering is also a field of contradiction, of renegotiation and dispute, biography and ideology. And memory – say in the form of DNA – can be unkind and (since it is a code) misleading, open to polysemy: transsexuals among others have every reason to distrust the pairings of amino acids in the double

helix, the material of genetic coding that determines biological sex. None the less, the raw material on which we work and the ways we know to work upon it are our common lot. Our work is then a common one, though riven through by contradiction at every level.

Within that field of contradiction there are nodes of power, institutionally-based discourses capable of regimenting the entire panjandrum – almost. As Enzensberger writes in 'A Critique of Political Ecology' (in Enzensberger 1988), the difference between materialist and ecologist is the determination on the part of the former that the distinction human/natural is inadequate to comprehend (accurately enough for successful action) the flux through and around the complex relations of people with their environments. In particular, human discourse is structured in dominance: we make our own histories but not in conditions of our own choosing. As the ecosystem must take account of every movement throughout its totality, however mediated by intervening actions, so we must work with the whole sphere of the social, but also with the weight of history. Video work is about difference, about dialogue, about place and about time.

Time has a particular set of relevances to video. The new medium belongs to the world described by Benedict Anderson (1983) as the era of print capitalism: a period in which the older circular time of agrarian societies gives way to the linear time of industrial society. Electronic media bolt this new temporal axis together with space. As Robert C. Allen argues (1985), electronic media tend towards paradigmatic rather than syntagmatic time, where the syntagm refers to the ordering of images and sound in linear time, but the paradigm operates a system of cross-referencing with other sights and sounds far more spatial in its orientation. The most familiar combined form is in machine memory, where a frame-store, for example, might hold not only the history of work on a particular project, but also all the other images which have been grabbed and manipulated in the process. But there are other forms of historical imagination: horror, the imagination of finality; the time of boredom and self-disgust most poignantly caught in the suicide note of the poet Mayakovsky: 'the love boat/ has crashed against the everyday' (quoted in Shklovsky 1972: 201); the intoxication of the endless paradigmatic present. To these we might also add Braudel's *longue durée*, the huge historical epochs over which climates, trade routes and modes of production change, and the awesome scale of astronomical time. What is productive is the

interplay of these timescales. It is essential to realise that the ancient scales persist, just as sailors still navigate with the Ptolemaic system, alongside the most recent. Machine memory, the Foucauldian archive of images as much as the computer frame-store, is largely information as opposed to knowledge, and to that extent the word memory is a misnomer. K. S. Gill (1986) argues that this conforms to a distinction between economic and social wealth creation, or between capitalist accumulation and the distribution of wealth. The point is to create the structures through which such information becomes knowledge, and to seize control of local knowledge.

This, of course, sits at the borders of legality. Hacking is a seed bed of the new electronic culture: the lure of William Gibson's hacker dystopias (1986; 1987; 1989) is the sense of entry into and disturbance of the hardware. On the one hand, we could argue with Whitby (1986) and Weizenbaum (1984) that 'One of the reasons someone might become a compulsive programmer is that a programmer has total and complete control over his/her program ... software engineers regard disobedient programs as very dangerous things (except perhaps from the extreme fringe of AI work)' (Whitby 1986: 120). This should remind us of Skirrow's (1986) thesis concerning video games and the maternal body: the narcissistic relation to video is one of power, and nothing is so frustrating to that emotional attachment to the VDU than a fault that interferes with the pleasures of mastery. At the same time, there is the lure of disobedience, and of the potential for unleashing unforeseen processes, the call of chaos. Paik entered these arenas in his early work. Yet the more advanced and user-friendly the machinery becomes, the less possible it is to gain entry to the programming software. Expensive paint systems, for example, will not let you determine the possibilities or shift their parameters. The future may belong to the treated image – the camera has never been the sole device for making moving-image media, and its role is diminishing daily – but there is no 'access' to the means of its treatment, other than forcible entry. A great deal of the future of electronic media will lie in the hands of engineers, software architects, programmers: it is easy to envisage a culture in which the aesthetic relation is no longer based on finished texts, but on the ways in which a programme can be manipulated by its users, so that the true computer art would not be like existing show-reels, but actual pieces of software for the user to create with. The designer of the Quantel Paintbox would be the real artist, not the producers of

flying logos and credit sequences that use it.

This new relation to the machine, however, opens another whole element in the theory of democratic media: the technological relation and the ways it relates to the extremities of human experience. Between the strangeness of our relations to ourselves, to each other and to the biosphere of local space, there subsists an instant of uncomprehending awe, the experience of the sublime that reframes and undercuts our comprehension of the Beautiful and the Good. The best, as Lacan observes (1986: 256), is the enemy of the good – and of goods. Sublimity puts us in awe – since the question persists after the death of God, in awe of what? – in awe of the mismatch between the poverty of the world we have created, and the wealth of the means at our disposal to change it.

Todorov's account of Bakhtin's 'philosophical anthropology' devolves upon the relation of self and other, the impossibility of solipsism. My perception of myself is necessarily partial: to be perceived as a totality, I depend on others, for example to witness my birth or my death:

> The very being of man (exterior as interior) is a *profound communication. Being* signifies *communication* . . . . Being signifies being for an other and, through them, for oneself. Man does not possess a sovereign internal territory, he is entirely and always on a frontier; looking inside himself, he looks *into the eyes of an other* or *through the eyes of another*.
>
> (Mikhail Bakhtin, 'Concerning the Revision of the Book on Dostoievsky', 1961; cited in Todorov 1981: 148)

The functions of this other, witness to life and to birth, had long been the province of divinity. In a secular world, the same function must be transferred to the totality of the human world, visibly manifest in the ecology of language, in which, as in the global ecosystem, each utterance only takes place as a result of, in concert with and in relation to, every other utterance. For us, however, the issue is one of the relation of this complex to the audio-visual media, the new complex of self, Other and machine that finds such popular expression in the horror genre.

If horror as a cultural affect continues to act consistently, it is because we still internalise and visit upon ourselves, our bodies and our planet – all now refigured in the guise of objects, of Others – in fantasy and reality, the fantastic wrath of the abandoned *infans*. The guards at Treblinka played at fort-da with human identity (and

indeed with the identities of the dogs they trained to attack men's genitals): in the cultural forms of horror we play the game with our own bodies – dismembered, returned to wholeness. Re-enacting compulsively the moment of loss on the figure of our bodies – and Whitehouse is quite wrong: identification is *always* with the victim, *never* with the perpetrator – we perform a psychic act of denial, a *Verneinung*, on our relations with ourselves.

Because film and tape have recorded what, in any decent world, should never have occurred; because this English language has been fouled with utterances – commands, remembrances, cries – that should never have been spoken; because uniforms clothe the torturers and smiles cover the tracks of gun-runners and arms dealers; because, all the same, we must speak, and work through images, and wear clothes and use the language of our bodies, because we are always already in the Symbolic, I must speak. And in speaking there is a virtually existential imperative to try to produce, even if it is only for myself, a way of speaking and acting that allows of respect, for my others and so for myself. The beautiful precision of these media – language, video – is marred, even invalidated by the uses to which they have been put. Perhaps this is the appeal of synthetic images generated by computer, the secret of their cleanness: that they emerge, or so it appears, from the mathematic universe of machine codes and Boolean algebra. They do not belong to us but to the dark interiors of the devices we have made, whose capabilities already exceed what uses we can make of them. In the new dialectic between the human and the machine that characterises the late twentieth century, replacing Lévi-Strauss's dialectic of nature and culture, it is the machine that is clean, and we ourselves the unclean.

Kristeva's work on abjection carries us further towards an understanding of what this might mean for us. The abject – which seems very close to *Das Ding* in Lacanian usage – is that which you try to expel in involuntary vomiting, but it is also your 'self' that you expel and abject. Abjection is therefore a kind of narcissistic crisis, as revulsion hurls us away from that which marks the limits of our being: birth, death, dirt. Two causes bring about this crisis:

A too great severity on the part of the Other, confounded with the One and the Law. And *the failure of the Other* which becomes apparent in the breakdown of objects of desire. In each case, the abject appears in order to uphold the 'I' in the Other. The abject is the violence of mourning for an object that is always already lost.

The abject smashes the wall of repression and its judgements. It resituates the ego at those abominable limits from which, in order to be, it had detached itself – it resituates it in the non-ego, in the drive, in death. Abjection is a resurrection which passes through death (of the ego).

(Kristeva 1980: 22)

In the wake of the cult of hygiene which blossomed in the mid-twentieth century, we have assumed all the dirt, leaving the machines clean: it is they, in some senses, who become our Other, confounded with the rule-giving, paternal figure of the One (whose unity underpins the ideologies of being, presence and identity) and the Law. In a moral order in which objects, having initially been produced as objects, are then categorised and hierarchised, the abject revolts at separation.

Yet via our technologies, we can be resituated at the brink of that loss. And it is in this nexus that the relation between the body, and its 'loathsome' interiors, with the machine enters into the play. At the limit between life and death arrives a third term, that which has never lived. The ambiguity recycles in android movies, the inside-out Freddy of the *Elm Street* series, in graphic novels and techno-pop. It emerges in fantasies of the future: cloning, for example, and the figure of the cyborg. And it is present in such areas as reproductive technologies (cf. Corea 1986) and medical practice generally. Corea argues that the control over birth acts also as a control over death, a bid for immortality through gene-cloning, prosthesis (cf. McLuhan's 'prosthetic media') and transplant surgery. We can thus arrive at a thesis of 'unmournable death' (Hayles 1987: 80), a refusal to accept death, the deaths of others or our own, which takes the form of unsuccessful repression, taken up and obliterated by the dominant media, which cannot provide a substitute for the older rituals through which our forebears laid their ghosts. Freud analyses unsuccessful mourning and melancholia alike as disguises for an unwillingness to come to terms with the hatred felt by a subject for its mourned object:

On the one hand a strong fixation to the loved object must have been present; on the other hand, in contradiction to this, the object cathexis must have had little power of resistance. As Otto Rank has aptly remarked, this contradiction seems to imply that object-choice has been effected on a narcissistic basis, so that the

object cathexis, when obstacles come in its way, can regress to narcissism.

(Freud (1917) 1984: 258)

A major function of new video will be to negotiate that mourning which we have never been able to conclude, to create forms in which the relation to death can be expressed, in which we can face the founding loss on which our culture and society is based. The alternative is a final act of mania, a withdrawal of the emotional bond to the objects of our affections ('object-cathexis') that returns us to a primary narcissism let loose in the nursery of universal destruction.

The centre-out model of broadcasting criticised by Enzensberger ('Constituents of a Theory of the Media', in Enzensberger 1988) is unable to handle process. Stuck in its eternal present, it has become static, able to increase quantitatively but not qualitatively through the addition of non-terrestrial channels. It seeks its novelties from the domain of video practice as narrowly defined: the world of community, campaign and artists' video provides the raw materials (and sometimes the personnel) for youth programming, advertising, pop video and new modes of documentary. It is in the margins that the nub of the culture now appears, a decentralised centre. The vital organs of the culture, the messy, vulnerable organs that keep us alive, are on the outside.

Video is not whole, though in its reference to reality it at times hypostatises a whole real preceding its activities, sometimes the real of television, sometimes that of the political world. Its wholeness and its reality however lie outside of each individual work, even outside the domain of video practice – including viewing – in general. Built in an aesthetics of difference, contemporary video practice encompasses as much as TV, and also includes TV itself, in a field of radical heterogeneity. The point of analysing it is not to restore it to wholeness, nor to celebrate the end of global modes of thinking, but to indicate its relation to the material absence of wholeness, and to the two routes which it takes to achieving some kind of alternate solidity, through intertextuality (and therefore intersubjectivity), and through reference to a common negativity vis-à-vis the accepted presentation of realities. Perhaps another route might be through what was described above (p. 170) as an ethical imperative, the critique of homogeneity as the apathetic acceptance of (the injustices which provide) comfort.

To take control of a means (but not the means) of production in this world is to make a qualitative shift from the ossifying forms of multinational and corporate capital in broadcasting to a more chaotic system, one whose 'organisation' exceeds the forms of previous systems through increasing levels of self-organisation. It is to assert with Whitehead the primacy of relations in the processes of innovation, that each new existent receives its identity from its relations with others, and adds to them all their new relations with itself (Whitehead 1969: 26ff.): that individual or small group activity is not without its significance, or the need to take responsibility for what is undertaken. This in turn implies again that relations are also relations of struggle, mapped through contradictions in the actual situations in which we act, not in abstract models of homogeneity.

Prigogine and Stengers note that

the specific form in which time was introduced into physics, as a tendency towards homogeneity and death, reminds us more of ancient mythological and religious archetypes than of the progressive complexification and diversification described by biology and the social sciences . . . . The rapid transformation of the technological mode of interaction with nature, the constantly accelerating pace of change experienced by the nineteenth century, produced a deep anxiety. This anxiety is still with us and takes various forms, from the repeated proposals for a 'zero-growth' society or for a moratorium on scientific research to the announcement of 'scientific truths' concerning our disintegrating universe.

(Prigogine and Stengers 1988: 116)

The often observed prevalence of pessimism as a cultural form in the 1980s has a longer heritage, which the previous quotation locates in the evolution of the theory of entropy. Such a pessimism undoubtedly underpins Baudrillard, and to some extent the claims of right-wing 'ecology' (the coca-colonialism of population control, the 'one-worldism' of Gorbachev): the crisis is now, 'we' must all pull in 'our' belts, we are all on this ship together (but some of the bastards are travelling first class). The mythologising of eco-disaster allows for a politics of crisis management in which social contradiction is pushed aside in favour of short-term solutions of often the most Draconian kind (cf. Ryle 1988).

Ecological disaster here stands in as the acceptable vision of the

death of God: here, someone must pay, but the someone is clearly anyone other than the global ruling class. In the Thatcherite version, it works as the otherwise unavailable mourning, undertaken in the spirit of a patrician stewardship of the Earth (the same rhetoric as employed by the aristocratic landowners of Norfolk in the East Anglian Filmmakers' documentary *The Poacher*). What we need to distinguish between are the rhetoric of 'green' policies (often driven through at the expense, for example, of Amazonian peasants or 'dirty'-industry workers), especially as they recruit from the pessimism of the nineteenth century or from the residual needs of populations for a sense of the sublime, and the possibility of building an ecological perspective on aesthetics, especially here in video. The first is a reaction to the 'failure of the Other' cited by Kristeva (1980: 22): the second is a response to the unavailability of the lost object, a readiness to face the physical and material reality of death, dirt and decay as the ambit within which the human subject operates, and a grasp on the intersubjectivity which makes us human.

Lyotard has spent some time examining the shape of the sublime in relation to death. In a 1984 catalogue essay he describes a suite of works by the American Barnett Newman:

> In 1966, Newman shows the fourteen *Stations of the Cross* at the Guggenheim. He gives them the subtitle *Lamma Sabachtani*, the cry of distress which the crucified Christ hurls towards God: why have You abandoned me? 'This question without a reply', he writes in the accompanying *Notice*, 'has been with us for so long – since Jesus – since Abraham – since Adam – it is the original question'. Jewish version of the Passion: the reconciliation of existence (and therefore of death) with signification has not taken place, The Messiah, bringer of meaning, always makes us wait. The only answer ever heard to the questioning of the abandoned is not *Know why*, but: *Be*.
>
> (reprinted in Lyotard 1988: 98)

The increasingly Kantian note which, as Meaghan Morris observes in her essay on 'Postmodernity and Lyotard's Sublime' (in Morris 1988), pervades his recent writings on politics and culture, is far removed from the realm of popular pleasures. The harsh return to a Greenbergian aesthetics of the purity of painting in and for itself denotes a severe elitism in his approach, one that moreover reaches its apotheosis in the instant, not of becoming, but of Being, that supremely metaphysical and monolithic state.

Maybe, in place of the sublime (a quality, it could be argued, of the art work itself), we should argue awe as the entity to be analysed, a quality of the subject/object relation in which the object loses its limits as object, invading the processes that constitute the subject, in a movement in which the subject also bleeds over into the object. Such a thesis would site horror as an effect in the imagination of one's own dissolution. One of the great truisms of popular wisdom is that if you dream of falling, you must wake before you hit the bottom: impact only occurs in the dream at the moment of the real dreamer's death. This tale is symptomatic of the relation of awe: the moving (*movance* – a movement defined not by the points from and to which it travels but by the activity of moving) between identification and loss of subjectivity beyond the exchange of ego for ego-ideal in visual pleasure: a horror which, in its finality, reduces to common humanity (beyond regimes, for example, of sexual and racial difference) while simultaneously insisting on the dreamer's own specificity, absolute difference.

I wonder whether Eisenstein's 'montage of effects' has re-emerged as the montage of affects in the pyrotechnic cinema of Spielberg and Lucas, and in the contemporary horror film. Their popularity would then be legible in terms of a loss of self which they offer in the spectacle of the destruction of objects, the imagination of finality, the engagement, not of knowledge, but of ignorance: destruction of the self in the eyes of others, an end in as well as of language. As mentioned above, every cinema usher knows that audiences identify with victims: fear is the attraction. That is the confrontation which Viola urges in *I Do Not Know What It Is That I Am Like* and its images of decay. This is me, in some sense which precludes (precedes?) meaning: awe in the face of the faceless. Beyond the postmodern play of identity is the unaddressed, unaddressable realm of non-identity: no dissolution into infinite semiosis, but the finality of one's own death, one's own birth, one's own fragile and passionate materiality: the zero-state of animal consciousness – no identity, no oneness, no incompletion, no entropy: the further side of experience that can only be spoken of in the negative.

Nor is this phenomenal obverse of the totalitarian nature of language and culture purely individual, though it starts in each different person and has its roots there in the most intimate hinterland between body and mind. Citing Fanon's dictum that 'it is to the zone of occult instability where the people dwell that we

must come' (Fanon 1967: 182–3), James Donald argues that the
politics of 'such a shadowy borderland' might learn from the
'sublime'

> an attention to the materiality and limits of representation, and to
> their inevitable inadequacy to the idea of totality, and so also a
> certain pragmatic modesty. And, not least, from the
> transgressive and creative aspects of popular culture it might
> learn not only the impossibility of political closure but also the
> critical possibilities of social and cultural heterogeneity for an
> aspiration towards community that always remains to be
> brought into being.
>
> (Donald 1989: 248–9)

The popular sublime demands just such a deference, not to the
theological command to 'Be', but, precisely, to the processes of
emergence and disappearance, of arrival and fading that mark video
as their own. Video cannot, and should not try, to imagine the
future – the traditional role of the final chapter of books on new
technologies – but to set up the terms on which the future might
emerge: to seize that initiative back from the 'global postmodern' (in
Stuart Hall's phrase in a talk at the 'Changing Identities' conference,
London, May 1989) which exists, in the main, precisely to halt the
emergence of the new through its proselytising theories of
sameness. Transgression, it should be recalled, is not some tidy
mess on the gallery floor, assimilable into the deft and inane
paradoxes of postmodernism, but potentially violent, ugly, foul,
disgusting: beyond the regimen of taste that regulates the tasteful
and the kitsch alike, it will above all not be nice. I think that I will
probably loathe it in its emergence.

There is, however, every risk of becoming prescriptive as to what
kind of video practice might be entailed by the strictures outlined in
this chapter. While recognising the issues in the impact of magnetic
media on the environment – energy-efficient? ozone-friendly?
biodegradable? safe work-stations? – what I have in mind is a
democracy of the media, in which management in all its forms –
corporate, governmental, psychic – gives way to a serious and
responsible play from which evolution, even through the kind of
radical instability described in Prigogine's chaos theory, can
produce the grounds on which cultural and technological means of
communication are opened up for play and for change. To do so, we
must give up the melancholia prevalent in the culture, finish

mourning the body of the all-knowing God who for so long legitimated religion and science, recognise the powers that oppress us for what they are and begin to dismantle them. The radical questioning at the heart of contemporary video practice is part and parcel of these processes.

The replicability of video, as it loses generations, means that, in art terms, it loses value: ubiquity at the price of unicity. But as it approaches the finite limit of lost generations, the valueless approaches the priceless. The moments, their transitoriness marked in the edits, the new metaphysical space of the image-generator, these do not promise a utopia. What can be said of an audio-visual culture in which the adverts cost more, use better equipment and compete seriously for talent with the programmes? Is this the rationale for the ascendancy of style over content and the deteriorating status of the referential?

And yet: work is being done. It is important to operate between impossibility and utopia: pessimism of the intellect, optimism of the will, in Gramsci's slogan. Video succeeds when it is heteroclite, when it moves by contradiction, from document to generation, from medium to material, from simple grapheme to complex lexicon and back. Video has already added to Metz's five codes of cinema (writing, speech, sound, music and image) with image-grabbing, treated images, multiple-perspective images, the interfacing of cel and stop-frame animation with computer technology, tapes based in photocopying technologies or ultra-sound scanning . . . . Video's strength is its ability to cut across the interstices, to play upon the contradictions, of the regimes of looking and hearing that structure the dominant audio-visual world. Its very weakness, its indefiniteness, becomes its field of possibility: the necessity of pluriform tactics, since no structure of power presents it with a strategy. Video is strong because it evades, is larger than, exceeds, avoids, slips by and away from, cannot be accounted for in the discourses (including this one) about it.

To resume: video is out of control, at least in the software zone. The hardware is still open to remaking, and a generation of artist–technicians is in the making, for whom software architectures and chip design will be potential areas for creative work. The problem is that such creativity is most immediately rewarded inside transnational corporations, rewarded in any case fiscally. You can't blame someone for accepting £40,000 a year as a paint-box editor in exchange for that creativity. But someone, somewhere has to

break the circuit: to be prepared for a culture of the one-off machine, owned and built outside the structures of corporate capital. Artists generally are getting access only to machinery a generation out of date. The few technician–artists working with the emerging generations are so constrained by the commercial imperatives of hugely expensive research and development programmes that the artistic potentials of the machines take second place, let alone their role as social rather than economic capital. We need a generation of image-generation for its own sake to break the cycle. It seems poignant to have to argue this tired ideology, and to have to suggest that through it alone, the full commercial potential of the new computers will be realised. Taking the longer view: capital demands, in the UK at least, returns in two or three years. Software applications call for a far further horizon. Finally, capital cannot deliver on its promises.

Cable, satellite, opto-electronics, 4D animation . . . the capability for so much and the delivery (not only in the peculiar circumstances of the United Kingdom) so trivial. Artists have ceased to be sources, have made themselves conduits: no longer the unacknowledged legislators, they are the unofficial magistrates of a cultural regime they are no longer invited to understand or to help make. The dominant is a stagnant and dying culture whose highest aim – and even this it lacks the courage to realise – is to become decadent, as if it imagined a moment beyond itself and its own barrenness, the grounds for a new and fundamentally alien growth.

To confound this depressing prognosis, video will in all probability become transfixingly lovely. The emergent Europe of the 1990s will enter a new and quite probably capitalist or metacapitalist phase that will throw up new Jimi Hendrixes, new Frieda Kahlos, new Pablo Picassos of the electronic image. For the best part of this century, the majority, if not indeed the totality, of artists worth the time of day have been profoundly at odds with the dominant presuppositions of capital and its workings, though most have had to make a virtue of coming to terms with the non-negotiable. At the time of writing, capital has rarely seemed more triumphant in attracting the best talent. If this situation continues, we are doomed to a bland, inhuman, sadistic and narcissistic spiral. It is so easy to deflect aspiration for the best into acceptance of the good(s); to redirect yearning for the sublime into nostalgia for the womb. Yet in its triumph, capital cannot help making enemies, and it is they who will provide the greatest contribution to the species, or

to whatever it might be that they will find to sing. The electronic media, for viewers as much as producers, like the social formation as a whole, is so productive of contradictions that there remains, in the absence of faith and of charity, that hope which baffles rational comprehension – hope that we could be surprised again, face the possibility of change so profound that nothing will ever be the Same again.

Bibliography

This bibliography contains all works cited in the text, plus a representative sample of writing on video in books, catalogues and journals. Other sources which have formed the background to my research are the magazines *Independent Media* (previously *Independent Video*), *Mediamatic* and *City Limits*. All translations are my own unless otherwise specified.

Acland, Charles (1988), '"Look What They're Doing on TV!": Towards an Appreciation of the Complexity of Music Video', *Wide Angle*, 10, n. 2.

Allen, Robert C. (1985), *Speaking of Soap Operas*, University of North Carolina Press, Chapel Hill, NC.

— (ed.) (1987), *Channels of Discourse: Television and Contemporary Criticism*, Methuen, London.

Almy, Max (1984), 'Leaving the Twentieth Century: Interview', *Camera Obscura*, 12.

Althusser, Louis (1965) *Pour Marx*, Maspero, Paris.

— (1971), *Lenin and Philosophy and Other Essays*, Monthly Review Press, New York.

Althusser, Louis, Etienne Balibar, Roger Establet, Pierre Macherey and Jacques Rancière (1971), *Lire le Capital*, 2nd edn, 4 vols, Maspero, Paris.

Alvarado, Manuel (1988), *Video World-Wide*, John Libbey/UNESCO, London.

Anderson, Benedict (1983), *Imagined Communities: Reflections on the Origin and Spread of Nationalism*, Verso, London.

Ang, Ien (1987), 'The Vicissitudes of "Progressive Television"', *New Formations*, 2, summer.

Armes, Roy (1985), 'Black African Cinema in the Eighties', *Screen*, 26, ns 3–4, May–August.

— (1988), *On Video*, Routledge, London.

Attali, Jacques (1985), *Noise: The Political Economy of Music*, Manchester University Press, Manchester.

Auguiste, Reece (1988), 'Handsworth Songs: Some Background Notes', *Framework*, 35.

Bakhtin, Mikhail (1968), *Rabelais and His World*, MIT Press, Boston, Mass.

— (1981), *The Dialogic Imagination: Four Essays*, University of Texas Press, Austin.

— (1986), *Speech Genres and Other Late Essays*, University of Texas Press, Austin.

Balio, Tino (ed.) (1976), *The American Film Industry*, The University of Wisconsin Press, Madison.

Barker, Martin (ed.) (1984), *The Video Nasties: Freedom and Censorship in the Media*, Pluto, London.

Barlow, Geoffrey and Alison Hill (1985), *Video Violence and Children*, Hodder and Stoughton, London.

Barnouw, Erik (1966), *A Tower in Babel: A History of Broadcasting in the United States; Volume 1 – to 1933*, Oxford University Press, New York.

— (1968), *The Golden Web: A History of Broadcasting in the United States; Volume 2 – 1933 to 1953*, Oxford University Press, New York.

— (1970), *The Image Empire: A History of Broadcasting in the United States; Volume 3 – from 1953*, Oxford University Press, New York.

Barthes, Roland (1970), *S/Z*, Seuil, Paris.

— (1973), *Le Plaisir du texte*, Seuil, Paris.

— (1975), *Roland Barthes par Roland Barthes*, Seuil, Paris.

— (1977), 'The Grain of the Voice', in Roland Barthes, *Image–Music–Text: Selected Essays*, Fontana, London.

— (1980), *La Chambre claire: note sur la photographie*, Gallimard, Paris.

Battcock, Geoffrey (ed.) (1978), *New Artists Video*, Dutton, New York.

Baudelaire, Charles (1968), *L'Art romantique*, Gallimard, Paris.

Baudrillard, Jean (1972), *Pour une critique de l'économie politique du signe*, Gallimard, Paris.

— (1975), *The Mirror of Production*, Telos Press, St Louis.

— (1983), 'The Precession of Simulacra', *Art & Text*, spring.

— (1986), 'The Year 2000 Will Not Take Place', in E. A. Grosz *et al.* (eds), *Futur*Fall: Excursions into Postmodernity*, Power Institute of Fine Arts, Sydney.

— (1988), *Selected Writings*, ed. Mark Poster, Stanford University Press, Stanford, California.

Bazalgette, Cary (1987), 'Screen Kids', *Media Education Journal*, n. 6.

Belloir, Dominique (1981), *Video Art Explorations*, Cahiers du Cinéma, hors série, Paris.

Bellour, Raymond (1983), 'Thierry Kuntzel and the Return of Writing', *Camera Obscura*, 11.

— (1985), 'An Interview with Bill Viola', *October*, 34, fall.

— (1988), 'Autoportraits', in Raymond Bellour and Anne-Marie Duguet (eds), *Vidéo: Communications 48*, Seuil, Paris.

Bellour, Raymond and Anne-Marie Duguet (1988a), 'La Question vidéo', in Raymond Bellour and Anne-Marie Duguet (eds), *Vidéo: Communications 48*, Seuil, Paris.

Bellour, Raymond and Anne-Marie Duguet (eds) (1988b) *Vidéo: Communications 48*, Seuil, Paris.

Benjamin, Walter (1969), 'The Work of Art in the Age of Mechanical Reproduction', in Walter Benjamin, *Illuminations*, Shocken, New York.

— (1979), 'A Small History of Photography', in Walter Benjamin, *One Way Street*, New Left Books, London.

Berger, John (1980), 'Why Look at Animals?', in John Berger, *About Looking*, Writers and Readers, London.

Berrigan, Frances J. (1974), *Access and the Media: New Models in Europe*, Middlesex Polytechnic, London.

BFI (1989), *The Corporate Plan 1989–93*, British Film Institute, WS/LD/C/3/8.2,

London, November.

Bhabha, Homi K. (1984), 'Of Mimicry and Man: The Ambivalence of Colonial Discourse', *October*, 28, spring.

— (1985), 'Sly Civility', *October*, 34, fall.

Bianchini, Franco (1987), 'GLC R.I.P. Cultural Policies in London 1981–1986', *New Formations*, 1, spring.

Blake, William (1966), *Collected Writings*, Oxford University Press, Oxford.

Boddy, William (1988), 'La Télé de guérilla revisitée', in Raymond Bellour and Anne-Marie Duguet (eds), *Vidéo: Communications 48*, Seuil, Paris.

Bode, Steven (1988), 'All that is Solid Melts on the Air – Art, Video, Representation and Postmodernity', in Philip Hayward (ed.), *Picture This: Media Representations of Visual Arts and Artists*, John Libbey/Arts Council of Great Britain.

Bódy, Gábor (1986), *Infermental 1980–1986*, Infermental, Cologne.

Bongiovanni, Michel (ed.) (1984), *2e manifestation internationale de vidéo de Montbéliard*, catalogue, Montbéliard.

— (ed.) (1985), *3e manifestation internationale de vidéo de Montbéliard*, catalogue, Montbéliard.

Bornemann, Ernest (1976), 'United States versus Hollywood: The Case Study of an Anti-Trust Suit', in Tino Balio (ed.), *The American Film Industry*, The University of Wisconsin Press, Madison.

Boulez, Pierre and Andrew Gerzso (1988), 'Computers in Music', *Scientific American*, 258, n. 4, April.

Boyden, Southwood (1989), *Developing the Independent Film and Video Sector*, report commissioned by Greater London Arts.

Boyle, Deirdre (1986), *Video Classics: A Guide to Video Art and Documentary Tapes*, Oryx Press, Phoenix, Arizona.

Brand, Stewart (1987), *The Media Lab: Inventing the Future at MIT*, Penguin, Harmondsworth.

Braverman, Harry (1974), *Labour and Monopoly Capital: The Degradation of Work in the Twentieth Century*, Monthly Review Press, New York.

Briggs, Asa (1979), *The History of Broadcasting in the United Kingdom: Volume 4: Sound and Vision*, Oxford University Press, Oxford.

Britton, Andrew (1984), *Katherine Hepburn: The Thirties and After*, Tyneside Cinema, Newcastle-upon-Tyne.

Brockbank, Steve (1987), 'Programming Languages: Structured Design and Speed. A Study of a Technological Field', Polytechnic of Central London.

Brown, Brian (1984), 'Exactly What We Wanted', in Martin Barker (ed.), *The Video Nasties: Freedom and Censorship in the Media*, Pluto, London.

Brunsdon, Charlotte (1982), 'Crossroads: Notes on Soap Opera', *Screen*, 22, n. 4, spring.

Burns, Gary (1988), 'Dreams and Meditation in Music Video', *Wide Angle*, 10, n. 2.

Carvell, John (1986), *Citizen Ken*, Chatto and Windus, London.

Caughie, John (1980), 'Progressive Television and Documentary Drama', *Screen*, 21, n. 3.

— (1981), 'Rhetoric, Pleasure and "Art Television"', *Screen*, 22, n. 4.

— (1984), 'Television Criticism', *Screen*, 25, ns 4–5, July–October, 109–21.

Chambers, Iain (1985), *Urban Rhythms: Popular Music and Urban Culture*, Macmillan, London.

— (1986), *Popular Culture: The Metropolitan Experience*, Methuen, London.

Changeux, Jean-Pierre (1986), *The Neuronal Man: The Biology of Mind*, Oxford University Press, London.

Chen, Kuan-Hsing (1986), 'MTV: The Disappearance of Postmodern Semiosis, or the Cultural Politics of Resistance', *Journal of Communication Inquiry*, 10, n. 1, winter.

Chesterman, John and Andy Lipman (1988), *The Electronic Pirates: DIY Crime of the Century*, Comedia/Routledge, London.

Clark, Katerina and Michael Holquist (1984), *Mikhail Bakhtin*, Harvard University Press, Cambridge, Mass.

Clarke, John and Chas Critcher (1985), *The Devil Makes Work: Leisure in Capitalist Britain*, Macmillan, London.

Cockburn, Cynthia (1983), *Brothers: Male Dominance and Technological Change*, Pluto, London.

— (1985), *Machinery of Dominance: Women, Men and Technical Know-How*, Pluto, London.

Comedia Consultancy (1988), *ACTT Franchised Workshops: An Assessment of the Operation of The British Film Institute's Regional Production Fund and the Impact of Its Funding*, report commissioned by five workshops, January.

Commission of the European Communities (1984), *Television Without Frontiers*, COM(84) 300 final, CEC, Brussels.

Conant, Michael (1976), 'The Impact of the *Paramount* Decrees', in Tino Balio (ed.), *The American Film Industry*, The University of Wisconsin Press, Madison.

Connor, Steve (1987), 'The Flag on the Road: Bruce Springsteen and the Live', *New Formations*, n. 3, winter.

Corea, Gena (1986), *The Mother Machine: Reproductive Technologies from Artificial Insemination to Artificial Wombs*, Harper and Row, New York.

Couchot, Edmond (1986), *Images: de l'optique au numérique*, Hermès, Paris.

— (1988), 'La Mosaïque ordonnée', in Raymond Bellour and Anne-Marie Duguet (eds), *Vidéo: Communications 48*, Seuil, Paris.

Cubitt, Sean (1984), '"Maybellene": Meaning and the Listening Subject', *Popular Music*, n. 4, Cambridge University Press, Cambridge.

— (1986a), 'Family Rot', *Media Education Journal*, n. 4.

— (1986b), 'Magic Hour: An Interview with Frank Abbott', *Framework*, 32–3.

— (1990), 'Innocence and Manipulation: The Politics of Censorship in the UK', in Alan Tomlinson (ed.), *Consumption, Identity and Style*, Comedia/Routledge, London.

Curtis, Dave (ed.) (1987), *The Elusive Sign: British Avant-Garde Film and Video 1977–1987*, Arts Council of Great Britain, London.

D'Agostino, Peter (ed.) (1985), *Transmission: Theory and Practice for a New Television Aesthetics*, Tanam, New York.

Davis, Douglas and Allison Simmons (eds) (1977), *The New Television: A Public/ Private Art*, MIT Press, Cambridge, Mass.

Davis, Mike (1987), '"Chinatown" Part Two?: The Internationalisation of Downtown Los Angeles', *New Left Review*, n. 164, July–August.

Dayan, Daniel (1974), 'The Tutor Code of Classical Cinema', *Film Quarterly*, fall.

de Certeau, Michel (1980), 'On the Oppositional Practices of Everyday Life', *Social Text*, 3, fall.

de Mèredieu, Florence (1988), 'L'Implosion dans le champ des couleurs', in

Raymond Bellour and Anne-Marie Duguet (eds), *Vidéo: Communications 48*, Seuil, Paris.

Department of Education and Science (1987), *National Curriculum 5–16: A Consultative Document*, London, July.

Derrida, Jacques (1967), *L'Écriture et la différence*, Seuil (Collection Points), Paris.

— (1976), *Of Grammatology*, Johns Hopkins University Press, Baltimore.

Dews, Peter (1987), *Logics of Disintegration: Post-Structural Thought and the Claims of Critical Theory*, Verso, London.

Docherty, David, David Morrison and Michael Tracey (1987), *Britain's Changing Film Audiences*, British Film Institute, London.

Donald, James (1989), 'The Fantastic, the Sublime and the Popular: Or, What's At Stake in Vampire Films' in James Donald (ed.), *Fantasy and the Cinema*, British Film Institute, London.

Dovey, John (1986), 'Copyright as Censorship – Notes on *Death Valley Days*', *Screen*, 27, n. 2, March–April.

Dowmunt, Tony (1987), *Video With Young People*, Cassell, London.

Dubois, Phillippe, Marc-Emanuel Mélon and Colette Dubois (1988), 'Cinéma et vidéo: interpénétrations', in Raymond Bellour and Anne-Marie Duguet (eds), *Vidéo: Communications 48*, Seuil, Paris.

Ducrot, Oswald and Tzvetan Todorov (1972), *Dictionnaire encyclopédique des sciences du langage*, Seuil (Collection Points), Paris.

Duguet, Anne-Marie (1979), *Vidéo – la mémoire au poing*, Hachette, Paris.

— (1988), 'Dispositifs', in Raymond Bellour and Anne-Marie Duguet (eds), *Vidéo: Communications 48*, Seuil, Paris.

Dungey, Jo and John Dovey (1985), *The Videoactive Report*, Videoactive, London.

Easley, Greg and Lauren Rabinowitz (1988), 'No Controles: Music Vide and Cultural Difference', *Wide Angle*, 10, n. 2.

Eco, Umberto (1962), *Opera Aperta – Forma e indeterminazione nelle poetiche contemporanee*, Bompiani, Milan.

— (1981), *The Rôle of the Reader: Explorations in the Semiotics of Texts*, Hutchinson, London.

— (1984), 'A Guide to the Neo-Television of the 1980s', *Framework*, 25.

Ellis, John (1982), *Visible Fictions: Cinema, Television, Video*, Methuen, London.

Elwes, Catherine (1985), 'Toys for the Boys', *Channel Five* (catalogue), LVA, London.

— (1988), 'Quiet Moments with Nature: An Interview with Bill Viola', *Independent Media*, 82, October.

Enzensberger, Hans Magnus (1988), *Dreamers of the Absolute: Essays on Ecology, Media and Power*, Radius, London.

Fanon, Frantz (1967), *The Wretched of the Earth*, Penguin, Harmondsworth.

Fargier, Jean-Paul (ed.) (1986), *Où va la vidéo? Cahiers du Cinéma*, hors série, Paris.

— (1988), 'Les Effets de mes effets sont mes effets', in Raymond Bellour and Anne-Marie Duguet (eds), *Vidéo: Communications 48*, Seuil, Paris.

Fenster, Mark (1988), 'Country Music Video', *Popular Music*, 7, n. 3, October.

Feuer, Jane (1983), 'The Concept of Live Television: Ontology as Ideology', in E. Ann Kaplan (ed.), *Regarding Television*, American Film Institute Monographs, 2, University Publications of America, Frederick, MD.

Finch, Mark (ed.) (1986), *ICA Video Library Guide*, ICA, London.

Fiske, John (1986), 'MTV: post structural post modern', *Journal of Communication*

Inquiry, 10, n. 1, winter.
— (1987), 'British Cultural Studies', in Robert C. Allen (ed.), *Channels of Discourse: Television and Contemporary Criticism*, Methuen, London.
— (1988), *Television Culture*, Methuen, London.
Flitterman-Lewis, Sandy (1987), 'Psychoanalysis, Film and Television', in Robert C. Allen (ed.) *Channels of Discourse: Television and Contemporary Criticism*, Methuen, London.
Forbes, Jill (ed.) (1984), *INA — French for Innovation: The Work of the Institut National de la Communication Audiovisuelle in Cinema and Television*, British Film Institute, London.
Forty, Adrian (1986), *Objects of Desire: Design and Society 1750–1980*, Thames and Hudson, London.
Foucault, Michel (1972), *The Archaeology of Knowledge*, Harper Collophon, New York.
— (1977), *Discipline and Punish*, Penguin, Harmondsworth.
Fountain, Alan (1989), *Workshop Policy in the 1990s: A Discussion Document*, Channel 4, London, April.
Freud, Sigmund (1961), *Beyond the Pleasure Principle*, trs. James Strackey, Livingstone, New York.
— (1976), *The Interpretation of Dreams*, Pelican Freud Library, vol. 4, Harmondsworth.
— (1984), 'Mourning and Melancholia', *Metapsychology: The Theory of Psychoanalysis*, Pelican Freud Library, vol. 11, Harmondsworth.
Frow, John (1988), 'Repetition and Limitation — Computer Software and Copyright Law', *Screen*, 29, n. 1, winter.
Furlong, Lucinda (1988), 'Electronic Backtalk: The Art of Interactive Video', *The Independent*, May.
Fusco, Coco (1988), *Young, British and Black*, Hallwells/Contemporary Arts Centre, Buffalo, NY.
Garratt, Sheryl and Sue Steward (1984), *Signed, Sealed, Delivered: True Stories of Women in Pop*, Pluto, London.
Geddes, Keith (1972), *Broadcasting in Britain 1922–1972: A Brief Account of Its Engineering Aspects*, HMSO, London.
Gheude, Michel (1988), 'Double Vue', in Raymond Bellour and Anne-Marie Duguet (eds), *Vidéo: Communications 48*, Seuil, Paris.
Gibson, William (1986), *Neuromancer*, Gratton, London.
— (1987), *Count Zero*, Gratton, London.
— (1989), *Mona Lisa Overdrive*, Gratton, London.
Gill, Karamjit S. (ed.) (1986), *Artificial Intelligence and Society*, John Wiley, London.
Gilroy, Paul (1987), *There Ain't No Black in the Union Jack*, Hutchinson, London.
Gilroy, Paul and Jim Pines (1988), 'Handsworth Songs: Audiences/Aesthetics/Independence — Interview with Black Audio Film Collective', *Framework*, 35.
Givanni, June (1988a), *Black and Asian Film List*, British Film Institute, London.
— (1988b), *Getting the Message Across: The Feasibility of a Black and Third World Film/Video Distribution Agency*, Vokhani Film Circuit, Wolverhampton.
Goodwin, Andrew (1987), 'Music Video in the (Post)Modern World', *Screen*, 28, n. 3, summer.
Gordon, David (1988), 'The Global Economy: New Edifice or Crumbling Foundation?', *New Left Review*, 168, March–April.

Gray, Ann (1986), 'Video Recorders in the Home: Women's Work and Boys' Toys', paper presented to the Second International Television Studies Conference, Institute of Education, London.

— (1987a), 'Behind Closed Doors: Women and Video Recorders in the Home', in Helen Baehr and Gillian Dyer (eds), *Boxed In: Women On and In Television*, Pandora, London.

— (1987b), 'Reading the Audience', *Screen*, 28, n. 3, summer.

Greenburg, Clement (1983), 'Modernist Painting', in Francis Frascina and Charles Harrison (eds), *Modern Art and Modernism: A Critical Anthology*, Paul Chapman Publishing, London.

Grossberg, Lawrence (1984), '"I'd Rather Feel Bad than not Feel Anything At All": Rock and Roll, Pleasure and Power', *Enclitic*, 8, ns 1–2, spring–fall.

— (1988), 'You (still) Have to Fight for your Right to Party: Music Television as Billboards of Postmodern Indifference', *Popular Music*, 7, n. 3, October.

Grundman, Heidi (ed.) (1984), *Art + Telecommunications*, Western Front, Vancouver and Blix, Vienna.

Haddon, Leslie (1988), 'Electronic and Computer Games', *Screen*, 29, n. 2, spring.

Hanhardt, John G. (ed.) (1986), *Video Culture: A Critical Investigation*, Peregrine Smith Books, Layton, Utah.

Hanson, Janice (1987), *Understanding Video: Applications, Impact and Theory*, Sage, London.

Haralovich, Mary Beth (1982), 'Advertising Heterosexuality', *Screen*, 23, n. 2, July–August.

Hardy, Thomas (1978), *Selected Shorter Poems*, Macmillan, London.

Harraway, Donna (1985), 'A Manifesto for Cyborgs: Science, Technology and Socialist Feminism in the 1980s', *Socialist Review*, 80.

Hartney, Mick (1983), 'Landscape/Video/Art: Some Tentative Rules and Exceptions', *Undercut*, 7–8, spring.

Haskell, Lisa (ed.) (1989), *Video Positive '89*, Merseyside Moviola, Liverpool.

Hayles, Katherine (1987), 'Cyborgs: Postmodern Phantasms of Mind and Body', *Discourse*, 9, spring–summer.

Hayward Gallery (1988), *Nam June Paik: Video Works 1963–1988*, South Bank, London.

Heath, Stephen and Gillian Skirrow (1977), 'Television: A World in Action', *Screen*, 18, n. 2, summer.

Hebdige, Dick (1983), 'Posing Threats . . . Striking Poses: Youth, Surveillance and Display', *SubStance*, ns 37–8.

— (1986), *Cut 'n' Mix: Culture, Identity and Caribbean Music*, Routledge, London.

— (1988), *Hiding in the Light: On Images and Things*, Routledge, London.

Holdstein, D. (1984), 'Music Video: Messages and Structures', *Jump Cut*, n. 29.

Horne, Larry (1984), 'On Video and Its Viewers', *On Film*, 13, fall.

Huffman, Kathy (ed.) (1984), *Video: A Retrospective*, Long Beach Museum of Art, Long Beach, California.

Huffman, Kathy and Dorine Mignot (eds) (1987), *The Arts for Television*, Los Angeles Museum of Contemporary Art/Stedelijk Museum, Amsterdam.

Huyssen, Andreas (1987), *After the Great Divide: Modernism, Mass Culture, Postmodernism*, Indiana University Press, Bloomington, Indiana.

Hyman, Anthony (1980), *The Mighty Micro*, New English Library, London.

IFVPA North of Ireland (1988), *Fast Forward: Report on the Funding of Grant Aided*

Film and Video in the North of Ireland, IFVPA/ACTT, Belfast.

Jacobus, Mary (1986), 'Madonna: Like a Virgin', in *Oxford Literary Review: Sexual Difference,* Southampton.

Jameson, Fredric (1988), 'La Lecture sans l'interpretation', in Raymond Bellour and Anne-Marie Duguet (eds), *Vidéo: Communications 48,* Seuil, Paris.

Jost, François (1984), 'New Tele/Visions', *On Film,* 13, fall.

Julien, Isaac and Kobena Mercer (1988), 'De Margin and De Centre', *Screen,* 29, n. 4, autumn.

Kaplan, E. Ann (ed.) (1983), *Regarding Television,* American Film Institute Monographs 2, University Publications of America, Frederick, MD.

— (1985), 'A Postmodern Play of the Signifier? Advertising, Pastiche and Schizophrenia in Music Television', in Phillip Drummond and Richard Patterson (eds), *Television in Transition,* British Film Institute, London.

— (1986), 'History, the Historical Spectator and Gender Address in Music Television', *Journal of Communication Inquiry,* 10, n. 1, winter.

— (1987), *Rocking Around the Clock: Music Television, Postmodernism and Consumer Culture,* Methuen, London.

— (ed.) (1988), *Postmodernism and its Discontents: Theories, Practices,* Verso, London.

Keen, Ben (1987), ' "Play It Again, Sony": The Double Life of Home Video Technology', *Science as Culture,* n. 1.

Kinder, Marsha (1985), 'Music Video and the Spectator: Television, Ideology and the Dream', *Film Quarterly,* 38, n. 1.

Klein, Melanie (1986), *The Selected Melanie Klein,* Peregrine, London.

— (1988a), *Envy and Gratitude and Other Works 1946–1963,* Virago, London.

— (1988b), *Love, Guilt and Reparation and Other Works 1921–1945,* Virago, London.

Krauss, Rosalind E. (1976), 'Video: The Structure of Narcissism', *October,* n. 1, spring.

— (1986), *The Originality of the Avant-Garde and Other Modernist Myths,* MIT Press, Cambridge, Mass.

Kristeva, Julia (1969), *Semeiotiké: recherches pour une sémanalyse,* Seuil, Paris.

— (1980), *Pouvoirs de l'horreur: Essai sur l'abjection,* Seuil, Paris.

Lacan, Jacques (1966), *Ecrits,* 2 vols, Seuil (Collection Points), Paris.

— (1973), *Le Séminaire, livre XI, Les quatres concepts fondamentaux de la psychanalyse,* Seuil, Paris.

— (1986), *Le Séminaire, livre VII, l'éthique de la psychanalyse,* Seuil, Paris.

Laing, Dave (1986), 'The Music Industry and the "Cultural Imperialism" Thesis', *Media Culture and Society,* 8, n. 3, July.

— (1988), 'Rocking Around the Clock: Music Television, Postmodernism and Consumer Culture by E. Ann Kaplan', *Popular Music,* 7, n. 3, October.

Larson, Judith K. and Everett M. Rogers (1984), *Silicon Valley Fever: Growth of High Technology Culture,* George Allen & Unwin, London.

Lewis, Lisa A. (1986), 'Female Address in Music Video: Voicing the Difference Differently', paper presented to the Second International Television Studies Conference, Institute of Education/British Film Institute, London.

Lewis, Peter M. (1978), *Community Television and Cable in Britain,* British Film Institute, London.

— (ed.) (1984), *Media For People in Cities: A Study of Community,* Media in the

Urban Context, UNESCO, COM.84/WS-7, London.

Linn, Pam (1985), 'Microcomputers in Education: Dead and Living Labour', in Tony Solomonides and Les Levidow (eds), *Compulsive Technology: Computers as Culture*, Free Association Books, London.

Lipman, Andy (1985), *Video*, Channel 4, London.

London, Barbara (1988), *Bill Viola*, Museum of Modern Art, New York.

London Video Arts (1978), *London Video Arts: 1978 Catalogue*, LVA, London.

— (1984), *London Video Arts: 1984 Catalogue*, LVA, London.

— (1985), *Channel Five*, LVA/IFVA, London.

Luce, Richard (1988), 'The Structure of Arts Funding', letter to Sir William Rees-Mogg, C88/5996, 8 December.

Lyotard, Jean-François (1984), *The Postmodern Condition: A Report on Knowledge*, Manchester University Press, Manchester.

— (1988), *L'Inhumain: Causeries sur le temps*, Galilée, Paris.

McGrath, John (1985), 'Strike at the Fiction Factories', *Edinburgh International Television Festival Magazine*, n. 10.

McLean, Martha (1988), 'Of Anthems and Reverse TV: A Critical View of Bill Viola', *Independent Media*, 82, October.

McLuhan, Marshall (1964), *Understanding Media*, Sphere, London.

McLuhan, Marshall and Quentin Fiore (1967), *The Medium is the Message: An Inventory of Effects*, Penguin, Harmondsworth.

MacRobbie, Angela (1977), 'Jackie: An Ideology of Adolescent Romance', Occasional Stencilled Papers, no. 27, Centre for Contemporary Cultural Studies, Birmingham.

Mandel, Ernest (1977), *Late Capitalism*, Verso, London.

Mann, Denise (1984), 'Staggering Towards Modern Times: The Video Art of Max Almy', *Camera Obscura*, 12.

Marris, Paul (1986), *The Regional Production Fund: A Discussion Document*, British Film Institute, London, December.

Marshall, Stuart (1978), 'Video Art, the Imaginary and the *Parole Vide*', in Geoffrey Battcock (ed.), *New Artists Video*, Dutton, New York.

— (1979), 'Video – Technology and Practice', *Screen*, 20, n. 1, spring.

— (1985), 'Video – From Art to Independence', *Screen*, 26, n. 2, March–April.

Marx, Karl (1973), *Grundrisse*, Penguin/New Left Books, London.

— (1976), *Capital*, vol. 1, Penguin/New Left Review, London.

Mellencamp, Patricia (1986), 'Uncanny Feminism: The Exquisite Corpses of Cecilia Condit', *Framework*, 32–3.

— (1988), 'Video Politics: Guerilla TV, Ant Farm, Eternal Frame', *Discourse*, X.2, spring–summer.

Mercer, Kobena (1986), 'Monster Metaphors: Notes on Michael Jackson's Thriller', *Screen*, 27, n. 1, January–February.

— (1988a), *Black Film, British Cinema*, ICA Documents 7, ICA, London.

— (1988b), 'Sexual Identities: Questions of Difference – Introduction', *Undercut*, 17.

Merck, Mandy (1987), 'Introduction – Difference and its Discontents', *Screen*, 28, n. 1, winter.

Metz, Christian (1977), *Psychoanalysis and Cinema: The Imaginary Signifier*, Macmillan, London.

Michaels, Eric (1986), *Aboriginal Invention of Television, Central Australia 1982–86*,

Australian Institute of Aboriginal Studies, Canberra.

Michaelson, Annette (1986), 'Heterology and the Critique of Instrumental Reason', *October*, n. 36, spring.

Mignot, Dorine (ed.) (1984), *The Luminous Image*, Stedelijk Museum, Amsterdam.

— (ed.) (1987), *Revision*, Stedelijk Museum, Amsterdam.

Montague, John 1972), *The Rough Field*, Dolmen, Dublin.

Morley, David (1980), *The Nationwide Audience*, British Film Institute, London.

— (1986), *Family Television: Cultural Power and Domestic Leisure*, Comedia, London.

Morris, Meaghan (1988), *The Pirate's Fiancée: Feminism, Reading, Postmodernism*, Verso, London.

Morse, Margaret (1983), 'Sport on Television: Replay and Display', in E. Ann Kaplan (ed.), *Regarding Television*, American Film Institute Monographs 2, University Publications of America, Frederick, MD.

— (1985), 'Postsynchronising Rock Music and television', *Journal of Communication Inquiry*, 10, n. 1.

— (1988), 'Artemis Aging: Exercise and the Female Body on Video', *Discourse*, X.1, fall–winter.

Moy-Thomas, Lucy (1985), 'TVEI', in *Media Education Initiatives*, SEFT, London, November.

Mulvey, Laura (1975), 'Visual Pleasure and Narrative Cinema', *Screen*, 16, n. 3, autumn.

— (1981), 'Afterthoughts on "Visual Pleasure and Narrative Cinema" Inspired by King Vidor's *Duel in the Sun*', *Framework*, 15–16–17.

Nichols, Bill (1988), 'The Work of Culture in the Age of Cybernetic Systems', *Screen*, 29, n. 1, winter.

Nigg, Heinz and Graham Wade (1980), *Community Media – Community Communication in the UK: Video, Local TV, Film and Photography*, Regenbogen Verlag, Zurich.

Ong, Walter J. (1982), *Orality and Literacy: The Technologising of the Word*, Methuen, London.

Oudart, Jean-Pierre (1977–8), 'Cinema and Suture', *Screen*, 18, n. 4, winter.

Paik, Nam June (1974), *Video 'n' Videology*, Everson Museum of Art, Syracuse, NY.

Pater, Walter (1912), 'The School of Giorgione', in *The Renaissance: Studies in Art and Poetry*, Macmillan, London.

Perrée, Rob (1988), *Into Video Art; The Characteristics of a Medium*, Con Rumore, Amsterdam.

Petley, Julian (1984), 'A Nasty Story', *Screen*, 25, n. 2, March–April.

Plant, Margaret (1988), 'Madonna in Venice', *Art & Text*, 30, September–November.

Poole, Mike (1984), 'The Cult of the Generalist: British Television Criticism 1936–1983', *Screen*, 25, n. 2, March–April.

Prigogine, Ilya and Isabelle Stengers (1988), *Order Out of Chaos: Man's New Dialogue with Nature*, Flamingo, London.

Roe, Keith and Monica Löfgren (1988), 'Music Video Use and Educational Achievement', *Popular Music*, 7, n. 3, October.

Ross, Christine (1988), 'Nan Hoover: Le Sujet vidéologique ou la réception', *Parachute*, 51, June–July–August.

Ryle, Martin (1988), *Ecology and Socialism*, Radius, London.

Saïd, Edward (1983), 'Opponents, Audiences, Constituencies and Communities', in Hal Foster (ed.), *Postmodern Culture*, Pluto, London.

— (1988), 'Identity, Negation and Violence', *New Left Review*, 171, September–October.

Sartre, Jean-Paul (1979 [1943]), *L'Être et le néant*, Gallimard, Paris.

Schneider, Ida and Beryl Korot (eds) (1976), *Video Art: An Anthology*, Harcourt, Brace Jovanovitch, New York.

Shklovsky, Viktor (1972), *Mayakovsky and His Circle*, Pluto, London.

Shore, Michael (1985), *The Rolling Stone Book of Rock Videos*, Sidgwick and Jackson, London.

Shukman, Ann (1984), *Bakhtin School Papers: Russian Poetics in Translation*, v. 10, RPT Publications, Oxford.

Siegel, Lenny (1979), 'Microcomputing Does Little for the Third World', *Pacific Research*, 10.

Skirrow, Gillian (1986), 'Hellivision: An Analysis of Video Games', in Colin MacCabe (ed.), *High Theory, Low Culture*, Manchester University Press, Manchester.

Slater, Phil (ed.) (1980), *Outlines of a Critique of Technology*, Inklinks, London.

Stam, Robert (1988), 'Bakhtin and Left Cultural Critique', in E. Ann Kaplan (ed.), *Postmodernism and its Discontents: Theories, Practices*, Verso, London.

Stevens, Wallace (1955), *Collected Poems*, Faber and Faber, London.

Stockbridge, Sally (1988), 'Music Video: Performance, Pleasure and Address', *Continuum*, 1, n. 2.

Straw, Will (1988), 'Music Video in its Contexts: Popular Music and Postmodernism in the 1980s', *Popular Music*, 7, n. 3, October.

Sturken, Marita (1988), 'Les Grandes Espérances et la construction d'une histoire', in Raymond Bellour and Anne-Marie Duguet (eds), *Vidéo: Communications 48*, Seuil, Paris.

Sweeney, Pat (1985), 'Casual Production', *Screen*, 26, n. 2, March–April.

Tamor, Sarah (1984), *National Video Festival*, catalogue, American Film Institute, Los Angeles.

Taylor, Ian (1987), 'Violence and Video: For a Social Democratic Perspective', *Contemporary Crises*, 11.

Tee, Ernie (1986), 'Music Videos: On Reality and Representation', paper presented to the Second International Television Studies Conference, Institute of Education/British Film Institute, London.

Tetzlaff, Dave (1986), 'MTV and the Politics of Postmodern Pop', *Journal of Communication Inquiry*, 10, n. 1, winter.

Todorov, Tsvetan (1981), *Mikhaïl Bakhtine: le principe dialogique, suivi de Écrits du Cercle de Bakhtine*, Seuil, Paris.

Toubiana, Serge (1981), 'Introduction', *Cahiers du Cinéma: Numéro Spéciale – Télévision*, n. 328, autumn.

Tunstall, Jeremy (1986), *Communications Deregulation: The Unleashing of America's Communications Industry*, Blackwell, Oxford.

Turim, Maureen (1983), 'Video Art: Theory for a Future', in E. Ann Kaplan (ed.) *Regarding Television*, American Film Institute Monographs 2, University Publications of America, Frederick, MD.

Turkle, Sherry (1984), *The Second Self: Computers and the Human Spirit*, Granada,

London.

UNESCO (1980), *Many Voices, One World (The MacBride Report)*, abridged edn, UNESCO/Kogan Page, London.

Vargaftig, Marion (1987), *Vidéo création en France*, Ministère des Affaires Etrangers/Intermédia, Paris.

Viola, Bill (1988),'Y aura-t-il copropriété dans l'espace des données?', in Raymond and Anne-Marie Duguet (eds), *Vidéo: Communications 48*, Seuil, Paris.

Virilio, Paul (1986), *Speed and Politics: An Essay in Dromology*, Semiotext(e), New York.

— (1989), 'La Lumière indirecte', in Raymond Bellour and Anne-Marie Duguet (eds), *Vidéo Communications 48*, Seuil, Paris.

— (1989), *War and Cinema*, Verso, London.

Volosinov, V. N. (1929) (1986), *Marxism and the Philosophy of Language*, Harvard University Press, Cambridge, Mass.

— (1987), *Freudianism: A Critical Sketch*, Indiana University Press, Bloomington, Indiana.

Wade, Graham (1980), *Street Video: An Account of Five Video Groups*, Blackthorn Press, Leicester.

— (1985), *Film, Video and Television: Market Forces, Fragmentation and Technological Advance*, Comedia, London.

Wallis, Roger and Krister Malm (1988), 'Push-pull for the Video Clip', *Popular Music*, 7, n. 3, October.

Weizenbaum, J. (1984), *Computer Power and Human Reason*, Pelican, Harmondsworth.

Welsh, Jeremy (1983), 'Creating a Context for Video', *Undercut*, 7–8, spring.

Whitby, Blay (1986), 'The Computer as Cultural Artefact', in Karamjit S. Gill (ed.), *Artifical Intelligence and Society*, John Wiley, London.

Whitehead, A. N.(1969), *Process and Reality: An Essay in Cosmology*, The Free Press, New York.

Wiener, Norbert (1948), *Cybernetics: or control and communication in the animal and the machine* (2nd edn 1961), MIT Press, Cambridge, Mass.

Willemen, Paul (1987), 'The Third Cinema Question: Notes and reflections', *Framework*, 34.

Willener, Alfred, Guy Milliard and Alex Ganty (1976), *Videology and Utopia: Explorations in a New Medium*, Routledge & Kegan Paul, London.

Williams, Raymond (1974), *Television: Technology and Cultural Form*, Fontana, London.

Williamson, Judith (1986), 'The Making of a Material Girl', *New Socialist*, October.

Wollen, Peter (1986), 'Ways of Thinking about Music Video (and Postmodernism)', Critical Quarterly, 28, ns 1–2.

— (1987), 'An Interview with Steve Fagin', *October*, 41, summer.

— (1988), 'Le Cinéma, l'américanisme et le robot' in Raymond Bellour and Anne-Marie Duguet (eds), *Vidéo: Communications 48*, Seuil, Paris.

Yeats, W. B. (1950), *Collected Poems*, Macmillan, London.

Young, Robert (ed.) (1986), *Oxford Literary Review: Sexual Difference*, Southampton.

Youngblood, Gene (1970), *Expanded Cinema*, Studio Vista, London.

Index

AIR Gallery 70
Abbott, F. 119–20
abjection 178–9
Academy of Video Arts 51
Accidents in the Home 103
advertising 7
aerobics 73–5, 77–8
aesthetics 125
Alexander, K. 137
algorythm 137
Allen, R. C. 99–100, 175
Almy, Max 96, 135–7
Althusser, L. 21
Amber 152
Anderson, B. 175
Ang, I. 19
Anthem 114–15
Armes, R. 37, 44, 88
art 171
Artificial Intelligence (AI) 176
Arts Council 166
Association of Cinematograph
    Television and Allied Technicians
    (ACTT) 152, 161
Atherton, W. 87
Attali, J. 45
auteurism 140
authenticity 64
authoritative 103–4
authorship 104

Bakhtin, M. M. 40, 57, 127, 172, 174,
    177
Barber, G. 68, 95
Barthes, R. 47, 138, 142

Bateson, Gl. 169
Battcock, G. 86
Baudelaire, C. 65
Baudrillard, J. 23–5, 121, 124, 127,
    173, 181
Bazalgette, C. 27
Beatles 45
Bellour, R. 122
Benjamin, W. 37, 57, 69, 124
Berger, J. 113
Berry, C. 48
Betamax 8
Bhabha, H. K. 120
Biggs, S. 70
Birmingham Film/Video Workshop
    152–3
Boulez, P. and Gerzso, A. 45–6
Bracknell 147
Braudel, F. 175
Braverman, H. 12
Brecht, B. 153
Bright, G. 159
British Board of Film Censors 159
British Board of Film Classification
    161
British Film Institute (BFI) 161, 166
British Telecom 28
Britton, A. 67
broadcast 27–8, 165
Brockbank, S. 17
Brunsdon, C. 6
Burns, Gl. 137
Byrne, D. 83, 110

Cabaret Voltaire 57, 89–90

Cage, J. 118
Cahen, R. 46, 100
Calling the Shots 129–30
Camera Lucida 142
campaign video 129
Candle TV 119
carnival 43, 55–6, 172
Caughie, J. 27, 46
Ceiber aka Penrhiwceiber: The Greatest Improvisers in the World 137, 152–3
censorship 157–61
Chambers, I. 53
Changeux, J–P 20
Channel 4 29, 86, 147, 161, 166
Chapter Workshop 151
The Chauffeur 57, 82
Chesterman, J. and Lipman, A. 156
Chott El-Djerid 112, 114
Clinton, Gl. 65–6, 90
Cockburn, C. 11
Coleridge, S. T. 3
colonialism 110
commodity 61
community video 128, 149–54
competence 5
computer-generated 178
Connection 117
Connor, S. 45
copying 105–6, 146, 157
copyright 4, 38, 156–8
Corea, G. 179
Crosby, B. 88
cultural industries 128, 154
Culture Club 47
cyborg 136–7, 179

Davis, M. 51
Dayan, D. 31
deconstruction 136
de Certeau, M. 172
Deleuze, G. and Guattari, F. 173
deregulation 171
Derrida, J. 22, 29–30, 36, 58, 61, 98, 136
Descartes, R. 34
Despite the Sun 110, 139
Despite TV 110, 137, 139, 151
Dews, P. 26, 131
dialect 88–9

digital audio tape (DAT) 17, 155
Dire Straits 82
Disneyland 24
distribution 150
documentary 139
Do Fries Go With That Shake? 65–7
Donald, J. 184
Don't Eat Today or Tomorrow 28
Dovey, J. 156
Duchess of York 133
Ducrot, O and Todorov, T. 5
Duguet, A–M. 86, 122
Duran Duran 57, 82
Duvet Brothers 95
Dylan, B. 45

Easley, G. and Rabinovitz, L. 51
ecology 174
editing 111, 146, 155
Education Reform Act 49, 171
Eisenstein, S. M. 183
Electronic Arts Intermix 140
Ellis, J. 39
Ellison, R. 141
The Elusive Sign 130
Elwes, C. 95, 107, 131–4
employment 151–2
engineering standards 7
entropy 144
Enzensberger, H. M. ix, 175, 180
Eurythmics 50, 79–81
The Evil Dead 159
The Extent of Three Bells 174

fading 143–4
Family of Robot 116–18, 121
Fanon, F. 183–4
Feuer, J. 16, 31, 35
Fenster, M. 51
Fish TV 117
Fiske, J. 38, 39, 52–7, 60
Flaxton, T. 145
Flitterman-Lewis, S. 16
Fonda, J. 73–4
Foucault, M. 131, 135, 173
Framed Youth 137, 138, 156
Franklin, A. 50–1
Frow, J. 17
Freud, S. 41, 58, 100, 106, 179

fort-da 41, 57–8, 177–8
funding 19

Garratt, S. and Steward, S. 83
Genaris, C. 166
Get It Shown 148, 166
Gibson, W. 176
Gill, K. S. 176
Gilroy, P. 9
Girl/Zone 153
Givanni, J. 109
Good Video Guide 150
Gorilla Tapes 95, 156
grab-frames 95
Gramsci, A. 185
Grateful Dead 45
Gray, A. 2, 6, 36, 41
Greenberg, C. 44, 114, 123, 182
Grossberg, L. 54
Gunther, I. 93

hacking 176
Hairspray 73
Hall, S. 184
Handsworth Songs 141
Hanhardt, J. G. 122
hardware 10, 17, 38, 39, 176, 185
Harraway, D. 135, 136
Hatoum, Mona 99
Hatsu Yume 114
Hawley, S. 174
Hayes Code 159
Hayles, K. 179
Heath, S. and Skirrow, G. 29
Heaven 17 51
Heavy Metal 75
heavy rotation 58
Hebdidge, D. 11, 64
hierarchy 6–7
high-band 151
Hill, G. 169
homeworkers 134
Horkheimer, M. and Adorno, T. 42
horror 177–9, 183
Huffman, K. 86
Huyssen, A. 53

identification 40
identity 141, 143

I Do Not Know What It Is I Am Like
    111–16, 121, 183
Idol, B. 63
Imaginary 39
Independent Media 149, 188
Institut Nationale de l'Audiovisuel
    (INA) 46
In the National Interest 147

Jackson, M. 54, 79, 84
Jameson, F. 122–4
Japan 114
Jean Genet Is Dead 166
Johnson, S. 48
Jones, H. 82
Julien, I. 109, 110, 141
Juste le temps 100

Kaplan, E. A. 51–7, 77
Keen, B. 37, 88
Keep Fighting Fit With No 2 Para 75
kitsch 83, 168
Klein, M. 40–3
Krauss, R. 87, 98
Kristeva, J. 129, 178–9, 182
Kuntzel, T. 106

Labour Party 52, 125
Lacan, J. 39–40, 72, 100–1, 126–7,
    169, 171–2, 177–8
Laing, D. 11
Landseer, W. 79
laser disc 155
Laughton, C. 75
Leavis, F. R. 1
Lester, R. 46
Lévi-Strauss, C. 36, 178
library service 147
light 72, 105
Lipman, A. 37
literature 1
Local Government Act 160
London Video Arts 140
long take 123
look 72
low-band 139, 151
Lucas, G. 183
Lyotard, F. 17, 24, 107, 174, 182

MTV 50–1, 82
MacBride Report 9
McGrath, J. 8, 35–6
machine/body relation 14–15
McLuhan, M. 21–3, 179
MacRobbie, A. 57, 62
Madonna 54–6, 60, 62, 74, 76–7
Mandel, E. 48
Marshall, S. 86, 108
Marx, K. 12–14, 33–4, 61
mass audience 50
Mass Observation 64
Material Girl 62, 76–7
Mayakovsky, V. 175
media education 3
melody 47
metaphor 101
metonmy 101–2
Metz, C. 16, 185
Mercer, K. 109, 141
Merck, M. 67
Michael, G. 51
microphone 47–8
Millions Like Us 172
The Miners' Campaign Tapes 137,
    139–40, 144, 147
mirror phase 39–40
Money for Nothing 82
Morley, D. 6, 16, 41–2
Morris, M. 116, 182
Morse, M. 36, 74–5, 79
MsTaken Identities 137
Muller, S. 79
multiscreen 69
Mulvey, L. 39, 112, 132

narcissism 170
negation 173–4
networking 150
'new realism' 161
Newman, B. 182
Nichols, B. 17
nightclubs 68
Nocturnal Emissions 95
North East Media Development
    Council 151

obscenity 160
Oedipus 39, 170

Ong, W. J. 22
Oudart, J–P. 31
Out of Order 153
outworking 134

Paik, N. J. 87, 99, 102, 108, 110,
    116–20, 121, 176
paint systems 176
Papa Don't Preach 54, 82
paradigm 99–100, 175
Passion Ration 105
Pater, W. 44
Pavarotti, L. 45
Perfect Leader 96, 135–7
Perree, R. 86
Pet Shop Boys 47
photocopiers 158
photomontage 98
playback 146
The Poacher 182
Pointer Sisters 50
Point of Light 119
Poole, M. 46
portraits 115
postmodern 49–50
presence 24, 29
Presley, E. 48
pretext 90–1
Prigogine, I. and Stengers, I. 181, 184
Prince 47
Private Dancer 79

radio 76
Radical Software 88
Rank, O. 179
reading 2
reality effect 138
Rebel Yell 63
Redman, Z. 105
Rembrandt 75
repetition 58, 92–5
reproductive technologies 179
Reverse TV 115
'riot money' 160
Road to Nowhere 110
rock 'n roll 11
Rockwell, N. 53
Roeg, N. 46
Romford Calling 147

Rotorama 93–4
Ryle, M. 181

Sade 48
Said, E. 168
Sartre, J–P. 77
Satellite Baby 118
Satellite Chair 118
Saussure, F. de 34–5, 97–8
Savage 79–81
scratch video 94–6, 99, 156
Screen 21, 109
sell-through 163
Sianel Pedwar Cymru 28
signifiance 48
silence 59, 113
Sinatra, F. 48
singing 47–8, 54
single-monitor 91–2
Sinn Fein 120
Sirk, D. 129
Skirrow, G. 40, 170, 176
social reader 2
Society for Education in Film and
    Television (SEFT) 162
software 11, 17
sound 8, 93–4, 112, 113–15, 185–6
Spector, P. 69
Spielberg, S. 183
Springsteen, B. 79
Stam, R. 127
star system 57, 73
Storytelling Giant 82–3
structuralism 23
struggle 6
sublimation 126
sublime 177, 182–4
suburbia 49–50
suture 31–2
Sweeney, P. 153
Symbolic 39–40
syntagm 97–175

TV Bra 118–19
Talking Heads 82–3
technological determinism 24
telephone 59
Territories 141
Thatcher, M. 5, 125, 160, 172, 182

Thing (Das Ding) 126–7, 178
This Is Not An AIDS Ad 141
Todorov, T. 174
Tommy 80
Top of the Pops 54
Toubiana, S. 32–3
Toussaint, A. 50
Trade Films 152
training 151–2
transnational corporations (TNCs)
    162
True Life Romance 96
Tunstall, J. 38
Turim, M. 122
Turner, T. 50, 79

Ugly George 120
Ultravox 62
underdeveloped nations 10

V–2000 8
VHS 8
Verneinung 178
vertical integration 18
Vertical Landscapes 92
Viola, B. 110, 110–16, 121, 183
video cassette recorder (VCR) 4,
    10–11, 17, 27, 38, 164–5
video culture 1
video projector 91
Video Recordings Act 38, 159–61
video rental 163–4
video walkman ('Watchman') 167
video wall 69–70
video workshops 149
Vienna 62
Virilio, P. 12, 48
Voloshinov, V. N. 26, 81, 174

The Wall 80
wall of sound 69, 71
Warhol, A. 53
Welsh, J. 87, 99, 129
Wenders, W. 146
Whitehead, A. N. 181
Whitehouse, M. 178
Who Killed Colin Roach? 110
Why Do Things Get In A Muddle?
    169–70

Wilcox, M. 129
Williams, R. 22, 29, 122
Williamson, J. 55, 60, 72, 74
Wilson, A. and St James, M. 96
With Child 131–3
Women's Film, Television and Video
    Network (WFTVN) 162
Wollen, P. 127
The World Within Us 145

writing 4, 22–3, 30

Yes Frank No Smoke 95
Young, G. 103
youth 61–2, 73

zapping 156
zipping 156